Building on a Solid Foundation

Building on a Solid Foundation

Examining Seven Topics
of the Catholic Faith

Mr. Daniel J. Daou
Rev. Father Antoine Bakh
Mr. Joseph Bakhos

To the mother of our Lord;
may the Son that she bore
be encountered in these pages.

Special Thanks to Mrs. Jacqueline Bakhos for the countless hours spent on grammar corrections and editing work.

Scripture excerpts from the New American Bible with Revised New Testament Copyright © 1986, 1970 by the Confraternity of Christian Doctrine, Washington, D.C. Used with permission. All Rights Reserved. No part of the New American Bible may be reproduced in any form without permission in writing from the copyright owner. Permission to use the New American Bible does not constitute endorsement or approval by the Confraternity of Christian Doctrine.

Imprimatur: The Most Rev. Robert Shaheen, Bishop of the Eparchy of Our Lady of Lebanon of Los Angeles

Nihil Obstat: Subdeacon Louis Peters, Censor Deputatus

The Imprimatur and Nihil Obstat are official declarations that a book is considered to be free of doctrinal error. No implication is contained therein that those who have granted the Nihil Obstat or the Imprimatur agree with the contents, opinions or statements expressed.

ISBN: 1-930314-04-3

Printed in the United States of America

All proceeds from this book will go to the Missionaries of Faith Foundation to be used to distribute this book and other material about the faith free of charge. If you wish to support the Missionaries of Faith Foundation in its faith endeavors, please send your donation to: Missionaries of Faith, P.O. Box 231820, Encinitas, CA 92023.

Contents

Introduction

For two thousand years, the Catholic Church has been bringing Christ to the world, witnessing to his death and resurrection and bearing his life to the faithful through the sacraments. Despite this lengthy tradition, a recent article from the *New York Times Magazine* describes the Catholic faith as the new counterculture in America—and it is![1] The ancient faith has not succumbed to centuries of worldly pressure but remains an ever new and challenging witness to the truth. For many Catholics the temptation to give in seems overwhelming. It would be so easy to concede on many points of faith and morals. But the consequences can be devastating, as many have learned from experience.

The authors of this book have chosen to concentrate on seven topics of the faith that are hardest hit by today's culture in order to build upon a solid foundation of rock. The intent is to provide the reader with biblical and rational support on topics often questioned. It is meant to invigorate Catholics to renew their commitment to the faith, because, as St. Paul warns us, "Our struggle is not with flesh and blood but with the principalities, with the powers, with the world rulers of this present darkness . . ." (Eph 6:12).[2]

First of all, we need to be convinced that dogma is important.

---

[1] Jennifer Egan, "Why a Priest?" *New York Times Magazine* Apr. 4, 1999: p. 30.

[2] Scripture excerpts from the *New American Bible with Revised New Testament* Copyright © 1986, 1970 by the Confraternity of Christian Doctrine, Washington, D.C. Used with permission. All Rights Reserved. No part of the *New American Bible* may be reproduced in any form without permission in writing from the copyright owner. Permission to use the *New American Bible* does not constitute endorsement or approval by the Confraternity of Christian Doctrine.

Many have the attitude that authority is not necessary. They may feel that Truth is self-evident. They may feel that anyone might simply use common sense to find the truth. It is true that human beings are given a natural capacity to distinguish between good and bad behavior. St. Paul even affirms this observation in his letter to the Romans when he points out that the gentiles have the demands of the law "written in their hearts" (Rom 2:15).

The problem is that human beings often beguile themselves. Many have made a shipwreck of their faith. Dogma is important as long as we care about being conscious of what we are doing. In contrast to the animal world of instinct alone, human beings are given the chance to mature into a state of freedom, where we can learn to distinguish between what we are inclined to do and what we ought to do. St. Paul makes this point very well in his letter to the Corinthians.

> When I was a child, I used to talk as a child, think as a child, reason as a child; when I became a man, I put aside childish things (1 Cor 13:11).

In this passage, St. Paul is warning us not to be satisfied with a child's knowledge of the faith. We must never stop striving to learn about God and the revelation that he imparted to us through the Church. The essence of dogma is clarification. It makes clear what the truth is. Unfortunately, dogma often stands in contrast to the pull of emotions and the tug of what "feels right." This is why it meets with so much resistance!

When friends or family want to discuss the Eucharist or the pope or our beliefs regarding purgatory or Mary, it is our duty to explain the faith in a helpful way (1 Pt 3:15). Oftentimes, if a person can be convinced that what the Catholic Church teaches about Jesus Christ is true, then belief in the moral teachings will follow. This is the meaning behind Christ's parable of the house built on a rock. The rock in this parable is the rock of right faith that provides us with stability when we are faced with a strong temptation to sin. In his letter to the Ephesians, Paul says that it is our duty to learn fully about the true faith, "so that we may no longer be infants, tossed by waves and swept along by every wind of teaching . . ." (Eph 4:14).

One way to grow in the faith is to read the Bible with understanding. This book should help towards that end, because it shows that the Bible is an integral part of the Church's testimony about God. While many people stay away from the inspired writings of the Old Testament because they are so difficult to understand, we have tried to show how these writings reveal how Jesus is the fulfillment of God's revelation of himself to his creation. They also help us to understand the full meaning behind Christ's words and deeds in the New Testament.

This book does not attempt to cover all there is about the faith. It serves as a compass to point out the right direction on seven topics that tend to cause confusion. The first chapter deals with the Triune Godhead. The Trinity, in one sense, is the beginning and end of the story, because it is the gift that Jesus came to give. The second chapter on the Eucharist tells how Christ is the Messiah who steps into his creation and gives his life to a dying world as the Way, the Truth, and the Life. The next chapter on salvation then explains what we must do to be saved. The fourth chapter on the Church reviews the primacy of Peter, but mainly it explains how we personally are joined to Christ in his Church. He has chosen not to appear to everyone in person but instead has arranged for the Church to imitate his mother in bearing him into the world for the generations to come. Later chapters on Confession and purgatory explain how the stain of sin can be removed so that the life of God can be restored to our souls. Finally, the chapter on Mary shows how she sums up salvation history as well as our vision of the future, when the New Jerusalem (the city of all God's children) will be drawn fully into the life of the Holy Trinity. Each chapter concludes with an appendix from the early Church Fathers (A.D. 70–450), so that you can trace for yourself the continuity of faith that extends across two thousand years. We hope these early writings will help you to look back with gratitude to the prior generations of Christians and that the book as a whole will inspire and encourage you to take part in passing on our Catholic faith to the next generation.

The Holy Trinity

Faith is foolishness if it is grounded in falsehood. The cornerstone of our faith is that Christ is true God and true man. If Jesus is not both God and Man, then we have been deluding ourselves for 2000 years. Therefore, if we cannot come to a definitive conclusion on this, then there is no point in calling ourselves Christian. We will not be saved merely by saying, "I believe in Jesus." What we believe about him matters. As Christians, all of us desire to have a personal relationship with the living Christ rather than some virtual Christ who does not really exist at all. St. Paul was so insistent on this point that he laid a curse upon anyone who would preach a false gospel about Christ.

> But even if we or an angel from heaven should preach [to you] a gospel other than the one that we preached to you, let that one be accursed! (Gal 1:8)

This leads us to ask, "Who is the correct Christ?" Who indeed is the Christ that Paul preached in the beginning? Paul and the other apostles showed by their teaching that Christ is God and Man. Leaving aside his humanity for a moment, let us ask the question that confuses many initial converts—namely, "How can the Father, Son, and Holy Spirit all be God if there is only one God?" Christ revealed this truth to the apostles, and the apostles handed it on, but Christianity grew into a fuller understanding of this mystery as time went on. Eventually, Christians used the word "Trinity" to describe the communion of three persons that we call God.

We will explore this topic in the way that it developed in the history of the Church. For example, early Christians began to understand something of the Trinity from thinking about Jesus Christ. They asked themselves, "How can he be distinct from and yet united to the Father?" A controversy arose in the early

fourth century about whether Christ was God. The bishops of
the world met in council in 325 in Nicea and formulated a Creed
regarding the divine identity of the Son.[1] They said that the Son
is "of one substance with the Father" and "eternally begotten,
not made."[2] They condemned the belief that the Son was created. Instead, they said that the Son was uncreated and had always been God along with the Father. (The Arian heresy had
depicted the Son as a created super-angel.) But just as a child
must mature in order to explain things better, so it was with
the Church. Before the Church could explain her belief in the
Trinity, she first had to explain what she meant by "the Son of
God." Likewise, our reflection on the Trinity in this chapter
begins with an examination of the divinity of Christ. With the
help of the Scriptures, we will then show how Christians came
to understand the divinity of the Holy Spirit.

Seeing God as a Trinity required a great leap of faith for the
earliest believers who were Jews by birth. For centuries upon
centuries, the Hebrew Scriptures had impressed upon the minds
of the chosen people the oneness of God. God had firmly and
emphatically declared himself the one and only God.

> Hear O Israel! The LORD is our God, the LORD alone! (Dt
> 6:4)

> I, the LORD, am your God, who brought you out of the land
> of Egypt, that place of slavery. You shall not have other gods
> besides me (Ex 20:2–3; cf. Dt 5:7).

> I am the LORD and there is no other,
> there is no God besides me (Is 45:5).

---

[1] "Creed" is from the Latin *credo*, which means, "I believe." The Creed
lists what one must believe in order to be called Christian.

[2] These phrases meant that the Son had always been God along with (but
coming out of) the Father and that Jesus was not a created being like some
sort of super-angel.

Turn to me and be safe,
all you ends of the earth,
for I am God; there is no other! (Is 45:22)

How difficult it must have been for the disciples to understand how Christ could also be God!

Jesus' Miracles, Words, and Actions Point to His Divinity

Whatever difficulties there might have been in understanding, the disciples believed that Jesus was divine because he revealed it to them. Just as the Scriptures make use of different genres and stories, the Lord Jesus also made use of many different ways to reveal that he was God—by his miracles, by his words, and by his actions. When he healed the blind, the deaf, and the lame, Christ was not only showing compassion for the individuals themselves, he was also establishing that he is God. This is why Christ referred to his miraculous deeds when John the Baptizer sent messengers to him to inquire whether he was the Messiah.

> Jesus said to them in reply, "Go and tell John what you hear and see: the blind regain their sight, the lame walk, lepers are cleansed, the deaf hear, the dead are raised, and the poor have the good news proclaimed to them" (Mt 11:4–5).

John recognized that these miracles fulfilled prophecies from the Old Testament:

> Here is your God,
>   he comes to save you.
> Then will the eyes of the blind be opened,
>   the ears of the deaf be cleared;
> Then will the lame leap like a stag,
>   then the tongue of the dumb will sing (Is 35:4–6).

John was probably the first to realize this central truth of Christianity: not only was Jesus the Messiah but also that the Messiah was God!

The healing of the man born blind also pointed to Christ's divinity. Christ could have simply laid hands on the man; instead, he mixed clay and applied it to the man's eyes. This calls to mind the genesis of Adam.

> The Lᴏʀᴅ God formed man out of the clay of the ground and blew into his nostrils the breath of life, and so man became a living being (Gn 2:7).

> "While I am in the world, I am the light of the world." When he had said this, he spat on the ground and made clay with the saliva, and smeared the clay on his eyes, and said to him, "Go wash in the Pool of Siloam" (which means Sent). So he went and washed, and came back able to see (Jn 9:5–7).

Just as God created life from out of the dust, so in this miracle, Christ showed that he possessed the power to restore the fullness of life (which includes sight) from out of mere mud and spittle. That Christ broke the Sabbath by kneading clay enraged the Pharisees, but only because they themselves were blind. Jesus also made use of this event to reveal himself as the fulfillment of God's first great declaration, "Let there be light" (Gn 1:3).

Christ also showed his Divine creative power by raising Lazarus from the dead. Doing this began to fulfill God's statement to Ezekiel that the day would come when God would cause dead bones to rise again.

> Then you shall know that I am the Lᴏʀᴅ, when I open your graves and have you rise from them, O my people! (Ez 37:13)

In raising Lazarus from the dead, Christ demonstrated that he could give life. Like God the Father in Genesis, chapter 9, Jesus is the source of all life.

The many physical acts of healing performed by Christ were also meant to make clear that he had the power to heal our spirits. Not many of us are literally blind, but all of us do have need for our eyes to be opened spiritually, so that we can see one another as God sees us. Likewise, few of us have a hearing problem, but all of us need God's grace to be able to hear his voice when he speaks to us in our hearts. Christ's healing miracles were performed to make it easier for us to believe in his divinity—and his divine capacity to heal our spirits and bring us to true life.

Other wonder miracles performed by Christ offer further scriptural proof that he was God. When Jesus walked on the water, for example, he showed himself worthy of receiving the same praise and honor that the prophets from the Old Testament reserved for God alone.

> He alone stretches out the heavens
> and treads upon the crests of the sea (Jb 9:8).

Furthermore, when Christ calmed the storm, the disciples were in evident amazement as they witnessed Christ perform what could only be understood as an act of God.

> What sort of man is this, whom even the winds and the sea obey? (Mt 8:27)

In each of the Gospels, the calming of the storm was included as proof that Christ was truly divine and that he fulfilled prophecies from the Psalms.

> They cried to the LORD in their distress;
> from their straits he rescued them.
> He hushed the storm to a gentle breeze,
> and the billows of the sea were stilled (Ps 107:28–29).[3]

> You still the roaring of the seas,
> the roaring of their waves and the tumult of the peoples (Ps 65:8).

> You rule over the surging of the sea;
> you still the swelling of its waves (Ps 89:10).

On several occasions, Jesus was able to know the secret thoughts of others.

---

[3] Please see appendix B.

> Now some of the scribes were sitting there asking themselves, "Why does this man speak that way? He is blaspheming. Who but God alone can forgive sins?" Jesus immediately knew in his mind what they were thinking to themselves, so he said, "Why are you thinking such things in your hearts?" (Mk 2:6–8)

Taken in the context of the paralytic's miraculous cure (as well as Jesus' assurance that the man was forgiven of his sins), the scribes should have understood that Jesus was giving them still more proof to believe that he was not just a man. In being able to perceive the secret thoughts of those around him, Christ fulfilled Old Testament depictions of God's omniscience.

> If we had forgotten the name of our God
>   and stretched out our hands to a strange god,
> Would not God have discovered this?
>   For he knows the secrets of the heart (Ps 44:21–22).

> The nether world and the abyss lie open before the LORD;
>   how much more the hearts of men! (Prv 15:11)

> O LORD, you have probed me and you know me;
>   you know when I sit and when I stand;
>   you understand my thoughts from afar.

> Even before a word is on my tongue,
>   behold, O LORD, you know the whole of it (Ps 139:1–2, 4).

Here and in other places, Jesus shows that he can read men's thoughts. But what was the limit of his knowledge as a man? On the one hand, since Jesus is one person, and this person is God, one might be tempted to say that he knew everything. On the other hand, men are limited. If Jesus was truly a man (not just pretending), then he must have had human limitations. Consider the following passages:

> Amen, I say to you, this very night before the cock crows, you will deny me three times (Mt 26:34).

> Seeing a fig tree by the road, he went over to it, but found nothing on it except leaves. And he said to it, "May no fruit ever come from you again" (Mt 21:19).

The first passage shows that Jesus could see into the future when he wanted to; he predicted Peter's betrayal. The second passage implies that Jesus could sometimes be unaware of certain natural facts, such as whether a tree had fruit on it or not. In trying to understand these apparent contradictions, we must follow the lead given by the early Christian councils when they affirmed that Jesus was fully God and fully Man. Though his manhood had the limitations experienced by every human being, Jesus could choose to have his human nature become aware of certain things that only his divine nature could possibly find out (such as Peter's future actions). His choice was not arbitrary; Jesus apprehended all knowledge necessary to fulfill his mission —all that was necessary for our salvation.

There were other times when Jesus denied knowing certain things in order to make a point. For example, he told the apostles that he did not know when the world would end because he wanted them to concentrate on God rather than worldly concerns (Mt 24:36). At other times, he chose not to know certain things in order to relate to us more as fellow human beings. He grew from infancy into youth by learning from his parents as other children did; he did not need to learn this way, but he chose to do so (Lk 2:51, 52). In other words, he waited until the proper time to reveal that he was divine. He began doing this at Cana.

At Cana and at the feeding of the five thousand, Christ demonstrated divine bounty by providing more than what was needed (Jn 2:1–11; Jn 6:1–14). At Cana, Jesus changed an astounding amount of water into wine—between one hundred and two hundred gallons! It was much more than they needed; especially considering that all the wine set aside for the wedding had already been served (Jn 2:3). In performing this miracle, Christ fulfilled prophecies from Amos and Joel that foretold the superabundance of the messianic times.

Yes, days are coming,
   says the LORD,

> The juice of grapes shall drip down the mountains,
>> and all the hills shall run with it (Am 9:13).

> And then, on that day,
>> the mountains shall drip new wine . . . (Jl 4:18).

The miracle of the wine symbolized the gift of the spirit—the new life in God. The superabundance and quality of the wine reflected the fullness of grace and the goodness of God's blessing. The wine also served as a symbol for the blood of Christ that would win redemption for the world. The wine was also a symbol of the wine of Holy Communion.

Jesus also fed the five thousand with five loaves and two fish (Jn 6ff.; Mt 14ff.). This miracle was meant to remind the Jews of the time when God provided them with manna in the desert. It was this miracle that drew the largest crowds and convinced many people that Jesus truly was the Messiah.

> When the people saw the sign he had done, they said, "This is truly the Prophet, the one who is to come into the world." Since Jesus knew that they were going to come and carry him off to make him king, he withdrew again to the mountain alone (Jn 6:14–15).

Christ chose precisely this moment in order to reveal to everyone that he was also God. As we will discuss more in the next chapter, he did this by promising eternal life to everyone who eats his flesh and drinks his blood (Jn 6:48–58).

Since ancient times, it was commonly believed that the blood of all living creatures was where a living thing's spirit was housed. Since death was inevitable once a certain amount of blood was lost, it was considered sacred. Based on this understanding, many pagan peoples would drink the blood of animals (and sometimes of other people) in order to receive extra strength or spiritual power. The Jews, however, were forbidden from consuming any meat that still contained traces of blood. Since the days of Noah, God's people remained faithful to this commandment.

> Every creature that is alive shall be yours to eat; I give them all
> to you as I did the green plants. Only flesh with its lifeblood
> still in it you shall not eat (Gn 9:3–4).

The reason why God strictly forbade the Jews from drinking the
blood of animals was because he wanted them to seek strength
and life from him alone. Therefore, when Christ began declaring publicly at the high point of his popularity that everyone
would have to drink his blood, this statement alone shows that
Christ believed himself to be divine. If Christ had been merely a
man, then the idea of having his disciples drink his blood would
have been a repulsive and decisive act of disobedience against
God's holy law. But since Jesus really was God, then he had every right to offer his blood for the Jews and Gentiles. In fact, to
offer his flesh and blood fulfilled the true meaning behind the
law—namely, that eternal life comes from God alone.

> Amen, amen, I say to you, unless you eat of the flesh of the
> Son of Man and drink his blood, you do not have life within
> you. Whoever eats my flesh and drinks my blood has eternal
> life, and I will raise him on the last day. For my flesh is true
> food, and my blood is true drink (Jn 6:53ff.).

Apart from this dramatic evidence that Christ was conscious
of his divinity, many of his comments and lessons affirm the
same truth. First of all, he revealed himself to be greater than
all the prophets and rulers of the Old Testament.

> At the judgment, the men of Nineveh will arise with this gen-
> eration and condemn it, because they repented at the preach-
> ing of Jonah; and there is something greater than Jonah here
> (Mt 12:41).

> At the judgment the queen of the south will arise with this
> generation and condemn it, because she came from the ends
> of the earth to hear the wisdom of Solomon; and there is some-
> thing greater than Solomon here (Mt 12:42).

Jesus also referred to himself as having a superior rank to that
of the angels. They ministered to him after his forty-day fast,
and in the Garden of Gethsemane, Jesus revealed to the disci-

ples that twelve legions of angels would come to serve him if he were to ask for their help (Mt 4:11; 26:53). Finally, when Jesus described the last judgment, he foretold how the angels would accompany him when he comes to judge the world.

> When the Son of Man comes in his glory, and all the angels with him, he will sit upon his glorious throne, and all the nations will be assembled before him. And he will separate them one from another, as a shepherd separates the sheep from the goats (Mt 25:31).

Such statements could only be made by God.

On other occasions, Christ directly revealed his identity as the Son of God, *who is God*. In his parable of the wicked tenants, for example, Christ reminded the scribes and Pharisees of Israel's ugly history of rejecting prophets of the Lord, and he foretold their own rejection of himself, the only Son of God.

> The owner of the vineyard said, "What shall I do? I shall send my beloved son; maybe they will respect him." But when the tenant farmers saw him they said to one another, "This is the heir. Let us kill him that the inheritance may become ours." So they threw him out of the vineyard and killed him (Lk 20:13–15).

After the chief priests captured Christ and brought him before the Sanhedrin, the high priest adjured Jesus to declare under oath whether or not he was the Messiah and Son of God. Christ spoke plainly and said, "I am" (Mk 14:62). Then, as if to underscore the truth that he was the fulfillment of all the Old Testament prophecies, Jesus stirred the anger of the high priest even further by referring to the prophecy from Daniel.

> and "you will see the Son of Man
> seated at the right hand of the Power
> and coming with the clouds of heaven" (Mk 14:62).

In calling himself "the Son of Man," Christ was implicitly declaring himself to be the fulfillment of Daniel's prophetic vision of the Messiah.

I saw
One like a son of man coming,
　　on the clouds of heaven;
When he reached the Ancient One
　　and was presented before him,
He received dominion, glory, and kingship;
　　nations and peoples of every language serve him.
His dominion is an everlasting dominion
　　that shall not be taken away,
　　his kingship shall not be destroyed (Dn 7:13–14).

The high priest was offended by Jesus' reference to Daniel, because Jesus was using the Scriptures to declare his equality with God. This was not the first time that he had done so. Jesus had already argued with them over the meaning of Psalm 110, where God says to the Messiah, "Sit at my right hand / till I make your enemies your footstool." At that time, Christ had silenced everyone by showing the Messiah in Psalm 110 could not be mere man or "son of David."

> While the Pharisees were gathered together, Jesus questioned them, saying, "What is your opinion about the Messiah? Whose son is he?" They replied, "David's." He said to them, "How then, does David, inspired by the Spirit, call him 'lord,' saying:
>
> > 'The Lord said to my lord,
> > 　"Sit at my right hand
> > until I place your enemies under your feet" '?
>
> If David calls him 'lord,' how can he be his son?" No one was able to answer him a word, nor from that day on did anyone dare to ask him any more questions (Mt 22:41–46).

From this earlier dispute, then, Jesus had proven for the scribes that the Messiah would have to be of divine origin. At his last encounter with the Sanhedrin, Christ reminded them that he was the Messiah who would be seated at God's right hand—and that they were his enemies who would serve as his footstool.

On this point also, Jesus had already warned the scribes and Pharisees when he explained what would happen to those who rejected him. The Gospels of Matthew, Mark, and Luke all mention this earlier encounter, where Jesus had explained the meaning of the Messianic prophecy in Psalm 118.

> But he looked at them and asked, "What then does this scripture passage mean:
>
> > 'The stone which the builders rejected
> > has become the cornerstone?'
>
> Everyone who falls on that stone will be dashed to pieces; and it will crush anyone on whom it falls" (Lk 20:17–20; cf. Ps 118:22; Mt 21:42; Mk 12:10).

In offering up this threatening interpretation of Psalm 118, Christ was drawing from the book of Daniel, where King Nebuchadnezzar is given a vision of the Messiah who is a rock with the power to destroy all earthly kingdoms. Here, it is Daniel offering up the interpretation.

> In your vision, O king, you saw a statue, very large and exceedingly bright. . . . While you looked at the statue, a stone which was hewn from a mountain without a hand being put to it, struck its iron and tile feet, breaking them in pieces. . . . But the stone that struck the statue became a great mountain and filled the whole earth.
> This was the dream; the interpretation we shall also give. . . . In the lifetime of those kings the God of heaven will set up a kingdom that shall never be destroyed or delivered up to another people; rather, it shall break in pieces all these kingdoms and put an end to them, and it shall stand forever (Dn 2:31–36, 44).

Thus, although the high priest tears his clothes when Jesus calls himself the Son of God, Jesus' Messianic claim to divinity was based on the Scriptures. The reference in Daniel to the stone that is "hewn . . . without a hand being put to it" is a prophecy that the Messiah literally will come from God. There are other references as well. The second Psalm, for example, promises a Messianic king who will be a son to God like no other.

> He who is throned in heaven laughs;
>   the LORD derides them.
> Then in anger he speaks to them;
>   he terrifies them in his wrath:
> "I myself have set up my king
> on Zion, my holy mountain."
>
> I will proclaim the decree of the LORD:
>   The LORD said to me, "You are my son;
>   this day I have begotten you" (Ps 2:4–7).

In Psalm 110, God's son is also described as having dwelled with the Father since before the beginning of time.

> Yours is princely power in
>   the day of your birth, in holy
>   splendor;
> before the daystar, like the
>   dew, I have begotten you (Ps 110:3).

Isaiah was another prophet who prophesied that the Messiah would be endowed with divinity:

> For a child is born to us, a son is given us;
>   upon his shoulder dominion rests.
> They name him Wonder-Counselor, God-Hero,
>   Father-Forever, Prince of Peace (Is 9:5).

The divine names that Isaiah attributes to the Messiah ("God-Hero" and "Father-Forever") could not be referring to God the Father, because the prophecy begins with a description of a child, and the rest of the prophecy refers to that child (Is 9:5). Another Messianic prophecy from Isaiah also ascribes to him the divine name of "Immanuel," which translates literally as "God is with us" (Is 7:14; Mt 1:23).

> Therefore the LORD himself will give you a sign: the virgin shall be with child, and bear a son, and shall name him Immanuel (Is 7:14).

Since the Son really did exist with God the Father before the beginning of time, it makes sense that he should claim to be the only one who knows the Father.

> All things have been handed over to me by my Father. No one knows who the Son is except the Father, and who the Father is except the Son and anyone to whom the Son wishes to reveal him (Lk 10:22).

When Jesus claims that no one knows the Son except the Father, he is implicitly declaring that he is infinite like the Father, since only the Father, who is infinite in knowledge, can know the Son in his infinity.

The Gospel of John presents the most insistent case that Christ's sonship is of a divine nature. The Gospel begins with a dramatic declaration of Christ's divine identity and his pre-existence with God in heaven.

> In the beginning was the Word,
>   and the Word was with God,
>   and the Word was God (Jn 1:1).

In saying that the Word was with God, John was explaining that the Son existed side-by-side with the Father, not merely as a part of God or an attribute of God. Rather, the Son was distinct from God the Father, even though he shared in the same divine essence. Again, in one of his epistles, John referred to the son with another divine title.

> No one has ever seen God. The only son, God, who is at the Father's side, has revealed him (Jn 1:18).

Again, we notice a distinction from the Father. Whenever Jesus talks about being "sent" from heaven or having a will separate from the Father's, we also notice the same distinction.

> I will not reject anyone who comes to me, because I came down from heaven not to do my own will but the will of the one who sent me (Jn 6:37–38).

> I came from the Father and have come into the world. Now I am leaving the world and going back to the Father (Jn 16:28).

Now glorify me, Father, with you, with the glory that I had with you before the world began (Jn 17:5).

The early Church did not have an easy time explaining how Christ could be distinct from the Father and yet be one with him. The present concept of a "person" did not even come into existence until the fifth century, when the Church was seeking a better way to talk about the Trinity. Nevertheless, it is clear from John's Gospel that Jesus revealed himself to be both distinct from and yet one with the Father. When Jesus was confronted at his last Feast of the Dedication (called *Hanukkah* in Hebrew), he left no doubt in their minds on this point.

> So the Jews gathered around him and said to him, "How long are you going to keep us in suspense? If you are the Messiah, tell us plainly." Jesus answered them, "I told you and you do not believe. The works I do in my Father's name testify to me. . . . The Father and I are one" (Jn 10:24–25, 30).[4]

Jesus implored the scribes to accept the testimony of his works as proof that he was divine.

> If I do not perform my Father's works, do not believe me; but if I perform them, even if you do not believe me, believe the works, so that you may realize [and understand] that the Father is in me and I am in the Father (Jn 10:37–38).

When the scribes complain about Jesus performing good works on the Sabbath, Jesus defends himself by explaining that, since God does not stop caring and upholding the world even on the Sabbath, neither should the Son of God.

> My Father is at work until now, so I am at work (Jn 5:17).

Jesus' audience obviously understood the point being made, because their response was to try and kill him.

---

[4] Concerning the use of the word "Jews": it should be kept in mind that Jesus, Mary, and all of the apostles were Jews. New Testament writers often used the term "Jews" to designate those of their race who did not believe.

> For this reason the Jews tried all the more to kill him, because he not only broke the sabbath but he also called God his own father, making himself equal to God (Jn 5:18).

Jesus also referred to his pre-existence and essential equality with God in an even more dramatic way by assigning to himself God's most sacred name, I AM (*Yahweh* in Hebrew). This name, which God first revealed to Moses at the burning bush, was so sacred that the Jews never spoke the word or wrote it down in whole. Jesus, a faithful Jew, used this title; he applied it to himself not only once, but several times.

> That is why I told you that you will die in your sins. For if you do not believe that I AM, you will die in your sins (Jn 8:24).

> When you lift up the Son of Man, then you will realize that I AM, and that I do nothing on my own, but I say only what the Father taught me (Jn 8:28).

> Abraham your Father rejoiced to see my day; he saw it and was glad. So the Jews said to him, "You are not yet fifty years old and you have seen Abraham?" Jesus said to them, "Amen, Amen, I say to you, before Abraham came to be, I AM" (Jn 8:56–58).

Again in the Garden of Gethsemane, Jesus referred to himself in the same way.

> Jesus, knowing everything that was going to happen to him, went out and said to them, "Whom are you looking for?" They answered him, "Jesus the Nazorean." He said to them, "I AM." . . . When he said to them, "I AM," they turned away and fell to the ground (Jn 18:4–6).

Finally, John's gospel ends the way it began, with an explicit affirmation of the divinity of Jesus. Thomas was anything but a doubter when he put his finger into the nail marks. He became the first human being to declare clearly and unambiguously, "My Lord and my God!" (Jn 20:28).

Although Jesus left it to his Church to "grow into" a more fully developed understanding of the Trinity, he did translate the fullness of his godhead into terms that would help us to understand his relationship with us. When Christ called himself "the Good Shepherd" and "the Light of the World," he was trying to help us understand how he came into the world as a gift for us from God. As "Good Shepherd," he promised to guide us to his Father, and as "Light of the World," he revealed the truth about God to a fallen world, darkened all the more by sinful living and willful ignorance.

Furthermore, when Christ called himself "the Way, the Truth, and the Life," he was attempting to translate for us how, in his person, he contained the source and summit of everything that is good. For those who think that a certain method or way of living will bring peace of mind (like modern "self-help" books), Jesus says, "I am the method, I am the way." For those who believe that the pursuit of knowledge is what matters most in life, Jesus says, "I am the Truth that matters most." Finally, to those who would pursue health and safety or comfort, Jesus says, "I am the life: whatever you are looking for, you will find it in me." How could a mere man point to himself as the one solution for all the problems of mankind?

The letters in the New Testament also proclaim the good news of the identity of Immanuel, "God with us," and his sacrifice of love for our sake. These letters deal with many problems that the early Christian communities encountered. Surprisingly, the First Letter of John deals with a problem that his gospel had inadvertently aggravated. John had provided such a striking account of Christ's divinity that Gnostic heretics used his gospel to show that Jesus only *appeared* human but was not human at all![5] John's first epistle was written to rebuff their dangerous arguments that threatened to reduce Christ's suffering and death into an illusion. John responded to the Gnostics by showing that, just as love of neighbor and avoidance of sin are signs of

---

[5] This group of sects sprang up in the first century, flourished for a time, but disappeared by about A.D. 500. They denied the humanity of Jesus. They also composed their own scriptures and said that matter was evil.

true Christian living, so also, the humanity of Christ and the Divinity of Christ are signs of true Christian teaching. To deny either one is to teach in the "spirit of the antichrist" (1 Jn 4:3).

> This is how you can know the spirit of God: every spirit that acknowledges Jesus Christ come in the flesh belongs to God, and every spirit that does not acknowledge Jesus does not belong to God (1 Jn 4:2–3).

> Whoever acknowledges that Jesus is the Son of God, God remains in him and he in God (1 Jn 4:15).

Paul made this same point when he wrote to the Colossians about Christ's divinity.

> He is the image of the invisible God,
>   the first-born of all creation.
> For in him were created all things in
>   heaven and on earth,
>   the visible and the invisible. . . .
>   all things were created through him
>   and for him.
> He is before all things,
>   and in him all things hold together. . . .
> He is the beginning, the firstborn from
>   the dead,
>   that in all things he himself might be
>   preeminent.
> For in him all the fullness was pleased
>   to dwell (Col 1:15–19).

The declarations "our great God and savior Jesus Christ" and "Christ God" are commonly used in the Greek Liturgy (the Mass) and other ancient Liturgies. Undoubtedly, these striking passages from the letters of Paul, written in Greek, have had some bearing on the use of these titles for worship:

> To them belong the fathers and out of them, so far as physical descent is concerned, came Christ who is above all, God blessed forever (Rom 9:5).[6]

---

[6] These two passages are from *The New Jerusalem Bible*, ed. Henry Wans-

waiting in hope for the blessing which will come with the appearing of the glory of our great God and Savior Christ Jesus (Ti 2:13).

The letter to the Hebrews takes up the same idea. This letter was intended to inspire Jewish Christians with an exalted understanding of Christ's priesthood. It does this by showing how Christ surpassed the angels and the prophets. It tells that Jesus established a new and perfect priesthood to replace the imperfect levitical priesthood of the Old Covenant. From the opening verses, it is obvious that the writer believed firmly and absolutely in the pre-existence and divinity of Christ.

In these last days, he spoke to us through a son, whom he made heir of all things and through whom he created the universe,

> who is the refulgence of his glory,
>   the very imprint of his being,
> and who sustains all things by his mighty word.
> When he had accomplished purification from sins,
> he took his seat at the right hand of the Majesty on high . . .
>   (Heb 1:2–3).

Hebrews 1:6–8 again ascribes to the Son psalms of praise that refer to God.

But of the Son:
    "Your throne, O God, stands forever and ever . . ."
        (Heb 1:8, cf. Ps 45:7).

Of old you established the earth,
    and the heavens are the work of your hands.
They shall perish but you remain
    though all of them grow old like a garment.
Like clothing you change them, and they are changed,
    but you are the same, and your years have no end
        (Ps 102:26–28).

---

brough (Garden City, N.Y.: Doubleday, 1985). This version better reveals the traditional understanding of the Greek texts quoted here. See appendix B for an explanation.

Finally, at the end of the book of Revelation Christ applies to himself words used by God in the beginning of the book.

> I am the Alpha and the Omega, the first and the last, the beginning and the end (Rv 22:13).

> "I am the Alpha and the Omega," says the Lord God (Rv 1:8).

While many other citations can be given from the Bible to show that Christ is divine, the selections that have been presented above are basic to any discussion on the subject.

The Holy Spirit Is Also God

Even though Jesus revealed himself as God and was believed by his disciples, there is no evidence anywhere in the New Testament that the Oneness of God was ever compromised or questioned. When a young man asks Jesus which commandment is the greatest, Jesus refers him to the great prayer from the book of Deuteronomy.

> Jesus replied, "The first is this: 'Hear, O Israel! The Lord our God is Lord alone! You shall love the Lord your God with all your heart, with all your soul, with all your mind, and with all your strength'" (Mk 12:29–30; cf. Dt 6:4–5).

Nowhere does Jesus ever seek to abolish this belief that God is one. Rather, he reveals the Father, Son, and Spirit to be united as one. He does this without compromising the truth that each "member" of the Trinity is also distinct. He describes the Holy Spirit, for example, as a distinct person with a distinct purpose and mission to accomplish. Jesus calls him an "Advocate" (meaning "helper" or "counselor") and he promises them that the Spirit will speak for them when they are called to witness to the truth.

> When they hand you over, do not worry about how you are to speak or what you are to say. . . . For it will not be you who speak but the Spirit of your Father speaking through you (Mt 10:19–20).

The Holy Spirit's title as "Advocate" shows that he is a unique person of the Trinity—with his own role of teaching, sanctifying, and guiding the Church on earth.

> And I will ask the Father, and he will give you another Advocate to be with you always, the Spirit of truth, which the world cannot accept . . . (Jn 14:16–17).

Jesus refers to the Holy Spirit as "another Advocate" *because he is another person.* Jesus says that he can "hear" and "declare," so the Spirit must be a distinct person, capable of knowing and willing.

> But when he comes, the Spirit of truth, he will guide you to all truth. He will not speak on his own, but he will speak what he hears, and will declare to you the things that are coming (Jn 16:13–14).

This is one of the most important prophecies made by Christ. First, it tells us that the Holy Spirit will instruct and help the Church "grow into" a fuller understanding of the truth with the passing of time. Secondly, this prophecy tells us that the Holy Spirit will never contradict himself. He might inspire and help everyone to love one another and do good works, but he will never inspire someone to believe in a false teaching.

In Jesus' final commandment to the disciples, we have one last saying from him showing that the Holy Spirit is God.

> All power in heaven and on earth has been given to me. Go, therefore, and make disciples of all nations, baptizing them in the name of the Father, and of the Son, and of the holy Spirit, teaching them to observe all that I have commanded you (Mt 28:18–20).

By declaring that all three persons share in the one "name," Christ affirms that Father, Son, and Spirit are God and that God is one.

This was the revelation that Christ gave to the disciples. As difficult as it was to comprehend, the disciples accepted his revelation as the truth. Paul, for example, clearly believed that Jesus was God, and yet he also continued to declare that there is only one God—especially when preaching to the Gentiles.

"There is no God but one" . . . yet for us there is

> one God, the Father,
>> from whom all things are and for whom we exist,
> and one Lord, Jesus Christ,
>> through whom all things are, and through whom we exist (1 Cor 8:4–6).

> For there is one God.
>> There is also one mediator between God and
> the human race,
>> Christ Jesus, himself human,
>> who gave himself as ransom for all (1 Tim 2:5).

I, then, a prisoner for the Lord, urge you to . . . preserve the unity of the spirit though the bond of peace: one body and one Spirit, . . . one Lord, one faith, one baptism; one God and Father of all, who is over all and through all and in all (Ephesians 4:1–4).

Throughout the Scriptures of the New Testament, there is a notable lack of philosophical discussion in regard to the Trinity. There is no place, for example, where Paul poses the question, "How can there be one God if the Father and the Son are both divine?" The word "Trinity" did not come into use until much later.

Instead of philosophizing about the Trinity, the first century disciples simply accepted both propositions that God is one and that the Father, Son, and Holy Spirit are all God. Thus, in regards to the Holy Spirit, the early Church also accepted this revelation and preached it as the solemn truth, while making references to the Holy Spirit in prayer and in blessings. The letters of the New Testament reflect this simplicity.

For the Spirit scrutinizes everything, even the depths of God. . . . No one knows what pertains to God except the Spirit of God (1 Cor 2:10–11).

Do you not know that your body is a temple of the holy Spirit within you, whom you have from God, and that you are not your own? (1 Cor 6:19)

Now the Lord is the Spirit, and where the Spirit of the Lord is, there is freedom (2 Cor 3:17).

The grace of the Lord Jesus Christ and the love of God and the fellowship of the holy Spirit be with all of you (2 Cor 13:13).

. . . in the foreknowledge of God the Father, through sanctification by the Spirit, for obedience and sprinkling with the blood of Jesus Christ: may grace and peace be yours in abundance (1 Pt 1:2).

Know this first of all, that there is no prophecy of scripture that is a matter of personal interpretation, for no prophecy ever came through human will; but rather human beings moved by the holy Spirit spoke under the influence of God (2 Pt 1:20–21).

Explanation of the Trinity

At this point in our discussion, we are ready to return to Church teaching about the actual dogma of the Trinity. First of all, we must acknowledge that no one will ever fully comprehend its mystery. Many early Fathers even shied away from philosophizing about the Trinity, out of respect for the sacredness of this special mystery. As a starting point, then, it might be easier to say what the Trinity is not, rather than what it is. First of all, the Trinity is not one person who puts on different masks for different purposes. Early on, there were some who proposed this false idea (called "Modalism"), by arguing that the Father, Son, and Holy Spirit are all really the same person who operates in different "modes" according to whatever he thinks is most helpful for human beings. The first objection to this idea concerns why God would ever need to wear a "mask" or go about "play-acting" in the first place. Secondly, if the Modalist theory of the Trinity were true, then God would be a liar. The prayers that Jesus offered up to the Father before the disciples and in the Garden of Gethsemane would have been deceitful, as well as Jesus' promise to the disciples that he would send the Advocate (Jn 16:7).

The other condemned theory about the Trinity is that the Father, Son, and Holy Spirit make up three different gods. The Church does not accept that each person of the Trinity is a distinct god. Instead, we believe that the Father, Son, and Holy Spirit are three distinct persons, each fully God, not parts of God. They are not three pieces that make up the whole. Rather, each is fully God. As three persons, however, they are still in relationship with one another: the Son comes from the Father because the Son is "begotten." The creed says that the Son is "eternally begotten, not made, one in being with the Father." Jesus can thus refer to his humanity by saying, "The Father is greater than I," and yet elsewhere say, "The Father and I are one" (Jn 14:28; 10:30). Similarly, the Holy Spirit comes from the Father and the Son. The Holy Spirit proceeds from them and is fully God.

Metaphors help explain what the Trinity might be like. One metaphor is that of a natural spring of water. Imagine water flowing like a fountain out of the ground. The spring is likened to the Son who reveals the hidden Father. When we see the spring, we can say there is water underground. We can know what it is like. This image helps us to comprehend how the Son is continuously begotten and not created at a single time.

The second metaphor is a little better. Imagine a candle flame. We know there is a flame because of the light that it gives off. Without the light, the flame cannot be seen. The light is the expression of the flame just as the Son is the expression (or Word) of the Father. The Holy Spirit can be thought of as the beauty of the candle flame or of the spring of water. Beauty attracts: just as the beauty of the candle attracts us to it, the beauty of the Holy Spirit draws us to God.

The best way to understand the Trinity is to understand Love, because, "God is love" (1 Jn 4:16). We are not talking about love as in, "I love ice cream" (here, love means "want" or "like").

But real "love" is like a mother's love. It is the complete, unconditional giving of self to the other for the sake of the other. It is the going out of one's self, leaving the self behind, making an empty space in the heart of one's being for the other's sake.

In the Trinity, the Father's very nature is to give. In the Father's action of going out of himself, the Son is begotten. The Son is the living "expression" or "Word" of the Father's love. Since God is perfect, he does not need many words to express his being, only one. In addition, because God is perfect, the perfect expression of his being cannot simply be like the image that we see of ourselves in a mirror; that image is lesser than us because it is not living. Rather, the perfect image of the Father's being must also be living and share fully in the divine essence of his being. This is why we say that the Son is the Word of God and the "Word is God." As the Son is continually begotten as the very essence of the Father's love, the Son reciprocates. There is an action of love that flows between them; the Holy Spirit is breathed. The Holy Spirit proceeds by the initial action of the Father, together with the reciprocal action of the Son. The three persons are distinguished only in the manner of their communion, not in any other way. It is possible to say then, that the Father loves, the Son is beloved, and the Spirit is Love.

How beautiful to know that God is not a lonely being.[7] He is more like a family or a society. Most astounding of all is that the Trinity wishes to share communion with us!

The Holy Spirit Binds Us into the Familial Love of the Trinity. A Reflection:

"Because I told you this, grief has filled your hearts. But I tell you the truth, it is better for you that I go. For if I do not go, the Advocate will not come to you. But if I go, I will send him

---

[7] In saying this, we are not trying to imply that God would be "lonely" (i.e., in need of someone) even if he were alone. Instead, we are trying to emphasize the beauty of thinking of God as a loving communion.

to you" (Jn 16:6, 7). This is one of the most mysterious remarks that Jesus made to his apostles. How could it possibly be better for us if Christ "goes away"? Why is it better for us to possess the Advocate?

If Christ had remained on earth as a visible King, he would have ruled over us, but only in an exterior fashion. Our obedience would have come from awe rather than love. Instead, we must accept Christ by employing his grace to love God, to love one another, and to withstand temptation. The presence of the Holy Spirit *within* us makes it possible to take part in this struggle. Thus we become joined to Christ both on the inside and on the outside. The invisible Spirit forms us into members of Christ's body.

Because the Holy Spirit is invisible and therefore hard to grasp, there are a multitude of material images for him in the Scriptures. He is described as the "breath" of God, as wind, fire, water, oil, etc. Each idea helps to reveal something about the mission and the power of the Holy Spirit, but the one single purpose revealed in all of these references is that of sanctification, e.g. making something holy so that it belongs to God. The Holy Spirit is the sanctifier, or dedicator, or animator of whatever he touches. The Holy Spirit assigns each thing its purpose. (After all, the word "Holy" means to "set aside for special use.") For example, in the book of Genesis, God is described as a spirit "hovering" over the waters (or in some translations, as "mighty" or "rushing" wind) (Gn 1:2). God is depicted this way in order to emphasize that all of creation is dedicated to his service.

The Garden of Eden represented man's simple physical communion with God on earth. The Spirit of life that God breathed into Adam and Eve dedicated them to his purpose in the Garden. Man's fall broke his communion with God and clouded his purpose; the Scriptures set forth how God used human history to call mankind back to his former purpose.

God chose the Hebrew people to be his instrument to accomplish this. The Spirit of God sanctified the minds and consciences of his prophets to renew humanity's dedication to God and their commitment to holiness. Just as the Spirit of God hovered over creation, so also the Spirit of God overshadowed the Hebrews as a visible and active presence. God delivered to Moses the Ten Commandments on Mount Sinai. After giving the people three days to prepare themselves, God caused lightning, thunder, and a dense cloud to settle over the mountain, so that everyone was afraid.

> But Moses let the people out of the camp to meet God, and they stationed themselves at the foot of the mountain. Mount Sinai was all wrapped in smoke, for the LORD came down upon it in fire. . . . Then God delivered all these commandments (Ex 19:17–18; 20:1).

The first great "overshadowing" occurred when the Spirit of God hovered over the waters in Genesis. At a second overshadowing, this same Spirit from Genesis settled over Mount Sinai and rededicated creation to God through the giving of the law. Although everyone had been invited by God to stand at the base of the mountain, their sins made them afraid to approach him.

> So they took up a position much farther away and said to Moses, "You speak to us, and we will listen; but let not God speak to us, or we shall die. Moses answered the people, "Do not be afraid, for God has come to you only to test you and put his fear upon you, lest you should sin." Still the people remained at a distance, while Moses approached the cloud where God was (Ex 20:18–21).

The fact that Moses was the only one to ascend the mountain and receive the law was a telltale sign of the Hebrews' unworthiness and inability to dedicate themselves totally to God. This is why God did not dwell in the people themselves, but instead chose to dwell in the Ark of the Covenant (Ex 40:34–38). The dense cloud that continued to overshadow the ark was also a sign that the Ark was wholly sacred to God. The many miracles associated with the Ark served as further signs and reminders of the power and glory of God. It was God's way of saying, "This part of creation belongs to me."

The third great overshadowing occurred at the Annunciation, when the infinite power of the Holy Spirit was made wholly manifest.

> The holy Spirit will come upon you, and the power of the Most High will overshadow you (Lk 1:35).

As we will see in the chapter devoted to Mary, she was the first creature since Adam and Eve to be wholly perfected and consecrated to God, and her relationship to the Holy Spirit was one of perfect obedience and love. For the next thirty years, the Holy Spirit dwelled in all fullness in both Mary and Jesus. During this time, the Holy Spirit was with Jesus, and at his baptism, he descended from heaven in the shape of a dove.

> After Jesus was baptized, he came up from the water and behold, the heavens were opened [for him], and he saw the Spirit of God descending like a dove [and] coming upon him. And a voice came from the heavens, saying, "This is my beloved Son, with whom I am well pleased" (Mt 3:16–17).

The presence of the dove is separate from the voice of the Father, as further evidence for the distinctness of the Spirit within the Trinity. He comes in the form of a dove bringing the promise of new life—like the dove that returned to Noah after the flood. At his baptism, Jesus did not need to be cleansed of any sin; instead, it is Jesus who sanctifies and purifies the baptismal waters. The hovering presence of the Holy Spirit over Jesus (and over the water) is a sign that he had been anointed by the Holy Spirit and had done his first great work.

The Holy Spirit prepares the apostles for their work by anointing them at Pentecost. It is true that the Holy Spirit had descended from heaven many times before (as when he inspired the prophets), but only on a temporary basis. This overshadowing at Pentecost, however, was unique. In the Old Testament, the Holy Spirit had overshadowed a consecrated box or ark, but at Pentecost, the Holy Spirit overshadowed a consecrated *people*, his Church (represented at Pentecost by Mary and the disciples). The reason why the Holy Spirit has never since departed from the Church is because the head of this Church is Jesus. As long as the Spirit dwells in Jesus, the Spirit will always dwell in the Church and in everyone who belongs to Christ.

> Remain in me, as I remain in you. Just as a branch cannot bear fruit on its own unless it remains on the vine, so neither can you unless you remain in me (Jn 15:4).

The Church is the means by which the Holy Spirit is poured out to humanity. She teaches in the name of Christ and administers the sacraments in his place. Some of these sacraments were foreshadowed in the Old Testament. For example, Moses was given special instructions regarding the oil that would be used for anointing.

> With this sacred anointing oil you shall anoint the meeting tent and the ark of the commandments, the table . . . the lampstand . . . and the altar of holocausts. . . . When you have consecrated them, they shall be most sacred; whatever touches them shall be sacred. Aaron and his sons you shall also anoint and consecrate as my priests. To the Israelites you shall say: As sacred anointing oil this shall belong to me throughout your generations (Ex 30:26–31).

The ancients knew nothing about the oxidation of carbon compounds; they only knew that light and heat were somehow "hidden" in oil. Thus, holy oil served as an appropriate symbol for the hidden presence of God in creation. When Moses anointed the priests with holy oil, they were both purified and prepared for a special mission. The Holy Spirit sanctified the water, oil, and fire and then made use of them to sanctify the priests and fill their souls with life and power from God. So it is with the sacraments of the New Testament. Outwardly, a person seems unchanged when he goes to Confession or Communion, but on the inside, his soul is filled with God's life. When the time is right, the light of Christ will shine forth.

Thus, whenever we participate in one of the seven sacraments, we are inviting the Holy Spirit to overshadow us, consecrate us to God, and give us the power to do his will and love as he loves.

The Holy Spirit draws us into the life of the Trinity. The Father, Son, and Spirit are distinct and yet one; the power of the Holy Spirit makes each person distinct and yet one with everyone else. First, each man or woman is anointed by the Spirit for a special place in creation that only he or she can fill, and then everyone is united as one by the Spirit who guides the Church into all truth.

Conclusion

We know that Jesus became man in order to make us one with God. But what does it mean to be united as one within the Trinity? Does it mean that we will all become God? Surely not. We will never be all knowing or all-powerful, and we will never be made into the God of our own universe. Nevertheless, because of the coming of Christ and the Holy Spirit, we can love one another with the same quality and purity as God's love. In other words, *we can love as God loves*. We hope that the coming chapters of this book will show how.

The Early Church Fathers
Speak on the Trinity

St. Ignatius of Antioch (A.D. 110): *Letter to the Ephesians* (v. 1, 42)

For our God, Jesus Christ, was conceived by Mary in accord with God's plan.

Eusebius (A.D. 125–200): *Letter to Diognetus* (v. 1, 98)

[The Father] sent the very Designer and Creator of the universe Himself, through whom He had made the heavens . . . by whom all things were ordered and bounded and placed in subjection: the heavens and the things in the heavens, the earth and the things on the earth, the sea and the things in the sea . . . yes, He it was that He sent to men.

The So-Called Second Letter of Clement to the Corinthians, A.D. 150. (v. 1, 101)

Brethren, we must think of Jesus Christ as God and as the Judge of the living and the dead.

Aristides of Athens in the *Apology*, A.D. 140. (v. 1, 112)

His disciples are called Christians. These are they who, above every people of the earth, have found the truth; for they acknowledge God, the Creator and Maker of all things, in the only-begotten Son and in the Holy Spirit. Other than Him, no god do they worship.

William Jurgens, *The Faith of the Early Fathers, Volumes I, II, and III.* (Collegeville, Minn.: The Liturgical Press, 1979). The first number in parentheses refers to the volume number of Jurgens' books. The second number refers to the reference number of the passage being quoted.

Tatian the Syrian in the *Address to the Greeks*, A.D. 165–175. (v. 1, 160)

We are not playing the fool, you Greeks, nor do we talk nonsense, when we report that God was born in the form of a man.

St. Melito of Sardes in the fragment of *Anastasius of Sinai, the guide*, ch. 13, A.D. 171–190. (v. 1, 189)

It is in no way necessary in dealing with persons of intelligence to adduce the actions of Christ after His Baptism as proof that His soul and His body, His human nature, were like ours, real and not phantasmal. The activities of Christ after His Baptism, and especially His miracles, gave indication and assurance to the world of the Deity hidden in His flesh. Being God and likewise perfect man, He gave positive indications of His two natures: of His Deity, by the miracles during the three years following after his Baptism; of His humanity, in the thirty years which came before His Baptism, during which, by reason of His condition according to the flesh, He concealed the signs of His Deity, although He was the true God existing before the ages.

St. Athanasius in the *Four Letters to Serapion of Thmuis*, A.D. 359. (v. 1, 780)

If the Holy Spirit were a creature, there could be no communion of God with us through Him. On the contrary, we would be joined to a creature, and we would be foreign to the divine nature, as having nothing in common with it. . . . But if by participation in the Spirit we are made partakers in the divine nature, it is insanity for anyone to say that the Spirit has a created nature and not the nature of God. Indeed, this it is whereby those in whom He is, are made divine; and if He makes men divine, it cannot be doubted that His is the nature of God.

St. Damasus I, Pope, in the *Tome of Damasus*, A.D. 382. (v. 1, 910k–910r)

If anyone does not say that the Holy Spirit is truly and properly of the Father, just as the Son, of the divine substance and true God: he is a heretic.

If anyone does not say that the Holy Spirit can do all things, knows all, and is everywhere, just as the Son and the Father: he is a heretic.

If anyone says that the Holy Spirit is a creature, or that He was made by the Son: he is a heretic.

If anyone does not say that the Father made all things, that is, the visible and the invisible, through the Son and the Holy Spirit: he is a heretic.

If anyone does not say of the Father, Son, and Holy Spirit, that there is one godhead, strength, majesty, and power, one glory and dominion, one reign, and one will and truth: he is a heretic.

If anyone does not say that there are three Persons of Father, and of Son, and of the Holy Spirit, equal, always living, embracing all things visible and invisible, ruling all, judging all, giving life to all, making all, and saving all: he is a heretic.

If anyone does not say that the Holy Spirit, just as the Son and the Father, is to be adored by every creature: he is a heretic.

Evagrius of Pontus in the *Dogmatic Letter on the Most Blessed Trinity*, A.D. 399. (v. 2, 914)

You call the Holy Spirit a creature. And every creature is the servant of its creator. . . . But if He is a servant, His holiness is acquired; and anything which acquires its holiness is capable also of evil. It is because the Holy Spirit is holy in substance, however, that He is called the "font of sanctification." The Holy Spirit, therefore, is not a creature. And if not a creature, He is consubstantial with God.

St. Basil the Great in the *Letter to Amphilochius, Bishop of Iconium*, A.D. 376. (v. 2, 926)

Essence and person differ as the general and the specific, as living being and particular man. In the Godhead, therefore, we confess one essence, so as not to give a varying definition of being; but we acknowledge a particularization of person, so that our notion of Father and Son and Holy Spirit may be unconfused and clear. For if we do not consider the separate qualities of each,—I mean paternity, filiation, and sanctification,—but confess God only, from the general concept of existence, we cannot possibly offer a sound explanation of our faith. It is necessary, therefore, to confess our faith by adding the particular to the general. Godhead is general, while paternity is particular. Joining the two, we must say: "I believe in God the Father." Again in our confession of the Son we must do the same, joining the particular to the general, to say: "I believe in God the Son." Likewise in the case of the Holy Spirit we must make our utterance conform to His appellation and say: "I believe also in the Divine Holy Spirit." This we do so that the [divine] unity may be safeguarded throughout by the confession of one Godhead, while the particularization of Persons is confessed in the distinction of the characteristics recognized in each.

St. Gregory of Nazianz in the *In Praise of Hero the Philosopher*, A.D. 370 (v. 2, 983)

The Holy Spirit is truly holy. No other is such, not in the same way; for He is holy not by an acquiring of holiness but because He Himself is Holiness; not more holy at one time and less holy another time; for there is no beginning in time of His being holy, nor will there ever be an end of it.

St. Ambrose of Milan in *The Holy Spirit*, A.D. 381. (v. 2, 1282)

If there is any grace in the water, it is not from the nature of water but from the presence of the Holy Spirit. . . . We were sealed, therefore, with the Spirit by God. For just as we die in Christ in order to be born again, so too we are sealed with the Spirit so that we may be able to possess His splendor and image and grace, which is indeed our spiritual seal. For although it is in our body that we are visibly sealed, it is truly in our heart that we are sealed, so that the Holy Spirit may imprint on us the likeness of His heavenly image.

St. Cyril of Alexandria in the *Tenth Festal Letter*, A.D. 422. (v. 3, 2063)

Sin, therefore, is condemned, put to death first by Christ and now about to be put to death in us, when we receive Him into our own souls by means of faith and the communion of the Spirit, who renders us conformable to Christ, by means, of course, of the quality of sanctification. For the Spirit of Christ our Savior is, as it were, His form, a divine stamp that in some manner leaves its imprint on us.

St. Cyril of Alexandria in the *Treasury of the Holy and Consubstantial Trinity*, A.D. 412. (v. 3, 2080)

If in being sealed by the Holy Spirit we are reshaped to God, how should the Holy Spirit be creature, when through Him the image of the divine essence is stamped on us, making us, making the seals of uncreated nature abide in us? For it is not, I suppose, after the fashion of a painter that the Holy Spirit depicts in us the divine essence, as if He Himself were foreign to it; nor is it in this way that He leads us to likeness with God. No, He who is God and who proceeds from God is invisibly impressed, after the fashion of a seal and as if in wax, on the hearts of those who receive Him through communion and likeness with Himself, painting a man's nature again in the beauty of the Archetype, and displaying the man anew according to the image of God.

Trinity Bible Study —
Scriptures Cited in the Chapter

Gal 1:8—No one can introduce a new Gospel.

Ex 20:2–3; cf. Dt 5:7, Is 45:5, and Is 45:22—There is only one God.

Is 35:4–6 and Mt 11:4–5—Jesus fulfills prophecies about the Messiah being a healer.

Gn 2:7, Gn 1:3, and Jn 9:5–7—Jesus uses clay to recall God's forming man from clay. Also, Jesus shown to be fulfillment of phrase "Let there be light."

Gn 9:5–6, Ez 37:13—God is source of life. Jesus gives life by raising the dead.

Job 9:8, Ps 107:28–29, Ps 65:8, Mk 2:6–8, and Mt 8:27—Jesus, like God of the Old Testament, controls weather and walks on water.

Mt 26:34—Jesus predicts future and reads minds. Here he predicts Peter's betrayal.

Mt 21:19—Jesus, by searching the fig tree, seems not to know that there were no figs.

Mt 24:36—Jesus says that only the Father knows when the end is coming.

Lk 2:51, 52—Jesus chose to grow and learn in the regular human way.

Jn 2:1–11; Jn 6:1–14—At Cana and at the feeding of the 5,000, Jesus provides bountifully.

Jn 2:3—The guests at Cana had already drunk freely.

Am 9:13 and Jl 4:18—Old Testament prophecies about the bounty of Messianic times.

Jn 6:14–15—The people wanted to make Jesus King after seeing these signs.

Jn 6:48–58—Jesus promises life to those who eat his flesh and drink his blood.

Gn 9:3–4—God forbids drinking of blood.

Mt 12:41–42—Jesus claims to be greater than Jonah and greater than Solomon.

Mt 4:11, 26:53—Jesus states that angels would come to help him if he wished it.

Mt 25:31—Jesus says he will judge everyone.

Lk 20:13–15—Parable of the vineyard that was leased out; the son is killed by tenants.

Dn 7:13–14 and Mk 14:62—Jesus tells the High Priest that he is both Messiah and the Son of God; in doing this, he fulfills prophecy from Daniel.

Ps 110 and Mt 22:41–46—Jesus explains meaning of Psalm where Messiah is shown to be a descendant of David yet having more authority than David.

Lk 20:17–20, cf. Ps 118:22; Mt 21:42; Mk 12:10—Jesus claims to be the stone that the builders rejected.

Dn 2:31–36, 44—Prophecy that a stone shall destroy earthly kingdoms and grow into a mountain that fills the whole earth.

Ps 2:4–7, Ps 110:3—Prophecies that show the Messiah as the Son of God.

Is 9:5, Is 7:14—Isaiah predicts that a child born among us by a virgin will become the Messiah and be named "Immanuel."

Lk 10:22—Jesus states he has authority from the Father and can show the Father to us.

Jn 1:1—John's Gospel opens by showing Jesus is God the Word.

Jn 1:18, Jn 6:37–38, Jn 16:28, and Jn 17:5—Jesus states he was always with the Father and will be returning to the Father.

Jn 10:24-25, 30, Jn 10:37–38, Jn 5:17, and Jn 5:18—Jesus states that he and the Father are One.

Jn 8:24, Jn 8:28, Jn 8:56–58, and Jn 18:4–6—Jesus calls himself "Yahweh," or "I AM."

Jn 20:28—Doubting Thomas says "My Lord and my God!"

1 Jn 4:21, Jn 4:15, Col 1:15–20, Rom 9:5, Ti 2:13, Heb 1:2–3, Heb 1:8. cf. Ps 45:7, Ps 102:26–28, Rv 22:12, and Rv 1:8—All of these passages contain explicit statements that show that Jesus Christ is God.

Mk 12:29, 30; cf. Dt 6:4–5—Love of God and neighbor sum up the Law.

Mt 10:19, 20, Jn 14:16, 17, and Jn 16:13–14—Jesus promises to send another Advocate, the Holy Spirit, to guide the Church.

Mt 28:18–20—Jesus commands baptism in the name of the Father, Son, and Holy Spirit.

1 Cor 8:4–6, 1 Tim 2:5, and Eph 4:1–4—These passages show that God is One; there is only one God.

1 Cor 2:10–11, 1 Cor 6:19, 2 Cor 13:13, 1 Pt 1:2, and 2 Pt 1:20–21—These passages show that the Holy Spirit is God; they also show that the Holy Spirit unites us to God and guides us to God.

Jn 14:28 and 10:30—Jesus says that the Father is greater, and then he says that he and the Father are one.

1 Jn 4:16—God is love.

Jn 16:6, 7—Jesus says it is better that he go, so that he can send the Holy Spirit.

Gn 1:2—Holy Spirit is the "mighty wind" over the waters at creation.

Ex 19:17–18 and 20:1; Ex 20:18–21—People frightened of God's awesome presence on the mountain. They want Moses to speak to God, because they are afraid to go near.

Ex 40:34–38 and Lk 1:35—God overshadowed Ark and God overshadowed Mary.

Mt 3:16–17—Holy Spirit present as a dove at Jesus' baptism.

Jn 15:4—Remain in Christ like branches must remain attached to the vine.

Ex 30:26–29—Anointing oil a symbol of the Anointing of the Holy Spirit.

The Eucharist

Why do Catholics walk into an empty church just to pray? After all, why not pray at home? For Catholics, the church is not empty. When the Eucharist[1] is there, God is there. This does not mean that Catholics are returning to the Old Testament worship that took place at the Temple. Jesus definitely ruled this out when he told the Samaritan woman that the day was coming when the proper worship of God was not going to be restricted to the Temple in Jerusalem. Rather, all people everywhere would worship God "in Spirit and truth" (Jn 4:23). What is the difference between Temple worship and the worship of the Eucharist in a Catholic church?

God gave Moses the pattern of the Temple in Exodus chapters 25 and 26.[2] The pattern conveyed two realities. The first reality was that we are separated from God because of sin. The second reality was that God wished to overcome this separation and allow us to return to the happy and innocent union with God that existed in Eden.

Every Christian is familiar with the story of Eden and how man's nature was corrupted when he ate of the forbidden fruit. Christians refer to this event as "the fall." It means that our nature has been marred by evil; we have a tendency to sin. The obvious result is that we cannot be near God. This is why Adam and Eve were cast forth from the garden and unable to eat of the "tree of life." In Genesis, the Tree of Life in Eden is depicted

---

[1] "Eucharist" means "Thanksgiving" and refers to the ritual of blessing that Christ performed upon the bread and wine during his Last Passover. See Luke 22:14–20. By his command, the apostles repeated this action and handed it on as a perpetual practice in the Church.

[2] The Sanctuary that contained the Ark was a tent until Solomon built the Temple based on the same pattern; in this book, we use the words "sanctuary," "tent," or "temple" interchangeably.

as still existing, but the path leading there is closed and guarded by the "cherubim and the fiery revolving sword" (Gn 3:24).[3]

God's instructions to Moses show the way back to unity with God. God's separation from man was represented by the Temple plan: there was an outer meeting tent enclosing an inner section called the "Holy Place." Another area inside the Holy Place was called the "Holy of Holies." In the Holy of Holies was kept the Ark of the Covenant that was overshadowed by the presence of God in the form of a dense cloud. It was forbidden for the people to enter the Holy of Holies because of their sinfulness. The only exception to this was the high priest, who could only enter it once a year, and then only after offering cleansing sin offerings for purification.

Once the Sanctuary was set up, God promised to dwell visibly among his people so long as they chose the law of life:

> I call heaven and earth today to witness against you: I have set before you life and death, the blessing and the curse. Choose life, then, that you and your descendants may live, by loving the LORD, your God, heeding his voice, and holding fast to him (Dt 30:19–20).

> I will take you as my own people, and you shall have me as your God (Ex 6:7).

This model of union with God did not last, however. Even when God dwelled visibly among the Hebrews, they could not live in perfect obedience to his law. They simply could not purify themselves by their own efforts. Instead, they were in need of *a real interior change*. Some five hundred years before Christ, Jeremiah prophesied of the day when God would bring this change about.

> The days are coming, says the LORD, when I will make a new covenant with the house of Israel and the house of Judah. It

---

[3] The cherubim are angels in the presence of God; they were depicted by golden statues on the Ark of the Covenant and are always associated with the throne of God (Ex 25:18 and Rv 4:6–9).

will not be like the covenant I made with their fathers the day I took them by the hand to lead them forth from the land of Egypt; for they broke my covenant and I had to show myself their master, says the Lord. But this is the covenant which I will make with the house of Israel after those days, says the Lord. I will place my law within them, and write it upon their hearts; I will be their God, and they shall be my people. No longer will they have need to teach their friends and kinsmen how to know the Lord. All, from the least to greatest, shall know me, says the Lord, for I will forgive their evildoing and remember their sin no more (Jer 31:31–34).

The Catholic Church teaches and believes that the Eucharist is the real physical and spiritual presence of Jesus Christ. When Adam and Eve ate the fruit from the forbidden tree, they were barred from paradise and from eternal life. When we eat the Eucharist, we can be saved because it is the fruit of the Tree of Life (Rv 2:7). By this fruit, God transforms us from within. We are joined to Christ by our faith expressed in our good works. We begin this new life in Christ at our baptism, and God continues to change and save us from within, nourishing us with the Eucharist so that we might persevere in our faith and good works. Through the Eucharist, God has come within us to dwell rather than dwelling in a Temple of dead stone.

Revelations 22:2 tells us that the Tree of Life has been found again and that its leaves are medicine for us. The way back to Eden has been opened for us: Jesus on the cross is the Tree of Life, and the Eucharist is the medicine by which God draws us back into communion with him.

Christ promised before he died, "And when I am lifted up from the earth, I will draw everyone to myself" (Jn 12:32). We know now what he meant by this prophecy. Christ was planning to offer himself up to God as the slain lamb (cf. Rv 5:6). It is in the form of the Eucharistic "slain lamb" that he draws everyone to himself and into himself. In assuming a hidden form under the appearance of bread and wine, God finally fulfilled his desire to dwell among his people and in his people.

This doctrine is a mystery, because the transformation of bread and wine into flesh and blood cannot be comprehended by human reason. This does not mean, however, that any effort we might make to think about the subject is a waste of time. It does require an act of faith to accept the Church's teaching on the Eucharist. But it helps to know exactly what that teaching is and where it comes from. Once all these teachings are understood, the nature of the mystery surrounding Holy Communion can appear as a truth that contains an inexhaustible fullness of meaning.

First, we believe that the Eucharist is the wellspring of grace around which all of the seven sacraments are oriented.[4] We believe this because the Eucharist is Christ giving himself to the Father on the cross. As such, it is the single greatest prayer that can be made. When we celebrate the Eucharist, we offer ourselves in union with Christ as a sacrifice of love to the heavenly Father. While it is true that anyone can say a prayer from the heart and have communion with God, we believe that God's ultimate goal is to bring about full unity between himself and mankind—and that the celebration of the Eucharist has the greatest power to achieve this purpose. In this mystery, an offering of bread and wine becomes the body and blood of Christ when the priest stands in the person of Christ and speaks for him, saying, "This is my body which will be given up for you" (cf. Mt 26:26). We believe that the bread and wine become Jesus Christ while retaining the appearance of bread and wine. Hence, we say that the bread and wine is no longer bread and wine. It has become the "Real Presence" of Christ. The Eucharist that we receive is the living, resurrected Jesus.

This has been the constant belief of the Church from her beginning—hence the accusations thrown out against early Christians that they were practicing cannibalism.[5] In response to this

---

[4] *Catechism of the Catholic Church* (hereafter CCC), trans. U.S. Catholic Conference, Washington, D.C.: Libreria Editrice Vaticana, 1997).

[5] Karl Keating, *Catholicism and Fundamentalism* (San Francisco: Ignatius

confusion, the Church explains that Jesus is not killed again in the Eucharist but rather gives life to those who receive him in faith. Jesus is present in a sacramental way. At the Last Supper, for example, Christ was present in a natural way (as were the other twelve apostles), but he was also present in a sacramental way (the way that he continues to be at every Mass). Some people question how the body and blood of Jesus can be present in so many different churches at the same time. To answer this concern, we have to look at the way Jesus himself stepped out of space and time when he first declared the doctrine. When our Lord said, "This is my body, which will be given up for you," his apostles probably wondered what he meant. How could he be offering to the disciples his body before it had been offered up on the cross?[6] The only way to make sense of this dilemma is to accept that Jesus somehow meant for this sacrament to extend beyond the ordinary boundaries of space and time.

To understand that the Eucharist can exist throughout space and time also helps to explain why we call our worship service "the sacrifice of the Mass."[7] Some people will ask, "Since Christ died once and for all, then why do you keep sacrificing him at every church service?" In response, we explain that Christ's death on the cross can also be made to extend through space and time. Christ died only once, but he continually offers up this one sacrifice to God through the prayers of the priest, who stands in the person of Christ and re-presents the one, eternal sacrifice to those who are present in the Church. The difference is that it is an unbloody sacrifice. Jesus does not die again. Instead, we are made present to his one sacrifice and we are able to join ourselves to him.

Press, 1988), 251. Christian apologists from the second century, Tertullian and Felix, defended the faith against this pagan misunderstanding.

[6] Jesus' entire life was a sacrificial offering to the Father. In this sense, the cross was the climax of a life-long offering.

[7] The Mass is actually composed of two parts; the Liturgy of the Word and the Liturgy of the Eucharist. It is the Liturgy of the Eucharist that is referred to as a "sacrifice."

How do we know that these teachings are consistent with what Christ taught to the apostles? Is it not possible that Jesus was speaking in metaphors? Did he not often use this method of teaching? For example, when the disciples came to Jesus, telling him, "Rabbi, eat," he said to them, "I have food to eat of which you do not know" (Jn 4:31–32). It turned out that he had been speaking metaphorically about doing the will of God (Jn 4:34). On another occasion, he warned his disciples, "Look out, and beware of the leaven of the Pharisees and Sadducees" (Mt 16:6). When they tried to interpret what he said in a literal way ("It is because we have brought no bread"), he made them to understand that he had been referring to false teachings (Mt 16:7). On both occasions and wherever Christ made use of difficult metaphors, he left no questions from the disciples unanswered.

Something very different happens in John, chapter 6.[8] Jesus performs the multiplication of the loaves and the fishes for the five thousand, who are left in a state of awe and wonder (Jn 6:11–15). He feeds them miraculously as God fed the Hebrews in the desert with manna from heaven (Ex 16). After the people begin proclaiming him to be their Messiah, Jesus warns them that their desire to have him become king is for the wrong reasons. He tells them, "You are looking for me not because you saw signs but because you ate the loaves and were filled" (Jn 6:26). Then he attempts to draw the crowd into a dialogue about a new kind of bread, different from manna, which "comes down from heaven and gives life to the world" (Jn 6:33). Just when the people seem wholly interested in what he has to say ("Sir, give us this bread always"), Jesus surprises them. He declares to the crowd, "I am the bread of life; whoever comes to me will never hunger, and whoever believes in me will never thirst" (Jn 6:34–35).

The people begin to complain and question every statement

---

[8] Many apologists take up this topic. See Frank Chacon and Jim Burnham, *The Beginners Guide to Apologetics* (Farmington, N.M.: San Juan Catholic Seminars, 1994), 8. See also Keating, 234–37.

that he makes from this point on. But instead of explaining to them that their confusion can be cleared up and that he was only speaking in metaphor, Jesus does the opposite. He affirms the teaching even more emphatically.

> Amen, amen, I say to you, unless you eat the flesh of the Son of Man and drink his blood, you do not have life within you. Whoever eats my flesh and drinks my blood has eternal life, and I will raise him on the last day (Jn 6:53–54).

With this statement, Jesus leaves no room for compromise. Some people (both then and now) might try to say that Jesus was referring to his words. Could a person metaphorically "eat the bread" by listening to the Gospel? No. This is ruled out by the fact that Jesus uses the future tense. He says: "The bread that I *will* give is my flesh for the life of the world" (Jn 6:51, emphasis added). At this point, he had been talking to the crowd for days; if his words were meant to be the metaphorical "bread" he was talking about, he obviously would not have referred to it as something he was going to be giving to them in the future.

He hears the people murmuring and ignores them when they complain, "This saying is hard; who can accept it?" (Jn 6:60). Having reached the height of his popularity only a few days before, he lets the crowd walk away over a doctrinal dispute! We can be sure that Jesus stands firm on this issue, because John tells us that from this point on, "Many [of] his disciples returned to their former way of life and no longer accompanied him" (Jn 6:66). Evidently, the only people who do not choose to walk away are the twelve apostles, but even they are put to the test. Jesus asks them, "Do you also want to leave?" (Jn 6:67). Peter is the only one who speaks up. The only answer that he can give is the only one there is to give.

> Master, to whom shall we go? You have the words of eternal life. We have come to believe and are convinced that you are the Holy One of God (Jn 6:67).

Peter does not claim to understand all that Jesus has just said, but he believes nevertheless. When he made that act of faith,

Peter did not have the luxury to consider almost 2000 years of Church teaching or the heroic examples of martyrs and other witnesses who believed. What he did know was that Jesus spoke only the truth and that to reject this new teaching would be to reject Christ himself.

It could be that Jesus privately calmed their concerns about becoming flesh-eating cannibals, but it was not until they had celebrated the Passover Supper that the disciples could understand the full significance of what Jesus meant when he called himself "the bread of life" (Jn 6:35).

Even now, we cannot fully understand the doctrine of the Eucharist except within the context of the Hebrew Passover ritual. It was during this meal that Jesus declared a new covenant between God and his people. In order to understand the Passover, we have to go all the way back to the time of Abraham, almost two thousand years before Christ!

During the time of Abraham and the patriarchs, the Hebrews practiced animal sacrifice as a way to atone for their sins and to offer worship and praise. The animal represented something valuable that would be given up in order to show true repentance. Taking the life of the animal showed both the seriousness of sin and the consequence of sin. Many of the surrounding nations practiced infant sacrifice as their way of making up for sins, but God showed the Hebrews his mercy when he commanded that the life of the animal should be substituted in place of a child.[9] Nevertheless, the life of the animal represented the life of a person, and the transferal of sin was accomplished only when the priest placed his hands upon the head of the animal. Afterward, the iniquities of the people would be atoned for when the animal was slaughtered.

The Feast of the Passover provides one of the most dramatic

---

[9] For example, when God said that the life of the first-born children and animals belonged to him, this meant that Hebrew families were required to go to the temple with their first-born child and sacrifice an animal, as a way of taking the place of the child (cf. Ex 13:11–16).

examples of animal sacrifice practiced by the Israelites (Ex 11–12ff.) The first Passover occurred when God freed the Hebrews from four hundred years of captivity under the Egyptians. This event was called the "Passover," because the Angel of Death "passed over" only those households where the blood of a lamb had been sprinkled over the doorway. In contrast, the Angel did not "pass over" the Egyptian households (who had not participated in the ritual), but instead took the life of every first-born animal and child. Even though the prior plagues showed God's decisive power over the "gods" of Egypt, Pharaoh would not acknowledge that the power of God was real until his own son died on the night of the Passover.[10] Finally he released the Hebrew slaves from their captivity (Ex 12:31–37).

The ritual surrounding the first Passover differed from the typical sacrifice not only because the families had been instructed to sprinkle the blood of the lamb over their lintels and doorposts, but also because they had been instructed to eat the lamb at a special meal.

> That same night they shall eat its roasted flesh with unleavened bread and bitter herbs (Ex 12:8).

Whereas most animals were destroyed or given to the priests as the portion due them, the Passover lamb was the only one that God commanded the people to eat with their families. The sacrificed lamb served not only to atone for their sins so that they might escape from the Angel of death, but it also fortified their bodies so that they could begin their flight from Egypt. The killing of a Passover lamb also differed from most sacrifices because God commanded the Hebrews to have this meal every year.

> This day shall be a memorial feast for you, which all your generations shall celebrate with pilgrimage to the LORD, as a perpetual institution (Ex 12:14).

---

[10] Turning the water of the Nile into blood demonstrated the symbolic slaying of the Nile god Osiris. The darkness demonstrated the symbolic defeat of the Sun-god, Amon-Ra, etc.

The meal was organized so that the event and its meaning could become present and relevant for the younger generation. In the second part of the meal, called the *Haggadah*, the youngest person would phrase his questions to the elder of the group, as if it were the night of the first Passover. For example, the first question, "What makes this night different from all the other nights?" would receive the elder person's response: "Tonight our LORD will set us free from slavery." The ritual not only helped to bind the families together and strengthen their identity as God's holy people, but it also helped remind them of the promise that God made to them when they were still in the land of Egypt.

> I will take you as my own people, and you shall have me as your God. You will know that I, the LORD, am your God when I free you from the labor of the Egyptians and bring you into the land which I swore to give to Abraham, Isaac, and Jacob. I will give it to you as your own possession—I, the LORD! (Ex 6:7–8)

One question worth asking, however, was why God ever permitted his chosen people to suffer under slavery in the first place—let alone for a span of four hundred years. It could be that God let this happen because he wanted the Hebrews to know that they could not gain freedom on their own. God wanted them to depend on him for that. Perhaps the captivity also served as a way to shape the outlook of his people, so that the issues of rebellion, slavery, obedience, and freedom would become the foremost concern in their lives. What we do know is that the Hebrews came to understand their slavery and freedom in a symbolic way. Their life in Egypt meant not only grueling work and humiliation, but it also symbolized the idol-worship and sinful living that the Hebrews had been practicing under the influence of the Egyptians. Similarly, the feast of the Passover came to represent a chance for the Hebrews to "pass over" from their old way of living into a new life with God. The parted water of the Red Sea that closed over the Egyptian charioteers was a sign "in water and blood" of a new birth. The Israelite nation was born, symbolically dying to the sin and slavery that they had left behind in Egypt.

Unfortunately, many Hebrews continued to live under the influence of the Egyptian idols long after they left Egypt. Therefore, instead of bringing the people directly to the Promised Land, God spent forty years with them in the desert so that they would have a chance to detach themselves fully from their past before entering into the Promised Land.

Nevertheless, even when the Hebrews were given the desired land and had divided it up among themselves, they did not completely give up their old ways. As part of their punishment, the Hebrews eventually lost all of the Promised Land to foreigners who conquered them. The Assyrians eliminated the ten tribes of the North; the Chaldeans from Babylon later conquered the South, and then, after the temple had been rebuilt under the Persian King Cyrus, the Greeks and Romans came and conquered the Hebrews once again.

Inspired by the prophets, many Hebrews hoped a "Messiah" would come ("Messiah" meaning "Anointed One"), who would bring them deliverance and political and material prosperity. Christ made it clear that the *true salvation* once promised to the Israelites in Egypt would indeed be won when he died on the cross. It was not the sort of salvation people had come to expect, but it was the one God had intended, and Christ was the one sent to win it for us.

Many at the time of Jesus, however, were like the Hebrew slaves in Egypt: when the Passover was at hand, they were not ready in their hearts to leave Egypt behind. Even though the nation of Israel had been celebrating and contemplating the Feast of the Passover for hundreds of years, they did not realize that the meal contained hidden meaning that would become clear when Jesus gave his life on the cross. They had studied the prophets but remained oblivious to the many pointers that were meant to help them identify the "Messiah" when he came.

While some prophecies pointed to the identity of the Messiah, others pointed to how the Messiah would fulfill the meaning behind the Passover—in other words, how he would make the redemption of mankind possible. An example of this can be found in Isaiah's visions of the suffering servant.

> Yet it was our infirmities that he bore,
>   our sufferings that he endured,
> While we thought of him as stricken,
>   as one smitten by God and afflicted.
> But he was pierced for our offenses,
>   crushed for our sins,
> Upon him was the chastisement that makes us whole,
>   by his stripes we were healed.
> We had all gone astray like sheep,
>   each following his own way;
> But the LORD laid upon him
>   the guilt of us all (Is 53:4–6).

This kind of prophecy shows that the work of the Messiah would be to fulfill the rituals of animal sacrifice. Throughout their history as a nation, the Hebrews had acknowledged that the consequence of sin was death, since sin was a denial of God, who is the source of life. This prophecy shows that the sacrifice of animals was not enough to make up for human sins. After all, the animal's blood cannot truly take away sin but must remain symbolic and await its fulfillment. It would take the sacrifice of the Messiah to do that. And if, prior to the coming of the Messiah, the animal sacrifices had been in any way efficacious, it must have been because they were dependent on the sacrifice of the Messiah—and the fact that God stood outside time and could see Christ's sacrifice coming in the future.

Another prophecy from Psalm 110 foretold that the Messiah would be a priest according to the order of Melchizedek: "The LORD has sworn, and he will not repent: /'You are a priest forever, according to the order of Melchizedek'" (Ps 110:4). In the book of *Genesis*, Melchizedek is described as "a priest of God Most High" who came to Abraham, offered up a sacrifice of bread and wine, and received a tenth of all that Abraham owned (Gn 14:18–20). The letter to the Hebrews draws out the mysterious elements from the Genesis account of Melchizedek: "Without father, mother, or ancestry, without beginning of days or end of life, thus made to resemble the Son of God, he remains a priest forever" (Heb 7:3). The priesthood of Melchizedek was greater than that of the Levites. The levitical priesthood was specific to a time and place (and was dependent upon a bloodline). The priesthood of Melchizedek, however, came before that of the Levites and was outside of time—or in the words of the Psalmist, it lasted "forever" (Ps 110:4). "If, then, perfection came through the levitical priesthood," the author of Hebrews asks, "what need would there still have been for another priest to arise according to the order of Melchizedek . . . ?" (Heb 7:11). The prophecy from Psalm 110 proves that Christ both fulfilled and abolished the need for a levitical priesthood based on animal sacrifice.

> He has no need, as did the high priests, to offer sacrifice day after day, first for his own sins and then for those of the people; he did that once for all when he offered himself (Heb 7:27).

Christ's sacrifice spans beyond the historical moment and is capable of redeeming everyone from the time of Adam until the end of time. To affirm this, the glorified Jesus appears to Thomas with open wounds. Jesus allows Thomas to examine the wounds. Thomas marvels (Jn 20:27–28). Christ's ongoing work of redemption is stressed still more in the book of Revelation (5:6). The heavenly visions mention the victorious "lamb that was slain" numerous times. Likewise, the celebration of the Eucharist as an unbloody sacrifice reflects this belief in the universal time-span of Christ's redemption.

There are still other kinds of prophecies that identify the true Christ—as well as the Real Presence of Christ in the Eucharist. The multiplication of the loaves and the fishes offers one example. By providing the crowd of five thousand with miraculous and superabundant bread, Jesus showed that he had the same authority and power as God, who had fed the Hebrews in the desert with bread from heaven, more than they could eat.

The story about the manna in the desert also serves as a symbol or type for the Eucharist. Like the manna, the Eucharist is more than enough to satisfy the hunger. It comes from heaven, and it is reliable, because one who eats of it will never hunger (cf. Ex 16:4, Jn 6:35).

One last pointer to the Eucharist comes from God's Passover instructions regarding the unleavened bread. Why is it, for example, that God did not simply allow the Hebrews to let their bread rise that evening? After all, they had been slaves for over four hundred years. What difference would a few more hours make? The point was that God accepted no questioning and no excuses. Instead, he demanded an immediate break with Egypt—and immediate, complete faith. Jesus also demanded this wholehearted commitment. He too, said, "No one who sets a hand to the plow and looks to what was left behind is fit for the kingdom of God" (Lk 9:62). St. Paul explains the connection between the unleavened bread and the Eucharist by urging the early Christians, "Let us celebrate the feast, not with the old yeast, the yeast of malice and wickedness, but with the unleavened bread of sincerity and truth" (1 Cor 5:8). With his reference to "the unleavened bread of sincerity and truth," Paul is warning them not to approach the Eucharist with hypocrisy, but instead with total commitment to God without any excuses. He returns to this idea with even more insistence later in the letter and warns them not to bring damnation upon themselves by partaking of the Eucharist when their soul is in a state of sin.

> Therefore whoever eats the bread or drinks the cup of the Lord unworthily will have to answer for the body and blood of the Lord (1 Cor 11:27).

One of the main reasons why the Church asks non-Catholics to refrain from taking communion is because of Paul's warning that, "Anyone who eats and drinks without discerning the body, eats and drinks judgment on himself" (1 Cor 11:29). To partake of the Eucharist "without discerning the body" refers to any situation where the soul is not prepared, such as when one does not know about or believe in the Real Presence of Christ in the Eucharist, or when a person is in a state of mortal sin. In any case, Paul's whole discussion about the Eucharist takes for granted Catholic teaching on the subject. If the Eucharist were only a symbol, then Paul's warnings would sound like nonsense, for how could a person "discern the body" or "drink judgment upon himself" if the body were not present? In a larger context, even the fact that the unleavened bread serves as a "pointer" to the Eucharist confirms our belief that the Eucharist is no mere symbol, for why would a symbol in the Old Testament point to something that is merely another symbol? The Old Testament "pointers" were meant to foreshadow something that would be fulfilled and made real with the coming of the Messiah.

The same could be said about the Old Testament commandments regarding the Passover lamb. They too serve as prophetic pointers to help identify the Messiah. Jesus was sinless and without blemish, just as God said the Passover lambs should be (Ex 12:5, 46). God also commanded the Hebrews not to break the legs of the sacrificed lamb, and this was seen as another pointer to Christ. St. John explains that, after being on the cross for several hours, Jesus was about to have his legs broken so as to hasten his death (Having the legs broken made it impossible for the crucified to breathe). However, when the centurions went up to Jesus, they found that he had already died, and so they did not break his bones (Ex 12:46, Jn 19:31–33). This detail also fulfills a prophecy from the Psalms, "He watches over all his bones; / not one of them shall be broken" (Ps 34:21). Furthermore, during the first Passover, God had commanded the Hebrews to use a branch of hyssop to mark their lintels (the crossbeam of the door) with the blood of the lamb (Ex 12:22). At the scene of the cross John purposely points out that someone raised a branch of hyssop, dipped in common wine, to Jesus on the cross (Jn 19:29). By bringing up this detail, the reader is reminded of the bloodied crossbeams from the first Passover. The Messiah had fulfilled the Passover by becoming the Passover lamb. In the book of Revelation, Jesus is referred to as "the lamb" or "the slain lamb" more than twenty-five times.

While the Gospel of John tries to convince us that Christ was the true lamb by drawing attention to Old Testament prophecy, Matthew conveys the same belief by portraying the Last Supper and the crucifixion as part of the same event. To understand this one must know a little about what the traditional Passover Supper was like.[11] (Today Jews still celebrate variations of this ritual.) The ceremony was divided up into a series of four prayers. Each of these series included a cup of wine, making four cups total. This is the order in which the Passover prayers were done: The opening blessing (or *Kiddush*) was first, concluded by a cup of wine that was passed around for everyone to drink from. The liturgy (*Haggadah*, or "the telling") was second. It included a song from Psalms 113 through 115 (called "the little *Hallel*"). The Haggadah was also concluded with its proper cup of wine. The blessing after the main meal (called "the second *Kiddush*") was third, followed by its cup of wine. Last was the concluding song taken from Psalms 116 through 118 (called the great *Hallel*). The fourth and final cup of wine, called the "Cup of Praise," always followed this concluding song. Drinking the fourth cup of wine signaled the end of the paschal meal. In his account of the Last Supper, Matthew shows how Jesus transformed the Passover feast. First of all, during the third part of the meal, Jesus tells them that the bread is his body and the wine is his blood (Mt 26:26). Secondly, Jesus interrupts the meal by telling the disciples that he will not be drinking the fourth cup that marks the end of the meal.

> I tell you, from now on I shall not drink this fruit of the vine until the day when I drink it with you new in the kingdom of my Father (Mt 26:29).

---

[11] "Passover," *The International Standard Bible Encyclopedia*, ed. G. W. Bromily, vol. 3 (Grand Rapids, Mich: W. B. Eerdman's, 1990), 675–78.

The meal ends abruptly. Matthew points out that, "After singing a hymn [the great *Hallel*], they went out to the Mount of Olives" (Mt 26:30).

From this point on, the "fourth cup" from the Passover ceremony comes to represent the passion of Our Lord. At the Garden of Gethsemane, for example, Jesus prays three times with great anguish, "Let this cup pass from me . . ." (Mt 26:39). When some wine is first offered to him at Golgotha, Jesus refuses to drink it (Mt 27:34). Not until his moment of death does Jesus accept the "fourth cup" and bring an end to the Passover meal.

> And about three o'clock Jesus cried out in a loud voice, *"Eli, Eli, lema sabachthani?"* which means, "My God, my God, why have you forsaken me?" Some of the bystanders who heard it said, "This one is calling for Elijah."[12] Immediately one of them ran to get a sponge; he soaked it in wine, and putting it on a reed, gave it to him to drink. But the rest said, "Wait, let us see if Elijah comes to save him." But Jesus cried out again in a loud voice, and gave up his spirit (Mt 27:46–50).

Jesus, drinking from the wine-soaked sponge while on the cross, concludes the Passover meal, and then dies, definitively connecting the Eucharist of the Last Supper with his own sacrifice as the Lamb of God.[13] By his act of complete self-donating love on the cross, Christ perfectly fulfilled the promises God had made in the past. By dying on the cross, he became the one, true, and eternal Passover lamb that all of the thousands of lambs before him had only symbolized.

The Jews offered Passover lambs for centuries in their liturgical celebrations. Jesus Christ, in the fullness of time, consummated these, thereby establishing the real Passover Liturgy for all of mankind. This is the reason God became man. It is the summit and point of all Creation. The Bible itself concludes

---

[12] Today's Passover celebration includes an empty setting and a cup of wine for Elijah; he is expected to appear (see Mal 3:23) announcing the coming of the Messiah.

[13] The vinegar of Mark 15 and John 19 is "sour wine."

with this theme in the book of Revelation. In Revelation, John uses symbolic imagery to show creation joined in the Eucharistic offering.[14]

First, John was "caught up in spirit" on the Lord's Day (Rv 1:10). It is possible that he went into a prophetic trance during the celebration of the Eucharist. Certainly, he uses symbols and proceedings to recall Jewish ritual and worship at the temple, as well as Christian worship at Mass. Consider some of the following.

The New Jerusalem, God's dwelling, is a perfect cube just as the Holy of Holies in the ancient temple was a perfect cube (Rv 21:16–17; Ez 41:4). There is an altar before the throne of God, corresponding to the altar of holocausts in the temple. There are martyrs underneath the altar, recalling the early Christian practice of saying Mass over the tomb of a saint or martyr (Rv 6:9–11). There were seven lamps in the Temple, and John writes of seven lamps representing the seven Asian churches in one instance and the seven spirits of God in another instance (Ex 25:37; Rv 1:20, 4:5). Clouds of incense are offered, just as in Temple worship (Ex 30:7–10; Rv 8:3–5). There are also traditional liturgical hymns being sung (Rv 4:8). Trumpets are used during key moments, just as was done in the Temple (Rv 8–11). There are readings from scrolls, just as in liturgical worship, both for Christians and for Jews. Jesus Christ, in the form of the Slain Lamb, is the only one found worthy to read the central scroll in Revelation (Rv 5:1–9). By his death and resurrection, the Slain Lamb transforms the Eucharistic celebration into the wedding feast that closes the book of Revelation (Rv 21:2, 3; 22:17).

This wedding feast is Jesus' new and everlasting covenant. In this covenant, Jesus does what only God could do: he transforms

---

[14] Scott Hahn discusses the book of Revelation as a symbolic re-enactment of the Catholic Mass in his book, *The Lamb's Supper* (New York, N.Y.: Doubleday, 1999). Our thanks to Linh Le, one of Dr. Hahn's students, for his help on this portion of the chapter.

simple bread into a new creation. This "new heaven and earth" exists outside of space and time, and everyone is invited to become part of it, in fulfillment of Isaiah's prophecy in which God makes a promise to his suffering servant (cf. Is 65:17; Rv 21:1).

> It is too little, he says, for you to be my servant,
>   to raise up the tribes of Jacob,
>   and restore the survivors of Israel;
> I will make you a light to the nations,
>   that my salvation may reach to the ends of the earth
>   (Is 49:6).

In this covenant, the Promised Land is the body of Christ, given up to God and given back to mankind so that all might partake of the "one loaf" and so become united to God and to each other (1 Cor 10:16–17). Our baptism makes us members of this "new heaven and new earth," and by our Communion we grow into it (cf. Is 65:17, Rv 21:1). Holy Communion is the "daily bread" that gives us what we need to give up our sins and live a new life with God and each other. We might study the Scriptures and hear Jesus himself speak to us, but like the disciples on the road to Emmaus, we will not recognize the true Christ except in the breaking of the bread.

> While he was with them at table, he took bread, said the blessing, broke it, and gave it to them. With that their eyes were opened and they recognized him, but he vanished from their sight (Lk 24:30–31).

It may be difficult to accept the Real Presence of Christ in the Eucharist. But for many, it would be more difficult to turn away if Jesus were to ask, "Do you also want to leave?" (Jn 6:67). When Jesus first spoke about "bread from heaven," he told the crowd only to believe and this bread would be theirs (Jn 6:32ff.) And to this day, when the bread is offered to us, all that Christ asks of us is to say, "Amen."

The Early Church Fathers
on the Eucharist

St. Ignatius of Antioch (A.D. 110): *Letter to the Ephesians* **(v. 1, 43)**

I will send you further doctrinal explanations especially if the Lord should reveal to me that all of you to a man, through grace derived from the Name, join in the common meeting in one faith, and in Jesus Christ, who was of the family of David according to the flesh, the Son of Man and the Son of God, so that you give ear to the bishop and to the presbytery with an undivided mind, breaking one Bread, which is the medicine of immortality, the antidote against death, enabling us to live forever in Jesus Christ.

Letter to the Romans (v. 1, 53a)

I am writing to all the Churches and I enjoin all, that I am dying willingly for God's sake, if only you do not prevent it. I beg of you, do not do me an untimely kindness. Allow me to be eaten by the beasts, which are my way of reaching to God. I am God's wheat, and I am to be ground by the teeth of wild beasts, so that I may become the pure bread of Christ.

Letter to the Smyrneans (v. 1, 64)

Take note of those who hold heterodox opinions on the grace of Jesus Christ that has come to us, and see how contrary their opinions are to the mind of God. For love they have no care, nor for the widow, nor for the orphan, nor for the distressed, nor for those in prison or freed from prison, nor for the hungry and thirsty. They abstain from the Eucharist and from prayer, because they do not confess that the Eucharist is the Flesh of our Savior Jesus Christ, Flesh which suffered for our sins and which the Father, in His goodness, raised up again. They who deny the gift of God are perishing in their disputes. It would be better for them to have love, so that they might rise again.

St. Justin the Martyr (A.D. 100/110–165): *Dialogue with Trypho the Jew* (v. 1, 134b)

The mystery, then of the lamb which God commanded to be sacrificed as the Passover, was a type of Christ. With its blood, by reason of faith in Him, they anoint their own homes, that is, they that believe in Him. . . . The two identical goats which were ordered to be offered during the feast, one of which was the scapegoat and the other for sacrifice, were a proclamation of the two comings of Christ: of the first coming, in which He was sent out as a scapegoat, when the elders of your people and the priests laid hands on Him and put Him to death; and of His second coming, when, in that same place in Jerusalem, you shall recognize Him who was dishonored by you, and who was a sacrificial victim for all sinners who desire to repent.

Didache or the Teaching of the Twelve Apostles (A.D. 140), (v. 1, 6–7)

In regard to the Eucharist—you shall give thanks thus: First, in regard to the cup:—We give you thanks, our Father, for the life and knowledge which you have made known to us through Jesus your Son. Glory be to you forever. As this broken bread was scattered on the mountains, but brought together was made one, so gather your Church from the ends of the earth into your kingdom. For yours is the glory and the power through Jesus Christ forever. Let no one eat or drink of the Eucharist with you except those who have been baptized in the name of the Lord; for it was in reference to this that the Lord said: "Do not give that which is holy to dogs."

After you have eaten your fill, give thanks thus: We thank you, holy Father, for your holy name, which you have caused to dwell in our hearts, and for the knowledge and faith and immortality which you have made known to us through Jesus your Son. Glory be to you forever. You, almighty Master, have created all things for your name's sake and have given food and drink to men for their enjoyment, so that they might return thanks to you. Upon us, however, you have bestowed spiritual food and drink, and eternal life through your Servant.

St. Irenaeus (A.D. 140–202): *Against Heresies* (v. 1, 232)

He taught the new sacrifice of the new covenant, of which Malachias, one of the twelve prophets, had signified beforehand: "You do not do My will," says the Lord Almighty, "and I will not accept a sacrifice at your hands. For from the rising of the sun to its setting My name is glorified among the gentiles, and in every place incense is offered to My name, and a pure sacrifice, for great is My name among the gentiles, says the Lord Almighty." By these words He makes it plain that the former people will cease to make offerings to God; but that in every place sacrifice will be offered to Him, and indeed, a pure one; for His name is glorified among the gentiles.

St. Cyprian of Carthage (A.D. 200/210–258): *Letter of Cyprian to a certain Cecil* (v. 1, 582–83)

We find that the cup that the Lord offered was mixed; and that what was wine, He called Blood. From this it is apparent that the Blood of Christ is not offered if there is no wine in the cup; nor is the Sacrifice of the Lord celebrated with a legitimate consecration unless our offering and sacrifice corresponds to the passion. . . .

I wonder, indeed, whence this practice has come, that, contrary to evangelic and apostolic Tradition, in certain places water alone, which cannot signify the Blood of Christ, is offered in the cup of the Lord. Because Christ bore us all, in that He bore our sins, we see that by the water, people are signified, while in the wine, indeed, the Blood of Christ is shown. And when the water is mixed with the wine in the cup, the people are made one with Christ, and the multitude of believers is coupled and joined to Him in whom it believes.

St. Ephraim (A.D. 306–373): *Homilies* (v. 1, 707)

Do not now regard as bread that which I have given you; but take, eat this Bread, and do not scatter the crumbs; for what

I have called My Body, that it is indeed. One particle from its crumbs is able to sanctify thousands and thousands, and is sufficient to afford life to those who eat of it. Take, eat, entertaining no doubt of faith, because this is My Body, and whoever eats it in belief eats in it Fire and Spirit.

St. Cyril of Jerusalem (A.D. 315–386): *Catechetical Lectures* (v. 1, 843, 845)

This one teaching of the blessed Paul is enough to give you complete certainty about the Divine Mysteries, by your having been deemed worthy of which, you have become united in body and blood with Christ. For Paul proclaimed clearly that: "On the night in which He was betrayed, our Lord Jesus Christ, taking bread and giving thanks, broke it and gave it to His disciples, saying, 'Take, eat, This is My Body.' And taking the cup and giving thanks, He said, 'Take, drink, this is My Blood.'" He himself, therefore, having declared and said of the Bread, "This is My Body," who will dare any longer to doubt? And when He Himself has affirmed and said, "This is My Blood," who can ever hesitate and say it is not His Blood?

Let us, then, with full confidence, partake of the Body and Blood of Christ. For in the figure of bread His Body is given to you, and in the figure of wine His Blood is given to you, so that by partaking of the Body and Blood of Christ, you might become united in body and blood with Him. For thus do we become Christ bearers, His Body and Blood being distributed through our members. And thus it is that we become, according to the blessed Peter, sharers of the divine nature.

St. Ambrose of Milan (A.D. 333/339–397): *The Sacraments* (v. 2, 1339, 1340)

You may perhaps say: "My bread is ordinary." But that bread is bread before the words of the Sacraments; where the consecration has entered in, the bread becomes the flesh of Christ. And let us add this: How can what is bread be the Body of Christ? By the consecration. The consecration takes place by certain words; but whose words? Those of the Lord Jesus. Like all the rest of the things said beforehand, they are said by the priest; praises are referred to God, prayer of petition is offered for the people, for kings, for other persons; but when the time comes for the confection of the venerable Sacrament, then the priest uses not his own words but the words of Christ. Therefore it is the word of Christ that confects this Sacrament. . . . Before it is consecrated it is bread; but where the words of Christ come in, it is the Body of Christ. Finally, hear Him saying: "All of you take and eat of this; for this is My Body." And before the words of Christ the chalice is full of wine and water; but where the words of Christ have been operative it is made the Blood of Christ, which redeems the people.

St. Gregory of Nyssa (A.D. 335–394): *The Great Catechism* (v. 2, 1035)

Since it has been shown that it is not possible for our body to become immortal except it be made participant in incorruption through communion with the Immortal, it is necessary to consider how it is possible for that One Body, though distributed always to so many myriads of the faithful throughout the world, to be whole in its apportionment to each individual, while yet it remains whole in itself. This Body, by the indwelling of God the Word, has been made over to divine dignity. Rightly then, do we believe that the bread consecrated by the word of God has been made over into the Body of God the Word. . . . In the plan of His grace He spreads Himself to every believer by means of that Flesh, the substance of which is from wine and bread, blending Himself with the bodies of believers, so that by this union with the Immortal, man, too, may become a participant in incorruption. These things He bestows through the power of the blessing that transforms the nature of the visible things to that of the immortal.

St. Augustine of Hippo (A.D. 354–430): *Sermons* (v. 3, 1524)

How is the bread His Body? And the chalice, or what is in the chalice, how is it His Blood? Those elements, brethren, are called Sacraments, because in them one thing is seen, but another is understood. What is seen is the corporeal species; but what is understood is the spiritual fruit.

Eucharist Bible Study—
Scriptures Cited in the Chapter

Jn 4:23—People everywhere will worship God in sincerity and truth.

Ex Chapters 25 and 26—God gives Moses the design of the Temple.

Gn 3:24—Cherubim guard the way back to Eden with a "fiery revolving sword."

Dt 30:19–20 and Ex 6:7—God's contract of life and death with the Hebrews and his promise, "I will take you as my own people, and you shall have me as your God."

Ex 25:18 and Rv 4:6–9—Cherubim are angels ministering before God.

Jer 31:31–34—The day when God will write the Law on our hearts.

Rv 22:2—Tree of Life has been found.

Jn 12:32—Jesus on the cross will draw everyone to himself (stretches out his arms).

Rv 5:6—Jesus is the slain lamb.

Mt 26:26—"This is my body."

Jn 4:31–32—"I have food to eat of which you do not know."

Mt 16:6–7 and Mt 16:12—"Beware of the leaven of the Pharisees and Sadducees."

Ex 16 and Jn 6:11–15—Miracle of the loaves and fishes recalls manna of Exodus.

Jn 6:26, Jn 6:32, and Jn 6:34–35—Jesus promises new kind of bread.

Jn 6:53, 54 and Jn 6:51—Jesus promises to give his own flesh and blood in the *future*.

Jn 6:60 and Jn 6:66—Crowd says "This saying is hard; who can accept it?" and many walk away from Jesus, no longer following him.

Jn 6:67—Jesus asks if the apostles also want to leave. Peter says that there is nowhere else to go.

Ex 11–12ff.—Old Testament animal sacrifice.

Ex 12:31–37—The night God freed the Hebrews from slavery in Egypt.

Exodus 12:8—Commandment to keep the Passover.

Exodus 12:14—Passover must be celebrated forever.

Ex 6:7–8—God promises Hebrews the land.

Is 53:4–7—Isaiah prophesies about the suffering servant.

Ps 110:4—Prophecy that the Messiah would be a priest according to the order of Melchizedek.

Gn 14:20—Melchizedek offers bread and wine on behalf of Abraham.

Heb 7:3—Paul hints that Melchizedek may have been Christ.

Heb 7:11 and Ps 110—Order of Melchizedek superior to levitical priesthood.

Heb 7:27—Christ abolishes animal sacrifice.

Rv 5:6 and Jn 20:27—Christ remains the slain lamb in heaven.

Ex 16:4 and Jn 6:35—Those who eat this new bread will not hunger.

Lk 9:62—Anyone who looks back is not fit for the kingdom.

1 Cor 5:8—New feast celebrated with the unleavened bread of sincerity and truth.

1 Cor 11:27 and 1 Cor 11:29—Eating or drinking unworthily makes one guilty of the body and blood of Christ.

Ex 12:5, 46—Passover lamb should be without blemish.

Ex 12:46, Ps 34:21, and Jn 19:31–33—Passover lamb not to have its bones broken.

Ex 12:22—Crossbeam to be smeared with the lamb's blood on hyssop branch.

Jn 19:29—Sour wine given to Christ on cross by using branch of hyssop.

Ps 113—The "little Hallel" of the Jewish Passover.

Ps 114–118—The "great Hallel."

Mt 26:29 and Mt 26:30—Jesus does not drink the cup that closes the Passover of the Last Supper. They sing the Hallel and go to the Mount of Olives.

Mt 26:39—At the Mount of Olives, Jesus prays that he not have to drink the closing cup.

Mt 27:33—When first offered a drink, Jesus refuses because the time had not come yet.

Mt 27:46–50—Jesus drinks the final cup and then dies.

Rv 1:10—John sees a vision on the Lord's Day, possibly during Mass.

Ez 41:4 and Rv 21:16–17—New Jerusalem, God's dwelling, is a perfect cube.

Rv 6:9–11—Masses said over the tombs of martyrs.

Ex 25:37, Rv 1:20, and Rv 4:5—Seven-branched lampstand.

Ex 30:7–10 and Rv 8:3–5—Clouds of incense offered.

Rv 4:8 and Rv 8–11—Liturgical hymns and trumpets.

Rv 5:1–9, Rv 21:2, 3, and Rv 22:17—Slain Lamb invites all to his wedding feast.

Is 65:17 and Rv 21:1—Suffering servant is raised as a light to the nations.

1 Cor 10:16–17—We are one body because we partake of the one bread.

Is 65:17 and Rv 21:1—Baptism and Communion make us part of the New Creation.

Lk 24:30–31—Christ recognized in the breaking of the bread.

Salvation

Are non-Christians saved? Is Christ necessary for salvation?[1] Are works necessary for salvation? Are you saved? Is there any need for salvation at all? These are questions people often wonder about. They are some of the most important questions that could be asked. After all, they have to do with our everlasting destiny.

First we must establish that there is need for salvation. Most people recognize that individuals are deficient and in need of something. No one can say, "I can stand alone and live forever by my own power; I am perfect." Aside from personal sin, the Judeo-Christian tradition recognizes a deficiency in man from the beginning. The Catholic tradition calls this "original sin."

All Christians agree that God loves us. He created us out of love, and he made us in his own image and likeness (Gn 1:26–28). Adam and Eve were in friendship with him. (For the correct interpretation of the book of Genesis please see appendix E.) The only law they had to keep—not to eat of the tree—gave them the capacity to say no to God. This possibility was precious; it distinguished them from the animals because the very ability to reject God is also the ability to love him. In order to love it is also necessary to be free. Love can never be forced. So

---

[1] This chapter addresses the issue of salvation as commonly understood by the laity—both Protestant and Catholic. The chapter does not consider the deeper theological dialogue currently underway between the Catholic Church and our separated brethren. For an example of this dialogue between churches, please see the Lutheran World Federation and the Roman Catholic Church, *Joint Declaration on the Doctrine of Justification* (Grand Rapids, Mich.: Eerdmans, 2000). See also Cardinal Edward Cassidy's press conference statement of June 25, 1998 in *Origins*, July 16, 1998: 128–30, as well as the Official Catholic Response to the draft of the Joint Declaration in the same issue of *Origins*, 130–32.

when they disobeyed the very God who gave them life, Adam and Eve lost the ability to have life with him in heaven, and they ended their life on earth by tasting the bitter fruit of death. They needed to be redeemed.

The evil of sin affects not only the person who sinned, but others as well, sometimes directly, sometimes indirectly. An arsonist damages his personal integrity by burning someone else's house, but the owner and other inhabitants are also affected. The owners lose sentimental possessions that are impossible to replace. The neighbors (and society in general) have to pay more for their insurance. In addition, the natural resources that are wasted would have to be replaced from out of a limited supply. Everyone suffers to some degree from the misdeeds of one person.

The same principle applies to sins that pass down from one generation to the next. Parents who do not raise their children with faith and morals are partly responsible for the misdeeds of their children as adults. A mother who is addicted to drugs passes on the addiction to her child. Likewise, the very nature of Adam and Eve's sin was especially severe because they did not have an inclination to sin as we do. Because of their sin, all of us now suffer from an inclination to do evil even when we know better. When Adam and Eve sinned, they were making a choice for their future and the future of their children. They chose to seek equality with God—the sin of pride. They did not know that the only way of being "equal" with God is to accept the love that only he can offer. Love is the very nature of God. The only way to possess love is to possess God. By love the most humble creature can be raised up to the level of God. Pride has the opposite effect.

Adam and Eve lost their original ability to share in the very nature of God and so did all their descendants. They squandered the inheritance that should have been passed on. From that point on, human beings lived in darkness and confusion, still seeking the good, but attracted to what they knew to be bad and looking forward only to a life of struggle, suffering, and death. Friendship with God was not spoken of or even heard of throughout the human race. Everyone sinned and personally endorsed the sin of Adam and Eve. Although God could still be known, knowledge of what he is like became darkened and confused until he intervened in human history. God revealed himself to the Hebrews. Little by little, he prepared them for the full revelation of himself that would come through his son.

When Christ came, he not only revealed the true nature of God the Father, but he also restored our friendship with God by offering his life in atonement for the sins of Adam and Eve and all of their descendants (Col 2:13–14). The grace that had been lost through the disobedience of Adam was restored through the obedience of Christ (1 Cor 15:21–22). St. Paul describes it this way:

> Just as through one transgression condemnation came upon all, so through one righteous act acquittal and life came to all (Rom 5:18).

St. Peter, the first pope, expressed the same idea when he said that, "There is no salvation in anyone else, nor is there any other name under heaven given to the human race by which we are to be saved" (Acts 4:12). All Christians agree on this point.

Does this mean that non-Christians are all going to hell? Some extremists will say so. Such Christians are actually preaching a falsehood that brings bad news instead of the good news. Concerning the fate of non-Christians, the Catholic Church teaches that,

> Those who, through no fault of their own, do not know the Gospel of Christ or his Church, but who nevertheless seek God with a sincere heart, and, moved by grace, try in their actions to do his will as they know it through the dictates of their conscience—those too may achieve eternal salvation.[2]

How can this be? Doesn't this contradict the belief in the need for Christ? Certainly not! Christ is truth; God is love (Jn 14:6

---

[2] Vatican II, *Lumen Gentium*, Nov. 21, 1964, no. 28, ch. 1, par. 16.

and 1 Jn 4:8). He who seeks truth and has love in his heart has something of Christ. His conscience will be his judge in the end. This is how St. Paul explains the judgment of those who are neither Christians nor Jews.

> For when the Gentiles who do not have the law by nature observe the prescriptions of the law, they are a law for themselves even though they do not have the law. They show that the demands of the law are written in their hearts, while their conscience also bears witness and their conflicting thoughts accuse or even defend them on the day when, according to my gospel, God will judge people's hidden works through Christ Jesus (Rom 2:14–16).

Paul's letter to Timothy also confirms the idea that a nonbeliever can be saved: "We have set our hope on the living God, who is the savior of all, especially of those who believe" (1 Tim 4:10).

So why do we need Christ? Everyone who goes to heaven must go through Christ. This is true even if they never know or believe in him during their life. This is why Paul points to Jesus as the "one mediator between God and / the human race" (1 Tim 2:5). It is true that anyone who rejects Christ will not be saved. Nevertheless, for this to happen, a person has to be conscious of what he is doing. For example, suppose a Christian came up to a tribesman in South America who has never heard of Christ. If the tribesman were immediately told that he must either accept Christ or be damned to eternal fire, his likely response would be to dismiss the Christian in anger and without a hearing. Would that tribesman be rejecting Christ? Of course not! He would be rejecting the messenger for his presumption, pride, and lack of compassion.

At this point, it might seem fair to conclude that God will save the tribesman as long as he does what is good. Not necessarily! There is no amount of doing "good" that can make up for our sins. Salvation is never earned; rather, it is pure grace won for us through the sacrifice of Christ. Yet, saving grace is available to all, for God "wills everyone to be saved" (1 Tim

2:4). This includes non-Christians who have love in their hearts but who, through no fault of their own, do not know Christ by name. Only God knows each person's heart; only he can judge the conscience.

So if the tribesman is to be saved, he must "accept Christ" in some hidden way that involves both faith and love. This mystery means that, for the tribesman or for anyone else, God's grace precedes initial acceptance of the truth. This is what Jesus meant when he said, "It was not you who chose me, but I who chose you and appointed you to go and bear fruit . . ." (Jn 15:16). In his letter to the Ephesians Paul makes the same point.

> But God, who is rich in mercy, because of the great love he had for us, even when we were dead in our transgressions, brought us to life with Christ . . . (Eph 2:4–5).

Not only does God's grace first make it possible to accept the faith, but his grace also makes a person righteous and pleasing in his sight, and therefore acceptable for heaven. The individual has to accept grace, even if he does not understand what grace is. The acceptance of this grace makes us good. Good works done in charity are a manifestation of grace. The main controversy within Christian circles revolves around the relationship between faith and works. How hard must we strive to be holy? How hard must we work to be saved? These are important questions that directly affect the way a person lives. The rest of the chapter will deal with these topics.

The Catholic position is that an authentic response to God's grace necessarily changes a person from within. *If the response is authentic, then God's grace will be made manifest.* An internal experience of God is not enough. A one-time outward response is not enough. Rather, Christ's presence is a living reality, moving and acting in the world, fulfilling the Scripture, "I will live with them and move among them . . ." (2 Cor 6:16). Christ gave a good metaphor describing this kind of relationship when he said, "I am the vine, you are the branches . . ." (Jn 15:5). The presence of Christ cannot be separated from a person's actions.

It is for this reason that Catholics should think of faith and good works as being inextricably bound up with one another, like the two sides of a coin.

Why would Jesus insist on the work—Baptism, for example? (Mk 16:16, 28:19) Those who believe in faith alone continue to baptize out of blind obedience without understanding. Baptism is not merely a symbol or a proclamation of faith. Baptism is the seal of faith and the embodiment of Christ. Infant souls can be baptized into the body of Christ, because their souls are open to God. When filled with his grace, baptized infants make manifest to the world Christ's own infancy. The sacrament of Baptism, like the other sacraments, concretizes the faith. No longer is Christ reduced to an abstract idea in the mind. Rather, he touches us and changes us. He permeates every aspect of our being. His presence in us becomes a wellspring of God's grace, flowing unto the whole body of Christ and into the world. From a pure heart, filled with his grace, we can help the poor, feed the hungry, shelter the homeless, minister to the sick and the lonely, and visit prisoners.

Although many Protestant theologians might agree with the idea that good works flow from God's grace, they would disagree that faith and good works are equally important responses to God's grace. Nor would they agree that faith and works are inseparable. Instead, most Protestants uphold their own doctrine that we are saved by grace alone through faith alone and not by grace alone expressed through our faith and works of love.

The familiar formulation is that, "If you repent of your sins and confess that Jesus Christ is your personal Lord and savior, then you will be saved." God adopts you as his son or daughter so that your inheritance in heaven is guaranteed. Furthermore, the performance of good works that occurs after this initial justification serves merely as a sign that a person has been saved. Salvation, then, is understood as a one-time event: God declares you righteous because of your faith and he covers over your sins with the blood of Jesus. Accordingly, being made holy is thought to be a separate phase that takes place after we have already been saved. (This is how Protestants define sanctification.)[3]

From this perspective, there is no real inner change that has to occur in a person before God will save him. Nor is it required that a person must necessarily become righteous by cooperating with God's grace in overcoming temptation and in doing good works. Instead, God simply declares a person to be righteous, although the sinful nature of the person has not really changed. From the Protestant perspective, neither good works nor an inward transformation is necessary in order to be granted eternal life. Most Protestants believe that they do good because God has commanded them to do so, not because they are afraid of being denied entrance into heaven.

One of the reasons why so many continue to uphold the doctrine of faith alone is because of their concern that the Catholic doctrine of salvation by faith and works leads people to believe that they can earn their way into heaven. Critics cite certain passages from St. Paul as proof that a person is saved by faith alone and not by faith and works. A careful review of Scriptures, however, will show that St. Paul does not always refer to the concept of "works" in the same way. Sometimes, the performance of works is seen as a hindrance to salvation, but other times, Paul makes it clear that God will judge us according to our works.

The only way that this discrepancy can be cleared up is to realize the three ways in which Paul refers to "works." Of these three types, Paul declares two of them to be useless (for salvation) because they stem from our own efforts. The two useless types of works are "works of the law" and works so that "one

---

[3] There are thousands of Protestant denominations; even some that refer to themselves as "non-denominational." Therefore, any general statement about their teaching is bound to be wrong in regards to at least some of them. When we use the word "Protestant" here, we mean the mainline churches descended from Luther, Calvin and Anglicanism.

may boast." We will explain a little about these two useless types of works before moving on to explain about the third, saving type that Paul endorses.

"Works of the Law" are the rituals and observances of Old Testament Law that were fulfilled by the death and resurrection of Christ. Paul criticizes the performance of these "works" because Christ's sacrifice made them unnecessary. In Paul's time, some Hebrew converts to Christ were continuing to follow the prescriptions of the Old Law, and so Paul wrote against them in order to convince them that it is Christ who will save them —and not their adherence to the Old Law. Part of his letter to the Galatians addresses this concern:

> Even we have believed in Christ Jesus that we may be justified by faith in Christ and not by works of the law, because by works of the law no one will be justified (Gal 2:16).

A few verses later in Galatians, Paul even warns that some will be damned for putting their faith in the Old Law rather than in Christ.

> You are separated from Christ, you who are trying to be justified by law; you have fallen from grace. For through the Spirit, by faith, we await the hope of righteousness (Gal 5:4–5).

The second type of useless works are the works done "so as to boast." Paul refers to these in a more general sense that could apply to any kind of good deed. Again, however, the word "works" carries a negative connotation, because in these instances, he is referring to works that are done for the wrong reason, whether for the sake of boasting or in order to earn one's way into heaven. In his letter to the Romans, Paul discusses the conflict between faith and these false "good works" at length. He argues that works performed as a way to earn salvation are of no value. Citing Psalm 14 ("There is not one who does good, not even one"), St. Paul explains that because no one has ever fulfilled God's law perfectly, no one can be justified (Rom 3:12).

No human being will be justified in his sight by observing the law; for through the law comes consciousness of sin (Rom 3:20).

St. Paul then points out that there is, however, a kind of righteousness that can save people when they have faith in Jesus (Rom 3:21–22). From this point, he concludes that whereas no one can boast about being able to save himself, everyone can boast about being saved by faith, because their faith has originated with God and not themselves.

What occasion is there then for boasting? It is ruled out. On what principle, that of works? No, rather on the principle of faith. For we consider that a person is justified by faith apart from works of the law (Rom 3:27–28).

Paul returns to the same critique of works in his letter to the Ephesians. In this passage, he explains that no one can earn saving grace.

For by grace you have been saved through faith, and this is not from you; it is the gift of God; it is not from works, so no one may boast (Eph 2:8–9).

Paul's purpose for writing these verses was to convince the Romans and the Ephesians that they are better off placing their faith in Christ rather than in themselves. His purpose was not to nullify the role of good works altogether. We know this because there are many other occasions in his letters when Paul refers to a third concept of "works" that are performed as an obedient response to God's grace. These works are works of love (charity). These works are completely different from the two useless types mentioned earlier, because these come from God's grace and are dependent on God's grace. We "accept" God's grace in the form of these works in the same way that we accept his grace in the form of faith in Christ. God's grace expressed as faith and God's grace expressed in works of divine love are the two hands by which we hold on to Christ. Since they do not come from our efforts, we do not boast of them.

In his letter to the Galatians, Paul describes the ideal faith not as a passive acceptance of the truth, but as an active response to God: "For in Christ Jesus, neither circumcision nor uncircumcision counts for anything, but only faith working through love" (Gal 5:6). Paul offers similar advice to the Philippians not to rely on faith alone: "Work out your salvation with fear and trembling" (Phil 2:12). Finally, in his letter to the Corinthians, St. Paul insisted on the necessity of works because some of the people were beginning to assume that their belief in Christ automatically assured them of salvation. They felt no need to reform but instead continued to practice the same sins as before. Paul's response was to make it clear that God will judge everyone according to their deeds.

> Do you not know that the unjust will not inherit the kingdom of God? Do not be deceived; neither the fornicators nor idolaters nor adulterers nor boy prostitutes nor sodomites nor thieves nor the greedy nor drunkards nor slanderers nor robbers will inherit the kingdom of God (1 Cor 6:9–10).

Although Paul's teachings have been used to affirm the doctrine of faith alone, it is obvious that Paul himself did not subscribe to this teaching. Neither did the other apostles. St. James, for example, goes through great effort to prevent anyone from dismissing the role that good works play in our salvation.

> What good is it, my brothers, if someone says he has faith but does not have works? Can that faith save him? If a brother or sister has nothing to wear and has no food for the day, and one of you says to them, "Go in peace, keep warm, and eat well," but you do not give them the necessities of the body, what good is it? So also faith of itself, if it does not have works, is dead (Jas 2:14–17).

It has been argued that James wrote about faith and works in order to prevent the faithful from misunderstanding Paul's letter to the Romans.[4] James realized that some of Paul's statements

---

[4] Scholars disagree about whether James' letter predates Romans; we hold

could be read out of context and used to support a "faith alone" doctrine—including Paul's statement, "For we consider that a person is justified by faith apart from works of the law" (Rom 3:28). Similarly, Paul's discussion of Abraham could also be misinterpreted as proof for a "faith alone" doctrine.

> Indeed, if Abraham was justified on the basis of his works, he has reason to boast; but this was not so in the sight of God. For what does the scripture say? "Abraham believed God and it was credited to him as righteousness" (Rom 4:2–3).

When James wrote his epistle, he specifically made mention of Abraham's good works in order to emphasize that a saving response to God involves both faith and works.

> Do you want proof, you ignoramus, that faith without works is useless? Was not Abraham our father justified by works when he offered his son Isaac upon the altar? You see that faith was active along with his works, and faith was completed by the works (Jas 2:20–22).

Paul and James do not contradict one another; they are merely emphasizing two different aspects of the one truth taught by Christ.

On the one hand, Christ demanded faith from his followers and was quick to show praise when he saw any evidence of it —even among the Gentiles. When the centurion approached Christ with his matter-of-fact request, "Only say the word and my servant will be healed," Christ responds to him with amazement: "Amen, I say to you, in no one in Israel have I found such faith" (Mt 8:8, 10). Also to the Canaanite woman who begs Jesus to heal her daughter, Christ declares, "O woman, great is your faith! Let it be done for you as you wish" (Mt 15:28). When he wished to encourage Jairus, the synagogue official whose daugh-

---

that Romans was written first. James' letter was intended as a clarification to ensure that no one could fall into the error of the "Faith Alone" dogma. It is instructive to note that Luther called the book of James an "Epistle of Straw" and argued that it should be taken out of the Bible.

ter had died, Jesus said, "Do not be afraid; just have faith" (Mk 5:36). Again, he encouraged another man whose son was possessed by demons with a similar entreaty: "Everything is possible to one who has faith" (Mk 9:23). Finally, Christ elsewhere appeals to the crowds not to place their faith in material wealth, but rather in God.

> Therefore I tell you, do not worry about your life, what you will eat [or drink], or about your body, what you will wear. . . . All these things the pagans seek. Your heavenly Father knows that you need them all. But seek first the kingdom [of God] and his righteousness, and all these things will be given you besides (Mt 6:25, 32–33).

With his own disciples, Jesus constantly put their faith to the test in matters small and large. He once left them wondering how they would feed a crowd of 5,000 after everyone had just spent three days together at an isolated place in the desert (Jn 6:6). When sending the disciples out to the villages to preach, Christ instructed them, saying, "Carry no money bag, no sack, no sandals; and greet no one along the way," because he wanted them to place their total faith in God (Lk 10:4). Finally, Christ's response to the doubting Thomas shows that true faith is a blessing from God.

> Have you come to believe because you have seen me? Blessed are those who have not seen and have believed (Jn 20:29).

There are many other examples of how acts of faith are required of us.

On the other hand, Christ demanded more than faith. In one of the simplest and strongest statements regarding the issue of faith and works, Christ warned his followers, "Not everyone who says to me, 'Lord, Lord,' will enter the kingdom of heaven, but only the one who does the will of my Father in heaven" (Mt 7:21). From the explanation that followed this warning, Christ made it clear that he would reject as worthless any "faith" or "good works" performed for a selfish reason.

Many will say to me on that day, "Lord, Lord, did we not prophesy in your name? Did we not drive out demons in your name? Did we not do mighty deeds in your name?" Then I will declare to them solemnly, "I never knew you. Depart from me, you evildoers" (Mt 7:22–23).

This teaching goes to the heart of the matter. Some people have "faith" and do "good works" for selfish gain or maybe to pat themselves on the back. But there are others who do good works in such a natural way that they do not even realize or count their deeds. They are completely selfless in their actions; their hearts are full of love:

Then the righteous will answer him and say, "Lord, when did we see you hungry and feed you, or thirsty and give you drink? . . ." And the king will say to them in reply, "Amen, I say to you, whatever you did for one of these least brothers of mine, you did for me" (Mt 25:37, 40).

In both cases, the saved and the damned demonstrated both faith and works! Christ showed us by this parable that faith by itself does not justify and works done without love will come to nothing. Both faith and works are dead without the purity of heart that comes from cooperating with God's grace.

Some people are scrupulous; they are always afraid that they are not doing enough. They are so focused on doing good works that they forget that they are saved by the freely given gift of grace that cannot be earned. On the other hand, some people presume on God's kindness by thinking that they can just say sorry before they die no matter how they lived. They mistakenly assume that their ultimate choice will be different from the habitual decision towards sin that they have been making for years. While it is true that there is hope for a sinner all the way until the moment of death, it is also true that the penitence must be real and heart-felt. Someone who pays lip service and cries, "Lord, Lord" at the end of his or her life should not expect to be acknowledged by Christ. Rather, it is someone who is granted the grace of a real, heart-felt change, like the thief on the cross. One must not assume that a presumptuous, flippant continuance in sin over the course of years will automatically be thrown aside by a few shallow gestures at the moment of death.

Jesus' parable of the ten virgins illustrates well the point that we cannot take salvation for granted. He uses imagery from a Jewish wedding feast. In his time, when there was a wedding feast, the groom would often arrive unexpectedly after all the guests had assembled. Virgins were assigned to announce the arrival of the groom and to escort him into the banquet. In some cases, the groom would appear late in the evening. Consequently, those who waited for him had to be ready with lighted lamps in order to escort him to the feast as soon as he arrived.

> Then the kingdom of heaven will be like ten virgins who took their lamps and went out to meet the bridegroom. Five of them were foolish and five were wise. The foolish ones, when taking their lamps, brought no oil with them, but the wise brought flasks of oil with their lamps (Mt 25:1-4).

First, Jesus called five of the virgins "wise" and five "foolish." The foolish ones can be compared to those who are expecting to gain entrance into the wedding feast of heaven just because they were invited (cf. Rv 19:8). When the bridegroom arrives, they suddenly realize that they are going to need more oil.

> The foolish ones said to the wise, "Give us some of your oil, for our lamps are going out." But the wise ones replied, "No, for there may not be enough for us and you. Go instead to the merchants and buy some for yourselves." While they went off to buy it, the bridegroom came and those who were ready went into the wedding feast with him. Then the door was locked (Mt 25:8-10).

The oil in the parable represents the grace of God that is given only to those who respond to him with faith and good works. The fact that it cannot be shared shows that Christ and the saints can help us, but only up to a point. In the parable, the foolish virgins run off to buy more oil, but it is too late. They come to the door crying, "Lord, Lord," but the bridegroom responds to them by saying, "Amen, I say to you, I do not know you" (Mt 25:11–12).

One of the more unfortunate consequences of accepting the doctrine of faith alone is that the sacrifice of the Mass and the other sacraments lose their importance. In fact, the entire role of the Church and the priests in helping people to attain salvation is downplayed as secondary, if not irrelevant. One could well argue that Martin Luther intended this to happen when he first devised the two doctrines of "faith alone" and "Scripture alone." Unfortunately, Luther did not like the idea of any person or institution having authority over him, so he formulated doctrines that would undermine that authority. His first doctrine of faith alone excluded all actions from playing any role in our salvation, including any participation in the sacraments. In order to defend this doctrine, he translated the Bible into German and changed Paul's letter to the Romans so that one of the verses would read, "For we consider that a person is justified by faith [alone] apart from works of the law" (Romans 3:28, with the word "alone" added). Luther also sought to exclude from his translation the letter of James and many other books of the Bible that had been accepted as part of the canon for more than a thousand years.

Secondly, by declaring his new doctrine of "Bible alone," Luther guaranteed that his "faith alone" doctrine would be reduced to "faith not from the Church." If Luther had only insisted upon the doctrine of "faith alone," then the Church would have continued to serve as the source of that faith. Therefore, in order to deny the Church any role whatsoever in the salvation of souls, Martin Luther coupled the two doctrines of faith alone and Bible alone. Together, the two doctrines served to "liberate" the faithful, so that each could approach the Scriptures as an individual, with an unspoken (*de facto*) guarantee of individual infallibility—as well as a guarantee that they had been saved regardless of how they behaved.

When people accept these teachings about salvation, the goal of sharing eternal life with God can easily become reduced to thinking of heaven merely as a place where we can be happy. The limitations of this kind of thinking become obvious when we remember that Satan was in heaven once and that he wasn't very happy. It is true that heaven is a place of peace, but it is also a state of being perfectly attached to God and perfectly obedient to his holy will.

In contrast to the denominations that undermine the authority (and consequently the unity) of the Church, the true teachings of Christ build up the individual members within the context of the whole body of Christ. Not only does our assent to faith open the doors to the Holy Spirit, but our assent to good works allows the grace of God to form us into the living stones of the one spiritual temple of Christ. When Christ performs good works through us, our hearts and minds undergo a real transformation. First of all, we undergo the painful process of detaching ourselves from sin and attaching ourselves to Christ. St. Paul expressed the nature of this transformation when he said that, "Whoever is in Christ is a new creation . . ." (2 Cor 5:17). Christ often spoke of the difficult conditions of discipleship.

> If anyone wishes to come after me, he must deny himself and take up his cross daily and follow me. For whoever wishes to save his life will lose it, but whoever loses his life for my sake will save it (Lk 9:23–24).

It is true that Christ never promised us that the path to heaven would be painless. What he did promise, however, is that he will be with us along the way. Catholics believe that Christ keeps his promise not only by inspiring us through the Scriptures, but also by imparting his life to us through the sacraments. They enable us to live "hidden with Christ," and the grace we receive from them explains why Paul had the confidence to declare in his letter to the Galatians, "I have been crucified with Christ; yet I live, no longer I, but Christ lives in me . . ." (Col 3:3; Gal 2:19–20). By our sufferings also, God works through us to transform us into the one, true body of Christ. St. Paul describes this mystery of suffering in his letter to the Colossians.

> Now I rejoice in my sufferings for your sake, and in my flesh
> I am filling up what is lacking in the afflictions of Christ on
> behalf of his body, which is the church . . . (Col 1:24).

Paul proclaims that the mystery once "hidden from ages and from generations past," (Col 1:26) has now been made manifest: it is the mystery of "Christ in you" (Col 1:27).

Christ must permeate every aspect of our being so that our every action is his action. Only then can we hope to bring Christ to the world. This is the essence of Christian witness that Christ is among us.

Conclusion: The Law Fulfilled in Jesus Christ

When Jesus was asked what is necessary to obtain eternal life, he answered, "Keep the commandments" (Mt 19:17). Another time, he was asked which is the greatest commandment. He responded by saying that we should love God with all our heart and mind and soul and love our neighbor as ourself (Mk 12:29–31). The refinement of the law, however, was still incomplete. St. John records one final and supreme commandment from Christ: "I give you a new commandment: love one another. As I have loved you, so you also should love one another" (Jn 13:34).

While Jesus focused the entire body of law on a single word —love—he did not abolish all that had been written before his coming. He assured the people that he had come, not to abolish the law, but to fulfill it (Mt 5:17). From this we can conclude that *love* is the fulfillment of the law.

The law of love crystallizes the Christian vocation. Christ told us to love others as he loves us; that means we must lay down our lives for them. In this supreme mandate, our Lord is asking each of us to become *another Christ* in the world. This is possible because of the transforming power of his grace and love at work within us. Through our justification, as adopted sons and daughters of the Father, we are given the gifts of grace necessary to help us conform, more and more, to the mind and heart of Christ. This "laying down of one's life" often takes place, in a figurative but very real sense, in the many daily ways we show charity and forgiveness to others.

Here is a story that helps to illustrate the essence of being transformed by his grace. There once was a musician who played a golden harp that he kept on display in the banquet hall in his house. An enemy broke into his house one night and spitefully broke the harp to pieces. He bent the frame, broke some strings, stretched others, and ruined the entire instrument. When the musician found the damaged harp the next day, he was angry, but he resolved to fix it, no matter what the cost. He set the parts in a storage room, determined that no one should see the harp until he should make it new.

He began his work with the frame. When unbent, it groaned in agony but submitted, out of desire to be restored. The musician then repaired the strings that could be repaired and threw out the ones that could not. By the time the harp was polished, tuned, and adorned with gems, it had become more splendid than ever before. When the harp was ready, the musician invited his friends to a great feast in order to celebrate. Once again he played music for his guests, and his word was rendered into song through the beautiful music of the harp, and everyone rejoiced in it.

What is the point of this story? The point is that when God saves us, he really saves us. We are like the broken pieces of the harp. The harp as a whole is like the Church. Salvation does not mean that he declares broken strings to be perfectly good strings. Salvation does not mean that he takes broken pieces of humanity into his hall (heaven) even though they do not deserve to be there. This is not salvation. God loves us, and he intends to fix us. Fixing us means he will make us perfect, as he is perfect (Mt 5:48). We will be in perfect harmony, both with him and with each other.

Neither is it salvation to think of ourselves as separate "parts" that will be placed in heaven. To be saved means to be joined to Christ. To be joined to Christ means to be part of his body. His body is the Church, and it is not simply a gathering of individual believers. It is ridiculous to think that parts of the harp could be "saved" without having a relationship to the harp as a whole. This would be akin to having the musician display the broken pieces of his harp as idle curiosities. To be related to the whole harp is part and parcel of being saved in the first place. The harmony, love, and beauty shared by the members of the Church with one another are all meant to display the Spirit of God, who is the animating spirit of his body. When they do this, the music of his word reverberates throughout.

The golden harp in this story represents the Church, while the parts of the harp represent us as individuals. In some ways, however, the musician's hall might better represent the Church, since the Church as a whole is God's dwelling. God is building the Church on the foundation laid by his Son, and her story is the subject of the next chapter.

The Early Church Fathers
on Grace and Baptism

Hermas (A.D. 140–155): *The Shepherd* (v. 1, 92)

They had need to come up through the waters, that they might be made alive; for they could not otherwise enter into the kingdom of God, except by putting away the mortality of their former life. These also, then, who had fallen asleep, received the seal of the Son of God, and entered into the kingdom of God. For before a man bears the name of the Son of God, he is dead. But when he received the seal, he puts mortality aside and again receives life. The seal, therefore, is the water. They go down into the water dead, and come out of it alive.

St. Irenaeus (A.D. 140–202): *Against Heresies* (v. 1, 220)

The Lord promised to send us the Paraclete, who would make us ready for God. Just as dry wheat without moisture cannot become one dough or one loaf, so also, we who are many cannot be made one in Christ Jesus, without the water from Heaven. Just as dry earth cannot bring forth fruit unto life, without the voluntary rain from above. Our bodies achieve unity through the washing which leads to incorruption; our souls, however, through the Spirit. Both, then, are necessary, for both lead us on to the life of God.

Arnobius of Sicca (A.D. 327): *Against the Pagans* (v. 1, 622)

But if Christ came as the Preserver of the human race, why does He not, with equal kindness, free all without exception? Well, does He not free all alike, when He calls all alike? or does He repel and thrust anyone away from the supreme benevolence, when He gives to all alike the power of coming to him—to men of rank, to common folk, to slaves, to women and boys? The fountain of life is open to all; nor is anyone turned away or denied the right to drink. If you are so fastidious as to spurn the kindness of the offered gift—nay, if you are of such superior wisdom that you term what Christ offers ridiculous and absurd, why should He keep on inviting you, when it is but His part to expose the fruit of His bounty to your own free choice? Plato says that God is not the cause of any man's choosing his lot in life; nor can anyone's will be rightly imputed to another, since the freedom of will is placed within the power of every one who wills.

Aphrahat the Persian Sage (A.D. 280–345): *Treatises* (v. 1, 699)

For great is the gift which He that is good has given to us. While not forcing us, and in spite of our sins, He wants us to be justified; and while He is in no way aided by our good works, He heals us that we may be pleasing in His sight. When we do not wish to ask of Him, He is angry with us. He calls out to all of us constantly. "Ask and receive; and when you seek, you shall find."

St. Cyril of Jerusalem (A.D. 315–386): *Catechetical Lectures* (v. 1, 808)

Just as those who are conscripting soldiers examine the age and physical condition of those being drafted, so also the Lord in enlisting souls examines their dispositions. If anyone harbors hypocrisy even in secret, He rejects that man as unfit for true service. But whoever is found worthy, to him he readily gives His grace. Holy things he does not give to dogs; but where he perceives a good conscience, there He gives the wondrous and salvific seal, at which demons tremble and which angels recognize. Thus are the former put to flight, while the latter gather about it, as something pertaining to themselves. They, then, who receive this spiritual and saving seal require also the dispositions pertaining to it. Just as a writing-pen or a dart has need of one to employ it, so also does grace have need of believing hearts. . . . It is God's part to confer grace, but yours to accept and guard it. Do not, therefore, spurn grace, because it is freely given; but having received it, guard it religiously.

The Church Fathers on
Justification and Sanctification

St. Justin Martyr (A.D. 100/110–165): *Dialogue with Trypho the Jew* (v. 1, 146)

If they repent, all who desire it will be able to obtain mercy from God. Scripture foretells that they shall be blessed, saying, "Blessed is he to whom the Lord imputes not sin." It means one who has repented of his sins, so that he might receive from God the remission of sins, and not, as you and some like you in this deceive yourselves, saying that though they be sinners, since they acknowledge God, the Lord will not impute sin to them.

St. Clement of Alexandria (A.D. 150–211/216): *The Instructor of Children* (v. 1, 412)

But that man in whom reason dwells is not shifty, not pretentious, but has the form dictated by reason and is like God. He is beautiful, and does not feign beauty. That which is true is beautiful; for it too, is God. Such a man becomes God because God wills it. Rightly, indeed, did Heraclitus say: "Men are gods, and gods are men; for the same reason is in both." That this is a mystery is clear: God is in a man, and a man is God, the Mediator fulfilling the will of the Father. The Mediator is the Word who is common to both, being the Son of God and the Savior of men.

Novatian (A.D. 251–258): *The Trinity* (v. 1, 607)

It is the Holy Spirit that effects with water a second birth. He is a kind of seed of divine generation and the consecrator of Heavenly birth, the pledge of a promised inheritance, and, as it were, a kind of surety bond of eternal salvation. It is He that can make of us a temple of God, and can complete us as His house; He that can accost the divine ears for us with unutterable groaning, fulfilling the duties of advocate and performing the functions of defense; He, that is an inhabitant given to our bodies, and a worker of holiness.

St. Methodius of Philippi (A.D. 311) *Against the Pagans* (v. 1, 613)

The illuminated take on the features and the image and the manliness of Christ. The likeness of the form of the Word is stamped upon them; and it is produced in them through sure knowledge of faith. Thus, Christ is born spiritually in each one. It is for this reason that the church swells and travails in birth until Christ is formed in us, as if it were that each of the saints, by partaking of Christ, were born a Christ. It is in this sense that it is said somewhere in Scripture, "Touch not my christs, and work no wickedness on my prophets" [Ps 105:15] those who are baptized in Christ become, as it were, other Christs, through a communication of the Spirit.

St. Athanasius (A.D. 295–373): *Discourses Against the Arians* (v. 1, 766)

God's love of man is such that to those for whom first He is the Creator, He afterwards, according to grace, becomes a Father also. The latter He does when men, who are His creature, receive into their hearts, as the Apostle says, the Spirit of His Son, crying, "Abba, Father." It is these who, by their having received the Word, have gained from Him the power to become the children of God; for, being creature by nature, they could not otherwise become sons than by receiving the Spirit of the natural and true Son. To bring this about, therefore, the Word became flesh—so that He might make man capable of divinity.

St. Cyril of Jerusalem (A.D. 315–386): *Catechetical Lectures* (v. 1, 813)

And if your piety is unfeigned, the Holy Spirit will come down upon you also, and from on high a paternal voice will sound over you, not, "This is My Son," but "This is now become My son." The "is" belongs to him alone, because "In the beginning was the Word, and the Word was with God, and the Word was God." To him belongs the "is", because always the Son of God he is. To you belongs the "is now become", because you have sonship not by nature, but have received it by adoption.

The Early Church Fathers
on Faith and Works

Pope St. Clement of Rome (A.D. 92–101): *Letter to the Corinthians* (v. 1, 16)

We, therefore, who have been called by His will in Christ Jesus, are not justified by ourselves, neither by our wisdom or understanding or piety, nor by the works we have wrought in holiness of heart, but by the faith by which almighty God has justified all men from the beginning. . . . What, then, shall we do brethren? Shall we cease from good works, and shall we put an end to love? May the Master forbid that such should ever happen among us; rather, let us be eager to perform every good work earnestly and willingly.

St. Irenaeus of Lyons (A.D. 140–202): *Against Heresies* (v. 1, 253)

Those men who are not bringing forth fruits of righteousness, being covered as it were by thorn bushes, if they observe diligence and receive the Word of God as if grafted on them, they will arrive at the pristine nature of men—that which was made in the image and likeness of God. . . . So when a man has been grafted through faith and receives the Spirit of God, certainly he does not lose the substance of flesh, but changes the quality of the fruit of his works and receives another name, signifying that which is a change for the better. He is no longer merely flesh and blood, but is a spiritual man and is called such.

(v. 1, 219)

Therefore He did also descend upon the Son of God made Son

of man, becoming accustomed with Him to dwell among the human race, to rest with men, to dwell in the workmanship of God, working the will of the Father in them, and renewing them from their old ways into the newness of Christ.

St. John Chrysostom (A.D. 344–407): *Homilies on the Epistle to the Hebrews* (v. 2, 1219)

Everything depends upon God, but not so as to hinder our free will. "But if it depends on God," someone will say, "why does He blame us." . . . It depends upon us and upon Him. We first must choose the good, and when we have chosen, then does He provide that which is His part. He does not anticipate our choice, lest violence be done to our free will. But when we have chosen, then great is the assistance He provides. . . . Even should you run, even should you strive earnestly, he says do not suppose that the good result is yours. For if you had not crucial help from above, all were in vain. It is perfectly clear, however, that with that help you will achieve what you earnestly strive for, so long as you also run, and so long as you will.

St. Ambrose of Milan (A.D. 333–397): *Commentary on the Gospel of Luke* (v. 2, 1302)

Fear the Lord and be confident in the Lord. . . . You see indeed, then, the strength of the Lord is cooperative in human endeavors, so that no one can build without the Lord, no one can preserve without the Lord, no one can undertake anything without the Lord.

St. Augustine of Hippo (A.D. 354–430): *Explanation of the Epistle to the Galatians* (v. 3, 1569)

In many passages (Paul) often bears witness to this, putting the grace of faith before works, not as if he wanted to put an end to works, but so as to show that works are the consequences rather than the precedents of grace. Thus, no man is to suppose that he has received grace because he has done good works but rather that he would not have been able to do those good works if he had not, through faith, received grace.

Salvation Bible Study—
Scriptures Cited in the Chapter

Gn 1:26–28—We are made in God's image.

Col 2:13–14, Rom 5:18, and 1 Cor 15:21–22—Jesus offered obedience to undo Adam's disobedience.

Acts 4:12—No salvation in anyone other than Christ.

Jn 14:6 and 1 Jn 4:8—Christ is Truth; God is Love.

Rom 2:14–16—Gentiles who do not know God still will be judged by their conscience.

1 Tim 4:10—Hint that Christ saves some who are not explicitly Christian: "savior of all, especially of those who believe."

1 Tim 2:5—One mediator between God and the human race.

1 Tim 2:4—God wills everyone to be saved.

Jn 15:16—"It was not you who chose me, but I who chose you."

Eph 2:4–5—Christ died for us while we were still sinners.

2 Cor 6:16—"I will live with them and move among them."

Jn 15:5—"I am the vine, you are the branches."

Mk 16:16 and Mt 28:19—Jesus insists on baptism as necessary for salvation.

Gal 2:16, Gal 5:4–5, Rom 3:20, Rom 3:27–28, and Eph 2:8–9 —Justification by faith, not works of the Law.

Rom 3:12—"There is not one who does good, / [there is not] even one."

Rom 3:21–22—There is a kind of righteousness that can save people when they have faith in Christ.

Gal 5:6—True faith works through love.

Phil 2:12—"Work out your salvation with fear and trembling."

1 Cor 6:9–10—Paul's warning that believers who practice immorality will not be saved.

Jas 2:14–17—Faith without works does not save because it is dead.

Rom 4:2–3 and Jas 2:20–22—Paul presents Abraham's faith as justification. James agrees but also says that Abraham's works justified him by completing his faith.

Mk 5:36 and Mt 15:28—Christ tells centurion and Canaanite woman that he has not found such faith in Israel.

Mk 9:23—Everything is possible for one who has faith.

Mt 6:32—"Seek first the kingdom [of God] . . . and all these things will be given you besides."

Jn 6:6—Tested the apostles' faith by asking them to feed the 5,000.

Lk 10:4—Sent the disciples out with no money, sack, or sandals.

Jn 20:29—Tells doubting Thomas: "Blessed are those who have not seen and have believed."

Mt 7:21—"Not everyone who says to me 'Lord, Lord!' will enter the kingdom of heaven. . . ."

Mt 25:37, 40—Those who have done works of charity (love) will be saved.

Mt 25:1–4 and Mt 25:8–10—Foolish virgins are like those who do not do good works.

Rom 3:28, with the word "alone" added—Luther changed this text by adding the word "alone" to his German translation.

2 Cor 5:17—"Whoever is in Christ is a new creation."

Lk 9:23–24—The followers of Christ must take up their cross daily.

Col 3:3 and Gal 2:20—We must be crucified with Christ if he is to live in us.

Col 1:24—Paul says he is filling up what is lacking in Christ's afflictions on behalf of Christ's body.

Col 1:27—The mystery of "Christ in you."

Mt 19:17 and Mk 12:29–31—Love of God and neighbor fulfills the Law.

Jn 13:34—Love one another as the New Commandment.

Mt 5:17—Christ came not to abolish the Law, but to fulfill it.

Mt 5:48—Christ will make us perfect, as he is perfect.

The Church

"She was created the first of all things . . . it was for her sake that the world was established."[1] So wrote Hermas, a revered second century Christian who had a vision concerning the Church. To understand this profound teaching is to grasp the essence of what the Church is! Still more astounding is the discovery that the whole of Scripture expounds on this theme.

People are often confused when they read the Bible for the first time. Most of us are not serious scholars of history or of ancient languages, and yet we are faced with a Bible that was written over a span of hundreds of years, in foreign languages, describing history and cultures alien to the modern mind. Because we are not familiar with this background, reading the Bible can be interesting but difficult to understand. Some stories might move us to reflect on events in our own lives, but once we notice the overarching theme of the Church, then we have found the path that helps make sense of the whole. Suddenly the Bible comes alive in a new and exciting way. Every line speaks to us of mysteries unfathomable yet enriching far beyond our needs.

The Church is everywhere we look, from the book of Genesis to the book of Revelation. Before Christ established her visibly, she already existed, since in the beginning (before the fall) the Church and creation were one and the same. When God created the universe, he intended that his creation would come to him in a covenant of love.[2] His creation was to be in harmony with him. God saw that it was good (Gn 1:31). He rested. This action of "resting" is in relation to his creation, since God does not need to rest and must continuously uphold the universe in

---

[1] Jurgens, v. 1, 82.
[2] A covenant is a kind of contractual agreement that forms an unbreakable family bond.

existence (Jn 5:17). The fact that he "rested" tells us the kind of relationship that God had with his creation. What kind of relationship did God intend it to be? The "rest" shared by God with his creation was meant to be that of spouses taking joy in one another's company. The Bible tells the story of divine courtship.

The Song of Songs vividly expresses this divine courtship in poetic imagery. It is a love song between God and his people, Israel. Here, the lushness of Lebanon speaks of breathtaking beauty. God planted the cedars there; they were used to build the temple (Nm 24:6; Ps 104:16).

> Come from Lebanon, my bride,
>   come from Lebanon, come!
>
> You have ravished my heart, my sister, my bride;
>   you have ravished my heart with one
>   glance of your eyes,
>   with one bead of your necklace (Sg 4:8–9).

The prophets also speak of God as "husband" and Israel (or Zion) as "bride." In the writings of Isaiah, for example, God takes on the role of a husband who will comfort and care for his people.

> No more shall men call you "Forsaken,"
>   or your land "Desolate,"
> But you shall be called "My Delight,"
>   and your land "Espoused."
> For the Lord delights in you,
>   and makes your land his spouse.
> As a young man marries a virgin,
>   your Builder shall marry you;
> And as a bridegroom rejoices in his bride
>   so shall your God rejoice in you (Is 62:4–5).

Jeremiah also believed that the Hebrew nation was betrothed to God. One of his first prophecies describes this betrothal from God's perspective: "I remember the devotion of your youth, / how you loved me as a bride, / Following me in the desert, /

in a land unsown" (Jer 2:2). Again, in one of Jeremiah's other prophecies, he encourages the people to find comfort in God's promise for them, "Again I will restore you, and you shall be rebuilt, / O virgin Israel" (Jer 31:4). The prophets spoke in this way to show God's deep and abiding love for his people and his desire to have them share in his life.

The creation that was intended to exist in a covenant with God includes all that is seen and unseen. The material universe, including all of the stars and planets, is part of the visible creation. All life on earth, including that of the plants and animals and mankind, is also part of the visible creation. In contrast, all the angels and saints in heaven make up the invisible part of creation. They are connected to the visible creation in a mysterious way that will be made clearer to us when we leave this life and go on to the next. Paul speaks of this when he quotes Isaiah:

> What eye has not seen, and ear has not heard,
> and what has not entered the human heart,
> what God has prepared for those who love him
> (1 Cor 2:9; cf. Is 64:3).

Both the visible and the invisible are included as parts of God's spouse, which is his Creation.

When Creation was first completed, God wished to rest with his spouse, that they might share love and joy with one another. Because God wished for a shared love, he did not limit himself to creating beautiful objects, such as rocks and trees. Instead, he made men and angels who possess a free will. They could have a loving relationship with God because they were free persons endowed with wills of their own.

Shared love is not possible without free will. Without free will, love becomes an expression of force and can no longer be called true love. Freedom does entail a certain risk, however. Freedom means that the creature is able to turn from God and even against God if it so chooses. The story of humanity's decision to reject God has already been recounted in the prior chapter on salvation. Here, we are concerned mainly with how God restored Creation to her proper place as his loving spouse. How did God take a creation that was broken and dying, missing some of her most important members, and transform her into something even more beautiful than she was in the beginning? This is the theme that is played out across the pages of the Bible. We will try to recount that story here, but in brief.

Recall that the fall of Adam and Eve does not end in their damnation. Instead, it brings a promise of redemption (Gn 3:15). God says that a future child of the woman would crush the serpent's head. Later, the story of the flood closes with God's promise that he will not solve the problem of sin by simply wiping out everything. Instead, God makes a covenant with Noah and his descendants. The rainbow is the sign of this covenant (Gn 9).

Because humanity continues to sin, God repeatedly renews his covenant. Through Noah's descendant Abraham, God begins forming a people who would know him and have communion with him (Gn 15). God promises Abraham two things. First, he promises him that his descendants would be as numerous as the stars in the sky. Secondly, he declares to Abraham, "All the communities of the earth / shall find blessing in you" (Gn 12:3).

The fulfillment of the first promise began soon after the time of the patriarchs.[3] The twelve sons of Israel (Abraham's grandson) became the Twelve Tribes of Israel, all of whom were descendants of Abraham. These were the Twelve Tribes who were led by Moses out of the slavery of Egypt. Moses led them to Mount Sinai to receive another renewal of the covenant. God descended upon the mountain in a great cloud, with thunder, lightning, and earthquakes. There he delivered to Moses a set of laws meant to form the Hebrews into a Holy Nation.[4]

---

[3] The time of Abraham, Isaac, and Jacob (whose name was changed to Israel).

[4] This set of laws is the first five books of the Bible, which are called the *Torah* in Hebrew and the *Pentateuch* in Greek.

The Hebrews tried God's patience by breaking his renewed covenant the moment it was made! They did this when they made the golden calf and worshipped it while Moses was still on Mount Sinai. God then purified the Hebrews by having them wander in the desert until the entire generation of calf-worshippers had died out. When this purification was accomplished, God allowed them to enter the Promised Land in order to establish the nation of Israel.

Four hundred years later, God formed a covenant with David and made him the King of Israel. Though God had described him as "a man after my own heart," David too broke faith with God and committed a great sin, just as his forefathers had done (Acts 13:22; 2 Sm). Nevertheless, God promised David that one of his descendants would be King and Priest forever (Ps 110). With each successive covenant, God expanded the number of possible participants: from Adam and Eve (as husband and wife), to Noah and his family, to Abraham and his clan, to the twelve tribes under Jacob/Israel, to Moses and the Hebrew nation, and finally to David and his kingdom, Israel.

This Kingdom of Israel was yet another new beginning for mankind. A fallen nature and a fallen mankind were to be re-sanctified by a special chosen nation, a nation of priests, mediating a blessing from God to humanity (Ex 19:6). Thus, God's relationship to Israel was to symbolize a marriage renewed.

This relationship was, however, more like a troubled engagement than a peaceful marriage. After David, mankind in general and Israel in particular proved that they would *never* be able to keep faith with God. Generation after generation continued the terrible trend. God renewed the covenant continually, and men broke it continually. Psalm 14 laments this fact with gripping insight:

> The LORD looks down from
>   heaven upon the children of men,
> to see if there be one who is
>   wise and seeks God.

> All alike have gone astray; they
>   have become perverse;
> there is not one who does
>   good, not even one (Ps 14:2–3).

The general tone of the Bible from the time of Solomon (David's son) until the time of Christ is one of despair and gloom. In the midst of this despair, however, there is always a ray of hope because the prophets begin to speak of a time when God would find a way to make a permanent covenant with mankind —an unbreakable covenant. Then Creation (often symbolized by Israel) would be restored to her former beauty. She would even surpass her former beauty, and God would once again delight in her.

The prophet Hosea writes, "On that day, says the LORD, / She shall call me 'My husband,' / and never again 'My Baal'" (Hos 2:18).[5] But how could this be? If humanity could not ever keep a covenant with God, then how could we ever find rest in a joyful marriage with him? Reading the Old Testament walks us through page after page of broken promises and spoiled covenants. It is not until the New Testament that we are told how this continuing tragedy is brought to an end.

God finally sent his own son to establish a new and everlasting marriage covenant. It was the fulfillment of all the past covenants. The bond of this covenant is freely given and yet unbreakable. It is sealed with the blood of Christ. Anyone who is bound to Christ in love can become a sharer in this covenant. It is international; it is universal; it is catholic.[6] We are made part of this covenant by being made new as members of his sacrificial body. His body is the Church, and Christ endured the trial through which she received new life.

---

[5] "Baal" referred to any local god worshipped in the Near East. One statue of Baal was made with an open mouth and large teeth. Fire was lit within. Children were thrown in alive as a sacrifice (Jer 19:5).

[6] The word "catholic" comes from the Greek *katholikos* and is translated as "universal."

His bride is the new creation, just as Zion was the bride of God, and the special part of his creation that he intended to be preserved immaculate.[7] Jesus refers to himself as the bridegroom (Mk 2:20). John the Baptist considered his own role to be the groom's best man (Jn 3:29).

What exactly does all this mean? Why is it so important? Simply put, the relationship between Christ and his Church is at the center of all that is Christian. God's communion with his creation is now possible to a far greater degree than it ever was before he became flesh. Just as God can become human, likewise, humanity can share in God's very nature. The second letter of Peter begins on this point: "He has bestowed on us the precious and very great promises, so that through them you may come to share in the divine nature . . ." (2 Pt 1:4).

This union between God and flesh is the culmination and purpose of his creation. In the end there will be a perfect communion of love. In Ephesians 5:32, St. Paul likens human marriage to the relationship Christ has with his Church and calls it a "great mystery." (Note that this "great mystery" is not a symbol of marriage but the other way around. The marriage of a man and a woman is a faint image of the greater reality.) For this reason Jesus proclaims that divorce is not what God intended from the beginning: "What God has joined together, no human being must separate" (Mt 19:6). Marriage is a symbol of the unbreakable communion of love between God and his creation in Jesus Christ.

When Adam declared, "This one, at last, is bone of my bones / and flesh of my flesh," we see in these words a prototype of the nature of Christ's union with his Church (Gn 2:23). The blood and water (signs of birth) that flowed from Christ's side while he slept in death on the cross were meant to call to mind

---

[7] Zion was the fortress conquered by King David that enabled him to capture Jerusalem (2 Sm 5:7). It became the site of the temple. Later, it became synonymous for the temple, for Jerusalem, and for Israel as the people of God.

the Genesis story of Adam's wife, when God fashioned her from the rib that had been taken from the sleeping Adam's side (Gn 2:22; Jn 19:34). The Church came out of the side of the New Adam, Jesus Christ. She is to be associated with his body, as St. Paul says on numerous occasions (Eph 1:23; Col 1:18). One day she will be revealed in her full glory, "as a bride adorned for her husband" (Rv 21:2). She will gleam "with the splendor of God" (Rv 21:11). God himself will be her light (Rv 21:23). For now, the full splendor of the Church on earth can only be seen through the eyes of faith.

This is because the Church is in some ways finished and complete, but in other ways, she remains incomplete. For example, St. Paul says that, "Creation itself would be set free from slavery to corruption and share in the glorious freedom of the children of God. We know that all creation is groaning in labor pains even until now" (Rom 8:21–22). In other words, the Church on earth still has trials and purification to undergo. She has not yet attained the full number of members or the complete perfection of each of them. Neither has she come to a complete fullness of understanding in regards to all the teachings that Christ imparted to the apostles.

On the other hand, the Church is finished, because Christ's death has made the covenant between God and his people complete. The Letter to the Hebrews explains that this covenant was unlike the old covenant with Moses. The covenant mediated by Moses still left the people in fear of their lives before God. The people were afraid to go anywhere near the Holy Mountain for fear that they would die (Dt 5:23–26). In contrast, the new covenant (as described by Paul and celebrated in the Mass) is complete and draws everyone close to God:

> You have approached Mount Zion and the city of the living God, the heavenly Jerusalem, and countless angels in festal gathering, and the assembly of the firstborn . . . and the spirits of the just made perfect, and Jesus, the mediator of a new covenant . . . (Heb 12:22–24).

We also know that the Church's identity as the bride of Christ is already sealed, because one of the final verses from the book of Revelation is addressed to the reader in present tense: "The Spirit and the bride say, 'Come'" (Rv 22:17). Christ and the Church exist together in perfect unity and invite us to "come" and be joined in union with them through the celebration of the Mass.

St. Paul tells us very clearly that the Church is the bride of Christ and that he died for her sake, "that she might be holy and without blemish" (Eph 5:27). Christ's Church is the "new heaven and new earth" promised by God (Is 65:17; 2 Cor 5:17; Rv 21:1). The Church is the new creation, and God's marriage to her shows that evil could not mar his plan forever. Instead, she has emerged from her trials more beautiful than ever, like gold tested in fire.

Until all of her members have been gathered in and perfected, the Church remains a loyal spouse waiting for Christ's visible return. She yearns for him and loves him with the divine love that is given her by the Holy Spirit. But why did Christ not remain visibly present to us here on earth?

The purpose behind the new covenant was not for God to force obedience from his people but rather to achieve full unity with them, just as he knew full unity with his son. When Jesus told the disciples, "It is better for you that I go," he meant that the world had seen enough of his power to know that he was God, and that it was time for the world to know him interiorly, or from the heart (Jn 16:7). He changed the form of his bodily presence into that of the Eucharist so that people's desire to follow him would be motivated from love rather than awe and fear. If he had continued to appear as the risen Christ whenever the Church desired to speak to him, the whole world might have been converted within a short time. If he ruled clearly, explicitly, and forcefully as God, then all of humanity would have given Christ absolute obedience immediately. But their obedience to Christ would have been shallow, and their unity with one another would not have been heart-felt.

Thus, Christ and the Church are united in the flesh and in the spirit, so that we can say with confidence that the Church is the body of Christ and the body of Christ is the Church. At the end of time, when all of the individual members have been perfected, then we will be able to say of the Church something even greater: "Christ is all and in all" (Col 3:11). This phrase from St. Paul perfectly expresses how the unity between the Father, Son, and Holy Spirit will be reflected perfectly in creation at the end of time.

Anticipating this ultimate end, the Church acts as our mother. She imitates Mary in bearing Christ to the world. She is our mother because she bears us into communion with the new life that is in Christ. Seeing the Church as our mother is perhaps the best way to understand what "Church" means. St. Paul regarded her in this way when he said, "The Jerusalem above is freeborn, and she is our mother" (Gal 4:26).

Just as it is the mother's job to teach and inspire her children to practice lives of purity and holiness, so the Catholic Church does her job when she encourages the faithful to seek and respond to God's love in specific and concrete ways. Not only does she provide a special place where her children can contemplate God through art and architecture or the perfume of burning candles and incense, but the Church also helps her people to increase their reverence and love for God through the Mass and the other sacraments. She joins all of humanity into one family of God. And, as both a physical and spiritual (and therefore living) entity, she transmits the truth and grace of God to the whole world.

The Church may also be thought of as an assembly of persons in communion with each other. Some of the people in this communion are visible to us, while others are not. The Father, Son, and Holy Spirit, Mary, and all of the angels and saints in heaven are not visible to us right now. We nevertheless believe that they are intimately connected to us. The Catholic Church calls the portion of her that is in heaven the *communion of saints*. They are described in Hebrews as "so great a cloud of witnesses" surrounding us (Heb 12:1). While this part of the Church in heaven must remain invisible until the end of time, Christ intended his Church on earth to be highly visible and easily recognizable to anyone seeking the truth about God.

How would the real presence of God be recognizable to the outside world, and how could the new Christian community itself be assured of his presence? Individuals might have powerful spiritual experiences through prayers, gatherings, speaking in tongues, or any number of other things. Any individual might claim to be animated by the presence of the Holy Spirit and seek out followers in the name of Christ. But how exactly can one tell the difference between someone who is *really* animated by the Holy Spirit and some pretender who merely *claims* to be animated by the Holy Spirit?

Fortunately, Christ gave us two ways to discern the presence of God in the real Church. These two ways are related to one another. One is by fruits, and the other is by a united love. Jesus said, "By their fruits you will know them" (Mt 7:16). By this, Jesus meant that people who are truly from God will give evidence by the way they act. When they do good to their fellow man, they show the presence of God in their hearts, and their good deed is evidence of their trustworthiness. Even those outside the visible Church on earth work in communion with the heavenly Church when they express love to their neighbor. For Christians, however, good deeds inspired by God's grace are only one way of proving truth and demonstrating God's presence.

The Church also demonstrates God's real presence in the unity of faith and love that is shared among her members. Consider the following passages:

> I pray not only for them, but also for those who will believe in me through their word, so that they may all be one, as you, Father, are in me and I in you, that they also may be in us, that the world may believe that you sent me (Jn 17:20–21).

> They went out from us, but they were not really of our number; if they had been, they would have remained with us. Their

desertion shows that none of them was of our number (1 Jn 2:19).

We know that we have passed from death to life because we love our brothers. Whoever does not love remains in death. . . . The way we came to know love was that he laid down his life for us. . . . His commandment is this: we should believe in the name of his Son, Jesus Christ, and love one another just as he commanded us (1 Jn 3:14, 16, 23).

From these passages, we see that the Christian Church is to be so unified in love that this unity will reflect the unity that exists in the Trinity. This visible unity between diverse members is why we call the true Church the "Catholic" Church.[8] The members of the Church are to love one another so clearly that the outside world will believe the saving message that we bear. How does one express love so powerfully?

The answer is a word that has practically become taboo in modern discussions about religion. That word is *organization*. This is shocking to some people. How often have you, the reader, heard one of the following?

"I believe in spirituality, but I'm just not into organized religion."

"I believe in a personal relationship with Christ, not in a religion."

"Religion is just a tradition of men."

The positive thing these statements are trying to say is that people do not like empty ritual. They do not like authorities who take their money, order them around, and then ignore them as an unimportant appendix. In this sense, their objection to what

---

[8] As mentioned above (n. 6), the Greek word for "universal" is *katholikos*. It was first used by Ignatius of Antioch around A.D. 107 to describe the one true Church that is present everywhere; the Church *katholikos* includes all nationalities and is rightly descended from Christ through the apostles. There may be many "local" churches, but they are all part of the *one* Church. The very word "universe" emphasizes the *oneness* of all created things, because every created thing is included in it. And since the Church is the New Creation, the Church is, in this sense, the New Universe.

they are calling "organized religion" might be valid. But in their haste to be rid of empty rituals and restrictions, they throw out the baby with the bath water.

Try to imagine any undertaking by God or human beings that is not organized. Take the human body as an example: the very word "organized" simply means that each organ is in its proper place and performing its proper function. Does not freedom from organization mean that an individual organ thinks it can stand on its own? Isn't this idea one that Paul explicitly condemns?

> Now the body is not a single part, but many. . . . If an ear should say, "Because I am not an eye I do not belong to the body," it does not for this reason belong any less to the body. If the whole body were an eye, where would the hearing be? . . . As it is, God placed the parts, each one of them, in the body as he intended. . . . The eye cannot say to the hand, "I do not need you" (1 Cor 12:14–21).

Now, all of us can sympathize with those who have been unhappy with a particular business or church. They may have been subjected to the authority of some tyrant in the organization. Nevertheless, people must learn to realize that the problem is caused by individual human sin. The problem is not caused by the idea of organization itself. Any mature person recognizes this in all other areas of life. Examples are so numerous that anyone can think of several without straining.

The organized classroom shows the concern that the teacher has for the students. A disorganized classroom shows that the teacher doesn't care. When a mother sets out a meal for her family, organization shows her attention to detail. She wants everything to be perfect. A good coach has an organized team. An owner devoted to his business organizes it. Even the natural environment expresses a highly organized system, with each life form having its own role to play in the ecology as a whole. It is precisely the interconnected and delicate balance within nature that draws us into the beauty of it all.

It is simply amazing therefore, that with all this evidence regarding the value of organization staring them in the face, perhaps the majority of people today are of the opinion that organization in religion somehow lessens the deep spirituality of it. This idea is completely false and runs directly contrary to basic life experience and to Christianity.

The truth is this: *Organization is simply the form that united love takes.* Loving as an individual is easier than loving in communion with others. But to love as a community is deeper and more enriching. It is the way that the Trinity loves us. Because of this, the Catholic Church sees her hierarchy as the loving union in God made visible to the faithful. The Church's hierarchy represents the united love of the people offered back up to God.

Each form of unified love in the Church is made possible by having a visible person who can direct it. There is nothing unusual in this; we experience it in our day-to-day lives. If another nation wanted to show honor to our nation, they might send a gift to the President of the United States. He would accept it on behalf of all the citizens. Likewise, if the united citizens of this country wanted to offer emergency aid to the victims of a natural disaster in another country, they would send their gift either through the president or else through a special ambassador who represents the nation as a whole.

In the Church, the pope, as successor to St. Peter, serves this function. He is the visible representative of the entire Church, and the entire Church loves with a *visible, witnessing* unity when it loves through the actions of the pope and those bishops who are in union with him.

Each bishop serves a similar purpose in his own diocese. Because he is joined to the pope, his people may be sure that their particular bishop has not veered off into a different religion of his own making. Because the bishops are the successors of the apostles, their people can be sure that they are passing on the true gospel in Scripture and Tradition. Bishops inspire awe of the Father in the sense that most of the time they are distant from the congregation (this is because a diocese is generally such a large unit), and their presence is experienced as something special. Bishops also represent the love of the Father to the parish congregations in a special way because the bishop imitates the Father in being the one who sends the parish priest to speak in his name.

Priests enable love as a parish unit. They represent the love of Jesus to the people and the love of the people to Jesus through the Eucharist. The priest is not his own witness and not his own authority; rather he imitates the Son by being sent from the bishop. He represents the authority of the bishop in the same way that Christ represents the authority of the Father. Under the authority of their bishops, it is generally through parish priests that God is offered an acceptable sacrifice universally.

Deacons represent the Holy Spirit among us. This is because they are closest to the people and act as a more interior directing of love. They make the parishioners conscious of how their personal acts of love may be joined to the Eucharist and inspired by the Eucharist; they are the intimacy of the Holy Spirit among the people. Through the deacons, every detail of the parish can be sanctified and included as an act of worship.

Through Christ and the action of the Holy Spirit, this form of hierarchy (bishop, priest, and deacon) has become a mark of the one true Church. This is because they represent the presence of the Trinity within the Church. A church that is without them is like an empty structure with nothing inside.

Did Jesus clearly establish this type of hierarchy? Is it evident in the Scriptures? We will now show scriptural proof for the hierarchy in general and the papacy in particular. Jesus knew that the unity of his followers could not be displayed without an organized church, and yet the hierarchy that he set in place was not an end in itself. Rather, it was a tool for expressing his unifying love to the members of his Church. He commissioned his apostles to carry out this very mission. They were sent forth by Christ with the authority to teach, guide, and minister to mankind. The apostles were believed by their initial converts because of their deeds and because of their unity with one another.

"Apostle" means "one who is sent." The bishops are the connection back to the original Church and the original apostles. They are the ones through whom we have apostolic succession, so we know that the Church we are in is the original Church historically.

Because of the apostolic bishops, the Church knows that Christ established her to be the one, true Church where he promised to dwell until the end of time. She has a conscious memory of the teachings that Christ imparted to her (the deposit of faith) and of all common beliefs and practices that have been passed down from generation to generation (the living Tradition).

The fact that Christ decided to found the Church on apostles tells us that he wanted his teachings to be preserved by an organized hierarchy. If Christ had not cared about establishing the Church, then he could have easily written down an exhaustive book about himself and all the teachings that the world would need to know in order to be saved. If Christ had wanted his authority to be placed into a book alone, then there would have been no need for him to train Peter to serve as the leader of the apostles. It was significant then, that Jesus chose not to write down a single word. Instead, he purposely (and publicly) placed his authority in a successor who would stand in his place and speak in his name.

For two thousand years, the Church has continued her practice of anointing apostolic successors. This is why every Catholic bishop in the world can trace his succession of authority back to one of the apostles. This practice insures that the historical eyewitness accounts at the heart of our faith and our Church will continue to remain intact.

The evidence for Peter's authority is so pronounced and definitive that all contrary arguments can easily be refuted. For example, some have tried to explain away the dramatic gesture made by Christ when he gave Peter a new name (Mt 16:18). When Peter first acknowledged that Christ was the Son of God,

Jesus said to him, "Blessed are you, Simon son of Jonah. . . . And so I say to you, you are Peter [*Petros*], and upon this rock [*Petra*] will I build my church, and the gates of the netherworld shall not prevail against it" (Mt 16:17–18). It is argued that since the word for "Peter" (*Petros*) is different from the word used for "this rock" (*Petra*), Christ could not have been saying, "You are Peter and on you, Peter, will I build my church."

But this is exactly what Jesus said. In the Aramaic language, Jesus used only one word for "Peter" and "this rock," and that word was *Kephas*. The modern confusion concerning whether Peter is or is not "this rock" arises from the fact that the Bible was written in Greek and that the Greek term for "large rock" (*Petra*) was a feminine noun that could not be used to refer to Peter. The New Testament writers used the word "*Petros*" as the closest approximation, even though this word means "small rock."

Jesus changed Simon's name to Peter for a purpose, and that purpose was to make clear to everyone that Peter was to serve as the foundation stone for the Church. Even now, when thousands of Christian denominations declare their church to be based on Christ, only one still follows the Tradition established by Christ himself, when he declared Peter to be the visible rock and foundation for his Church. It is understood, of course, that Christ is the ultimate invisible head of the Church. Christ, in this sense, is the ultimate Rock of Salvation (cf. Ps 62:3), and Peter exercises his office in a way that is dependent on and subject to Christ.

Christ's intention to have his authority passed on becomes most evident when he quotes to Peter a passage from the Old Testament where a scribe was being given an office that would last from generation to generation (Is 22:22).

> I will give you the keys to the kingdom of heaven. Whatever you bind on earth shall be bound in heaven; and whatever you loose on earth shall be loosed in heaven (Mt 16:19).

Any faithful Jew listening to Jesus at that moment would have known that he was quoting from Isaiah's promise to Eliakin that he and his descendants would serve as prime ministers for the King of Judah from generation to generation.

> On that day I will summon my servant
>> Eliakin, son of Hilkiah;
> He shall be a father to the inhabitants of Jerusalem,
>> and to the house of Judah.
> I will place the key of the House of David on his shoulder;
>> when he opens, no one shall shut,
>> when he shuts, no one shall open.
> I will fix him like a peg in a sure spot,
>> to be a place of honor for his family;
> On him shall hang all the glory of his family:
>> descendants and offspring,
>> all the little dishes, from bowls to jugs (Is 22:20–24).

The job of the Prime Minister was to be spokesman for the king, and so the office was second in importance only to that of the king. Therefore, when the Jews heard Christ promise the keys of the Kingdom to Peter, they understood that Christ wanted Peter to serve as his Prime Minister and that Peter's office would have no end. It is not surprising that the writings of the early Church fathers confirm this. St. Clement (Bishop of Rome in the first century) wrote that it was common practice for the early leaders of the Church to appoint their own successors, in case they were taken away to become martyrs.[9]

Many other passages should convince someone that Peter was the leader over the other apostles. First, whenever the twelve apostles are listed, Peter is named first as their head (Mt 10:2, Mk 3:16, Lk 6:14, Acts 1:13). Peter's primacy was not restricted to his office. It was expressed as well in simple details in the gospels. For example, Peter and his brother Andrew are the first apostles to be chosen by Christ (Mt 4:18). Peter (along with James and John) is chosen to witness the Transfiguration of Our Lord on the Mount of Olives. Peter asks to walk on the water (a sign that his faith was greater than the others) (Mt 14:28–31, 17:4).

---

[9] Jurgens, v. 1, 21.

Many other examples appear in Scripture in order to emphasize Peter's primacy. After Christ rose from the dead, Peter was
the first to enter the holy tomb (Lk 24:12). Later that week,
when Jesus appears to them on the shore of the Sea of Tiberius
and tells them they should cast out their net once more, Peter
swims to the shore before anyone else in order to meet him (Jn
21:7–9). When Jesus asks to see the fish, Peter swims out and
drags back a net by himself that is bursting with 153 large fish
(Jn 21:11). The fact that Peter could pull them in by himself
was a sign that he would be given supernatural strength to bring
in all the nations to the shores of heaven. Later on, when the
Holy Spirit descends upon the disciples at Pentecost, it is Peter
who gives the first sermon that converts the first three thousand
to the faith (Acts 2:41).

An earlier incident in the gospels also shows that Peter was
recognized as the leader among the apostles. When taxes had
to be paid, even the outside authorities knew that Peter was the
one to approach (Mt 17:24). Christ then assigned Peter the job
of catching the fish that held the coin needed to pay the tax
—strong evidence that Peter was seen as the provider for the
others (Mt 17:27).

That the outside authorities should approach Peter raises an
important point. Suppose a non-religious person was looking at
the worlds' religions one by one, trying to decide which one (if
any) taught the truth. Who would they ask to get the "official"
Christian version? Would it be enough to simply give such a
person a copy of the Bible? The Bible says not. Consider the
interaction between the apostle Philip and the Ethiopian eu-
nuch.

> There was an Ethiopian eunuch, a court official . . . reading
> the prophet Isaiah. . . . Philip ran up . . . and said, "Do you
> understand what you are reading?" He replied, "How can I,
> unless someone instructs me?" (Acts 8:27–31)

This passage should make it clear that the Bible was not meant
to replace the voice of God's appointed shepherds. Instead, the

Scriptures were handed down to us as an aid in helping the Church proclaim the good news. Leaving aside the question of witnessing to outsiders, there is still the question of dissension within the Church herself. If an occasional bishop or group of bishops were to begin promoting some controversial new doctrine, how could we know which faction, if any, was representing the one true faith? Would God leave his Church vulnerable in this way to any heretic who happened to come along? All of this argues for having a visible head as well as an invisible one.

When occasional critics of the Church come to admit that, "Yes, Peter was the leader of the apostles," they still cannot accept that Peter's unique authority was meant to be passed on to someone else—let alone to a succession of people. We cannot know whether Christ said to Peter, "Pass on your authority to a proper successor." We can, however, be sure that he intended for this succession to occur. Christ not only gave to Peter "the keys of the kingdom" so that all the Jews would apply to Peter the same rule of succession that once applied to Eliakin (as was mentioned earlier in this chapter), but he affirmed this point on other occasions as well. For example, Jesus shows that Peter is the head of the other apostles in the following passage from Luke:

> Simon, Simon, behold Satan has demanded to sift all of you like wheat, but I have prayed that your own faith may not fail; and once you have turned back, you must strengthen your brothers (Lk 22:31–32).

Peter confirms this special office when he opens a speech to the other Church leaders in this way: "My brothers, you are well aware that from early days God made his choice among you that through my mouth the Gentiles would hear the word of the gospel and believe" (Acts 15:7).

Without a "speaker of the house," there is nothing but the chaos of competing voices. So Christ spent three years teaching the disciples and preparing them to receive the divine authority they would need in order to build up the Church. Just as God entrusted great authority to Moses and the priests of Aaron, Jesus entrusted his authority to Peter and the other apostles who would serve as bishops and priests for the new Church. Because the priesthood of the New Covenant was based on Christ's sacrifice, it perfected and completed the priesthood of Aaron and the Levites (Heb 7–8ff.)

The authority given to the priests of the New Covenant would be even greater and more powerful, because they would be standing in the person of Christ himself. This is why we always see Jesus building up the authority of his disciples, and especially the authority of Peter, who was to stand in the place of Christ to an even more perfect degree, in order to insure the perfect unity of the Church.

The old levitical priesthood was fulfilled and replaced by the Priesthood of Christ. The Old Law was fulfilled and replaced by the New Law of Love. This love was not to be random and disordered, however. It was to unite the faithful in a rational way. The hierarchy of the Church enables her to teach her members what true love is. Because the Holy Spirit teaches through the pope (and the bishops in union with him) with one voice, the faithful are guaranteed that their teaching on matters of faith and morals is the correct one. Simply put, we need the authority of the Church to keep us from deceiving ourselves. Although Christ left us with one simple command ("Love one another"), the application of this principle is sometimes far from simple.

Consider, for example, a young girl who is pregnant and trying to decide whether to have an abortion. One friend might say to her, "You shouldn't have a baby that you can't properly support, so it would be more loving for you to terminate the pregnancy now rather than introduce the baby into a life of poverty." Someone else might tell her, "Love means sacrifice; you have no right to kill the baby and must care for it as best you can."

Now, on the surface both statements may seem plausible to

her. How is she to decide between them? Loving within the context of a community lends support by providing a common view of what love is.

> I have much more to tell you, but you cannot bear it now. But when he comes, the Spirit of truth, he will guide you to all truth. He will not speak on his own, but he will speak what he hears, and will declare to you the things that are coming (Jn 16:12–13).

For many Christians, the issue of abortion is easy to answer. But what about something like contraception? Until the 1930s, Christians (all Catholics and all Protestants) agreed that it was contrary to Scripture and sinful. This is no longer the case. Many denominations accept contraception as a part of a loving family life. The Catholic Church holds to the original teaching (that it is sinful). Who is right? How are we to know?

We can see in Scripture that Christians always have had questions about such things. Scripture also shows that Christians have always had a visible authority to whom they could turn. At that first council in Jerusalem, for example, the early Church was caught up in a dispute as to whether Gentile converts needed to follow the Law of Moses (and so be circumcised) in order to be saved (Acts 15:1–12). The Old Testament made it clear that circumcision was necessary, but Christ himself had said nothing on the matter. The issue had begun to create divisions within the Church, and so they decided to deal with the problem at the council of Jerusalem.

After everyone had spoken at length, it was Peter who finally resolved the dispute and pronounced definitively that the Old Law would not be imposed upon the Gentiles (Acts 15:10–11). We are told that after Peter spoke, everyone at the council remained silent (Acts 15:12). They accepted his word as the last word. Just as it does today, the Holy Spirit spoke through Peter to pronounce true and correct teaching that was faithful to Christ. Church unity was the result.

Many ask: "If the united Church (the one identified by the pope and the bishops in union with him) is so good, then why have so many of her leaders sinned?" Here we have to make an important distinction. The Church as the body of Christ is not capable of sinning any more than Christ was. She is holy. But her members on earth, like the apostle Judas, are capable of betrayal and sin. Jesus likened the Church to a tree or a grapevine. Every tree has branches that need pruning because they dry out or do not bear fruit. Jesus said that the Father "takes away every branch in me that does not bear fruit, and every one that does he prunes so that it bears more fruit" (Jn 15:1–2).

What may bother some is the idea that a wicked pope can claim infallibility. But apart from the fact that a pope's infallibility applies only to his official statements about Catholic faith and morals, it must be understood that the validity of priesthood does not rest on the sanctity of the office-holder. Christ himself upholds the office when a sinful priest does not. Peter's threefold denial of Christ before the servant girl teaches this lesson well (Mt 26:69–74). Christ responded to Peter's failure not by sending him away but by lifting him up again with forgiveness and encouragement. He gave Peter the chance to make up for each denial (asking him three times, "Do you love me?"), and then he affirmed that Peter's authority was still in place by conferring upon Peter the title of shepherd that Jesus had once reserved only for himself! (Jn 21:15–18) In short, being partly human means that the Church can still be subject to scandal from the leadership and laity, but being partly divine insures that her doctrines will never be subject to error or falsehood.

As for the question concerning how the pope (even a bad pope) can speak infallibly, we need only keep in mind the three promises of Christ. First, he promised that he would be with the Church until the end of the world (Mt 28:20). He identified himself so closely with the Church, that when he appeared to Saul on the road to Damascus, he did not question why Paul was persecuting his Church. Instead he said, "Saul, Saul, why are you persecuting me?" (Acts 9:4). Furthermore, when Jesus sent forth the disciples, he said, "Whoever listens to you, listens to me. Whoever rejects you rejects me" (Lk 10:16). It was Jesus' own idea to have the disciples speak in his name, just as the pope does now, whenever he speaks in union with the bishops on matters of faith and morals. And so, if Jesus spoke infallibly and gave his full authority to Peter and the disciples, then why should their successors not also be given the authority to speak infallibly when they speak in his name?

A second reason why we can believe that what the Church teaches is infallible is that Christ promised that the Holy Spirit would lead us into all truth (Jn 16:13). Christ entrusted his disciples with a body of knowledge, but this knowledge was compact and not always easy to understand. When Christ said to the disciples, "I have much more to tell you, but you cannot bear it now," he was referring not to some large body of new doctrine, but rather to the full and complete understanding (including all the moral implications) of what he had already said and done (Jn 16:12). And so it has been the work of the Holy Spirit to guide the Church in the process of developing and declaring the doctrines of Christ with ever greater clarity and force.

Thirdly, we should believe in the Church's infallibility, because when Christ founded his Church, he promised that the gates of hell would not prevail against it (Mt 16:18). As much as the devil might try to attack the Church (even through priests and bishops), Jesus promised that these attacks would not harm the Church any more than the buffeting of the wind and the rain harmed Noah's ark. As for the sinfulness of individual persons and priests within the Church, Christ said that we should respond to scandal with patience. In his parable of the tares among the wheat, Jesus explained why the good and the bad must be allowed to remain in the Church until the end of time: "If you pull up the weeds you might uproot the wheat along with them" (Mt 13:25–29). It will be the work of Jesus and his angels to separate the two at the end of time.

The Church is being built by her Builder to last until the end of time and beyond. The presence of her Builder, Jesus Christ, is continued invisibly by the action of the Holy Spirit. Like all living bodies, the Church has been endowed with a spirit. Just as a person's spirit animates his body, so the Holy Spirit animates the Church. She was first animated as a united body at Pentecost. St. Luke tells us that the disciples were all of one accord, in one place, when this happened (Acts 2).

When the Holy Spirit came to rest upon the disciples, the life of God was being breathed into the Church, anointing the disciples with power to become teachers, prophets, and priests. When the disciples began to speak in tongues, the Holy Spirit miraculously interpreted their words into each person's native language. (Families had come for the Pentecost from all over the Diaspora.) This was a sign to everyone that the Holy Spirit came to bring unity to the disciples and everyone who would listen to them (Acts 2:6–12).

In Hebrew tradition, the feast of the Pentecost (meaning "fifty days") occurred fifty days after the Passover. Not only did the Hebrews take this time to celebrate God's gift of the "first fruits" from the harvest, but they also celebrated God's giving of the Ten Commandments to Moses on Mount Sinai. Thus it was significant that the birth of the Church should occur on this feast. In the Old Testament God had come down from heaven and written his law upon the stone tablets given to Moses (Ex 31:18). At Pentecost, the new law of Love (the Holy Spirit) was written on the hearts of the members of the Church.

When writing about the first Pentecost, it is certain that St. Luke intended to emphasize unity as a mark of the one true Church. We can be sure of this by the strong **contrasts** he makes with the account of the Tower of Babel in Genesis.

> And suddenly there came from the sky a noise like a strong driving wind, and it filled the entire house in which they were. Then there appeared to them tongues as of fire, which parted and came to rest on each one of them. And they were all filled with the holy Spirit and began to speak in different tongues, as the Spirit enabled them to proclaim (Acts 2:2–4).

> The whole world spoke the same language. . . . While men were migrating in the east, they . . . said to one another, "Come, let us mold bricks and harden them with fire." . . .

Then they said, "Come, let us build ourselves a city and a tower with its top in the sky, and so make a name for ourselves; otherwise we shall be scattered all over the earth."

. . . Then the LORD said: ". . . Let us . . . confuse their language, so that one will not understand what another says." Thus the LORD scattered them from there all over the earth, and they stopped building the city. That is why it was called Babel, because there the LORD confused the speech of all the world (Gn 11:1–9).

At Babel, men hardened bricks with fire to build a tower for themselves. At Pentecost, the apostles were hardened by the fire of the Holy Spirit, and they were built into a united Church. (For a vision of the apostles as building stones, consider Rv 21:14.) At Babel, all of humanity was united in sin. God confused them in their pride and scattered them. At Pentecost, the Church is given the capacity of "tongues" to reach all men in all nations and gather them back in. This time, the union would be based on the love of God, rather than pride.

Ever since the birth of the Church at her first Pentecost, the one, holy, catholic (literally, "universal"), and apostolic Church has been sent to sanctify people of every nation. Every person from every culture is invited to join, and every nation's culture can be adapted into Catholicism. This does not diminish the diversity among believers, but instead enables their differences to become more profound and meaningful, while at the same time uniting them into a deeper communion of love. The rich unity of the Church offers testimony to her Builder. Her unity silences the "babel" spouted by her critics. This should be pointed out to anyone who does not understand the need for "organized religion."

The Early Church Fathers
on the Pope

Pope St. Clement of Rome (Pontificate A.D. 92–101): *Letter to the Corinthians* (v. 1, 20)

The Apostles received the Gospel for us from the Lord Jesus Christ . . . receiving their instructions and being full of confidence on account of the resurrection of our Lord and confirmed in faith by the word of God, they went forth in the complete assurance of the Holy Spirit . . . and they appointed their earliest converts, testing them by the spirit, to be the bishops and deacons of future believers.

(v. 1, 21)

Our Apostles knew through our Lord that there would be strife for the office of bishop. For this reason . . . having received perfect foreknowledge, they appointed those who have already been mentioned, and afterwards added the further provision that, if they should die, other approved men should succeed to their ministry.

St. Ignatius of Antioch (A.D. 110): *Epistle to the Magnesians* **(v. 1, 44)**

Take care to do all things in harmony with God, with the bishop presiding in the place of God and with the presbyters in the place of the council of the Apostles, and with the deacons who are most dear to me.

(v. 1, 47)

Take care, therefore, to be confirmed in the decrees of the Lord and of the Apostles, in order that in everything you do, you may prosper in body and soul, in faith and love, in Son and in Father and in Spirit, in beginning and in end, together with your most reverend bishop; and with that fittingly woven spiritual crown, the presbytery; and with the deacons, men of God. Be subject to the bishop and to one another, as Jesus Christ was subject to the Father, and the Apostles were subject to Christ and to the Father, so that there may be unity in both body and spirit.

(v. 1, 65)

You must all follow the bishop as Jesus Christ follows the Father, and the presbytery as you would the Apostles. Reverence the deacons as you would the command of God. Let no one do anything of concern to the Church without the bishop. Let that be considered a valid Eucharist that is celebrated by the bishop, or by one who he appoints. Wherever the bishop appears, let the people be there; just as wherever Jesus Christ is, there is the Catholic Church.

St. Irenaeus, Bishop of Lyons (A.D. 190): *Against Heresies* (v. 1, 210)

. . . [P]ointing out here the successions of the bishops of the greatest and most ancient Church known to all, founded and organized at Rome by the two most glorious Apostles, Peter and Paul, that Church which has the Tradition and the faith which comes down to us after having been announced to men by the Apostles. For with this Church, because of its superior origin, all Churches must agree, that is, all the faithful in the whole world; and it is in her that the faithful everywhere have maintained the Apostolic Tradition.

St. Ephrem (A.D. 306–373): *Songs of Praise* (v. 1, 706)

Simon, My follower, I have made you the foundation of the holy Church. I betimes called you Peter, because you will support all its buildings. You are the inspector of those who will build on earth a Church for Me. If they should wish to build what is false, you, the foundation, will condemn them. You are the head of the fountain from which my teaching flows; you are the chief of my disciples. Through you I will give drink to all peoples. Yours is that life-giving sweetness which I dispense. I have chosen you to be, as it were, the first-born in my institution, and so that, as the heir, you may be executor of my treasures. I have given you the keys of my kingdom. Behold, I have given you authority over all my treasures.

St. Jerome (A.D. 347–419): *Letter of Jerome to Pope Damasus* (v. 2, 1346)

I follow no leader but Christ and join in communion with none but Your Blessedness, that is, with the chair of Peter. I know that this is the rock on which the Church has been built.

The Early Church Fathers on the Work of the Church

Pope St. Clement of Rome (Pontificate A.D. 92–101): *Second Letter of Clement of Rome to the Corinthians* (v. 1, 105)

The living Church is the body of Christ . . . and the Apostles declare that the Church belongs not to the present, but has existed from the beginning. She was spiritual, just as was our Jesus; but was manifested in the last days so that He might save us. And the Church, being spiritual, was manifested in the flesh of Christ.

Origen (A.D. 185–253): *Hom. in Ezech.* (CCC 817)

Where there are sins, there are also divisions, schisms, heresies, and disputes. Where there is virtue, however, there also are harmony and unity, from which arise the one heart and one soul of all believers.

St. Cyprian of Carthage (A.D. 200–258): *The Unity of the Catholic Church* (v. 1, 557)

The Bride of Christ cannot be defiled. She is inviolate and chaste. She knows but one home, and with a chaste modesty she guards the sanctity of one bedchamber. It is she that keeps us for God, she that seals for the kingdom the sons whom she bore.

St. Cyril of Jerusalem (A.D. 315–386): Catechetical Instruction (*Liturgy of the Hours*, Wednesday, 17th Week of Ordinary Time)

The Church is called Catholic or universal because it has spread throughout the entire world, from one end of the earth to the other. Again, it is called Catholic because it teaches fully and unfailingly all the doctrines which ought to be brought to men's knowledge, whether concerned with visible or invisible things, with the realities of Heaven or the things of earth. Another reason for the name Catholic is that the Church brings under religious obedience all classes of men, rulers and subjects, learned and unlettered. Finally, it deserves the title Catholic because it heals and cures unrestrictedly every type of sin that can be committed in soul or in body, and because it possesses within itself every kind of virtue that can be named, whether exercised in actions or in words or in some kind of spiritual charism.

St. Augustine of Hippo (A.D. 354–430): *En. in Ps.* [Ps 74:4] (CCC 796)

This is the whole Christ, head and body, one formed from many . . . whether the head or members speak, it is Christ who speaks. He speaks in his role as the head (*ex persona capitis*) and in his role as body (*ex persona corporis*). What does this mean? "The two will become one flesh. This is a great mystery, and I am applying it to Christ and the Church." And the Lord himself says in the Gospel: "So they are no longer two, but one flesh." They are, in fact, two different persons, yet they are one in the conjugal union, . . . *as head, he calls himself the bridegroom, as body, he calls himself "bride."*

Contemporary Writings
on the Church

Constitution on the Church, VII *The Pilgrim Church* (*Lumen Gentium* 48) [10]

Christ lifted up from the earth, has drawn all men to himself (cf. Jn. 12:32). Rising from the dead (cf. Rom. 6:9) he sent his life-giving Spirit upon his disciples and through him set up his Body which is the Church as the universal sacrament of salvation. Sitting at the right hand of the Father he is continually active in the world in order to lead men to the Church and, through it, join them more closely to himself. . . .

Constitution on the Church, I *The Mystery of the Church* (*Lumen Gentium* 8) [11]

The Church, "like a stranger in a foreign land, presses forward amid the persecutions of the world and the consolations of God" [St. Augustine] announcing the cross and death of the Lord until he comes (cf. 1 Cor 11:26). But by the power of the risen Lord she is given strength to overcome, in patience and love, her sorrows and her difficulties, both those that are from within and those that are from without. . . .

Decree on Ecumenism *Catholic Principles on Ecumenism* (*Unitatis Redintegratio* 3) [12]

[I]n subsequent centuries much more serious dissensions appeared and large communities became separated from full communion with the Catholic Church—for which, often enough, men of both sides were to blame. However, one cannot charge with the sin of the separation those who at present are born

---

[10] Austin Flannery, ed., *Vatican Council II: The Conciliar and Post Conciliar Documents, New Revised Edition* (Northport, N.Y.: Costello Publishing Co., 1984) 407.

[11] Ibid., 358.

[12] Ibid., 455.

into these communities [that resulted from such separation] and in them are brought up in the faith of Christ, and the Catholic Church accepts them with respect and affection as brothers. For men who believe in Christ and have been properly baptized are put in some, though imperfect, communion with the Catholic Church.

A Brief Summary of the Ecumenical Councils

325 — Nicea I (Pope Sylvester I)

Declared against Arius that the Son was of the same "substance" as the Father. The priest Arius had been teaching falsely that Christ was a sort of super-angel.

381 — Constantinople I (Pope Damasus I)

Clearly defined the divinity of the Holy Spirit.

431 — Ephesus (Pope Celestine I).

Declared against Nestorius that the Blessed Virgin Mary may be called the Mother of God, since Jesus is one person not two, and he is God.

451 — Chalcedon (Pope Leo I)

Declared that Jesus has two natures, divine and human.

553 — Constantinople II (Pope Vigilius)

Affirmed the dogma of the general council of Chalcedon. Named and condemned those who had taught a contrary doctrine.

680–681 — Constantinople III (Pope Agatho, Pope Leo II)

Declared that Christ has two wills. His human will is distinct from, but not opposed to his divine will.

787 — Nicea II (Pope Adrian I)

Allowed the veneration of sacred images. Affirmed the value of the intercessory power of the saints.

869–870 — Constantinople IV (Pope Adrian II)

Settled a quarrel over the legitimate patriarch of Constantinople and normalized relations between the Byzantine church and Rome.

1123 — Lateran I (Pope Callistus II)

Decreed that all elections of bishops must be made freely without the interference of secular authority.

1139 — Lateran II (Pope Innocent II)

Ended a papal schism, condemned various heresies, issued thirty-two canons dealing with disciplinary and moral matters.

1179 — Lateran III (Pope Alexander III)

Regulated the election of popes, annulled acts of three anti-popes, instituted various disciplines and reforms. Twenty-seven canons were issued.

1215 — Lateran IV (Pope Innocent III)

A clarification of the Catholic teachings on faith and morals. A clarification of the universal nature of the Church, outside of which there is no salvation. First use of the term "transubstantiation" regarding the Eucharist.

1245 — Lyons I (Pope Innocent IV)

Deposed Emperor Frederick II for trying to make the Church a department of the state. Disciplinary legislation.

1274 — Lyons II (Pope Gregory X)

Reunited the Greek and Roman Church. (This attempt later failed.) A clarification that the Holy Spirit proceeds from both the Father and the Son.

1311–1312 — Vienne (Pope Clement V)

Affirmed that the rational soul is the form of the human body. Condemned quietism (which teaches that one can be so holy that one can give free reign to fleshly desires). Disciplinary decrees.

1414–1418 — Constance (Pope Martin V)

Ended the Great Western Schism. Also condemned John Wycliffe and John Huss.

1438–1445 — Basel-Ferrara-Florence (Pope Eugene IV)

Reunited the Greek churches and some Middle-Eastern churches with Rome. (This was only partially successful.)

1512–1517 — Lateran V (Pope Julius II, Pope Leo X)

Spoke on the authority of the pope in relation to an ecumenical council, the immortality and individuality of the soul, and enacted some reforms.

1545–1563 — Trent (Pope Paul III, Pope Julius III, Pope Pius IV)

The Council responded to the Protestant Reformers and condemned the heresies of Luther, Calvin, and others. The Council also re-affirmed Church teaching on marriage, purgatory, indulgences, and religious images. Issued various decrees on the Mass and sacraments.

1869–1870 — Vatican I (Pope Pius IX)

Issued two dogmatic constitutions:

1. The Church guides the interpretation of the Scriptures and is herself guided by the Holy Spirit.
2. The primacy of the pope over the whole Church. A confirmation of the pope's infallible authority.

It also spoke of the relationship between faith and reason.

1962-1965 — Vatican II (Pope John XXIII, Pope Paul VI)

Produced four constitutions, nine decrees, and three declarations dealing with:

—The Church
—Revelation
—The liturgy
—The Church in the modern world
—The relation of the Church to other Christian denominations and other world religions.

Church Bible Study—
Scriptures Cited in the Chapter

Gn 1:31—God declares creation to be good.

Jn 5:17—Jesus reveals that God continually works (even on the Sabbath) to keep creation in existence.

Nm 24:6 and Ps 104:16—Lebanon is beautiful and the source of the cedars used to build the Temple. It is also the scene of the garden in the Song of Songs.

Sg 4:8—Love song calling God's bride from Lebanon.

Is 62:4–5—God is bridegroom and his people are his bride. He promises to restore them.

Jer 2:2—"You loved me as a bride, / Following me in the desert."

Jer 31:4—God promises to restore Israel.

1 Cor 2:9; cf. Is 64:3—What heaven will be like: "What eye has not seen. . . ."

Gn 9—Rainbow is a sign of God's covenant.

Gn 15—God's promises to Abraham. A people will be formed from him.

Gn 12:3—"All the communities of the earth / shall find blessing in you."

Ps 110—David's descendant will be King and Priest forever.

2 Sm 5:7—Zion is a fortress in Jerusalem that David conquers.

Ex 19:6—Israel is to be a nation of priests.

Ps 14:3—"[T]here is not one who does good, not even one."

Mk 2:20 and Jn 3:29—Christ is the bridegroom and John the Baptist is the best man.

2 Pt 1:4—We will share in God's nature. We will become like him.

Eph 5:32—Paul says that the Church is Christ's bride and that "This is a great mystery."

Mt 19:6—Christ on divorce: "What God has joined together, no human being must separate."

Gn 2:23—"This one, at last, is bone of my bones / and flesh of my flesh."

Gn 2:22 and Jn 19:34—God fashioned Eve from the rib that had been taken from the sleeping Adam's side. Water and blood from Christ's side show that Church came to be through his sacrifice as he lay sleeping in death on the cross.

Eph 1:23 and Col 1:18—The Church is Christ's body.

Rv 21:2, Rv 21:11, and Rv 21:23—One day the Church will be revealed in her full glory, "as a bride adorned for her husband." She will gleam "with the splendor of God." God himself will be her light.

Rom 8:22—"All creation is groaning in labor pains even until now."

Dt 5:23–26—The people were afraid they would die if they went near the holy mountain.

Heb 12:22–24—At Mass, on the other hand, people are free to approach God and the assembly of the saints.

Rv 22:17—"The Spirit and the bride say, 'Come.'"

Eph 5:27—Christ will make the Church "without spot or wrinkle or any such thing."

Is 65:17 and Rv 21:1—Christ's Church is the "new heaven and . . . new earth."

Jn 16:7—"It is better for you that I go." Christ's promise to send the Advocate.

Col 3:11—"Christ is all and in all."

Gal 4:26—"The Jerusalem above is freeborn, and she is our mother."

Heb 12:1—The *communion of saints*. Paul describes them as "so great a cloud of witnesses" surrounding us.

Mt 7:16—"By their fruits you will know them."

Jn 17:21—Jesus prays that Christian unity will testify to the truth of his message.

1 Jn 2:19—"They went out from us, but they were not really of our number."

1 Jn 3:14, 16, 23—Christ's new commandment is that we should love one another.

1 Cor 12:14–21—Each of us is to be part of the body. Each of us has a role to play.

Mt 16:18—Christ gives Simon a new name: "Rock" (Peter).

Mt 16:17–18—"Upon this rock will I build my church, and the gates of the netherworld shall not prevail against it."

Jn 1:42 and 1 Cor 15:5—Kephas is an Aramaic word that means "Rock," and this is what Christ called Peter.

Ps 62:3—Christ is the ultimate rock of salvation.

Is 22:22 and Mt 16:19—Giving Peter keys means Peter is the prime minister of his kingdom on earth.

Mt 10:2, Mk 3:16, Lk 6:14, and Acts 1:13—Peter is always first when the apostles are listed.

Lk 22:31–34—Peter instructed to strengthen the others.

Acts 15:7—God chose Peter to teach the gentiles.

Mt 4:18—Peter and his brother Andrew are the first apostles to be chosen by Christ.

Mt 14:28–31; 17:4—Peter asks to walk on the water.

Lk 24:12—Peter was the first to reach the tomb.

Jn 21:7–9—Peter swims to the shore before anyone else in order to meet Christ.

Jn 21:11—Peter swims out, and drags back a net by himself that is bursting with 153 large fish, representing all the known nations at that time.

Acts 2:41—Peter gives the first sermon that converts the first three thousand to the faith.

Mt 17:24—Even authorities outside the Church knew that Peter was the one to approach.

Mt 17:27—Christ assigned Peter the job of catching the fish that held the coin needed to pay the temple tax.

Acts 8:27–31—The Ethiopian tells Philip that one cannot understand the Scriptures unless one has someone to give instruction.

Heb 7–8ff.—The priesthood of the New Covenant, based on Christ's sacrifice, has perfected and completed the priesthood of Aaron and the Levites.

Jn 16:12–13—Jesus promises that the Spirit of Truth will come and guide the Church.

Acts 15:1–12—Argument in the early Church about whether converts needed to be circumcised.

Acts 15:12—Peter gives final decision.

Jn 15:1–2—God will prune branches that do not bear fruit.

Mt 26:69–74 and Jn 21:15–18—Christ calls for Peter to give a threefold affirmation in order to erase his threefold denial of Christ earlier.

Mt 28:20—Christ promised to be with the Church until the end of the world.

Acts 9:4—Christ asks Saul "Why are you persecuting me?"

Lk 10:16—"Whoever listens to you listens to me. Whoever rejects you rejects me."

Jn 16:12—"I have much more to tell you, but you cannot bear it now."

Mt 16:18—The gates of hell will not prevail against the Church.

Mt 13:25–30—The good and the bad must be allowed to remain in the Church for the time being because, "If you pull up the weeds, you might uproot the wheat along with them."

Acts 2—The Holy Spirit overshadows and animates the Church at Pentecost.

Ex 31:18—Pentecost recalls the giving of the Law on Mount Sinai that formed the Hebrews into a new nation.

Gn 11:1–9 and Acts 2:2–4—Parallels and contrasts between the spirit of confusion at the tower of Babel and the Spirit of unity at Pentecost.

Rv 21:14—apostles as stones upon which the building of the Church is based.

Confession and Reconciliation

Many people do not feel comfortable going to Confession because they are confessing to another human being who can also sin. They also feel that it is enough to confess to God in the secrecy of their own heart. In this chapter, we will discuss the virtue of confessing our sins to a priest and why this very act witnesses to, testifies to, and confesses our faith. The outward confession of sin demonstrates our faith in Christ's merciful presence in his Church as signified by the person of the priest. Speaking our sin outwardly to the priest thus becomes a proclamation of the good news of salvation. The act of faith that we make at Confession gives evidence that we believe in his presence and in his power to heal us. Confession celebrates Christ's choice to manifest himself in his Church and act through her ministers even if they are imperfect. This should be a sign of hope to all.

Once we come to the understanding that confession of sin is not only an act of faith but also a confession of faith, we can begin to appreciate the sacrament. When we confess, we testify to the truth. As if in court, we acknowledge that God is our ultimate judge and that we have sinned against him. The Scriptures are filled with images of God as the absolute judge over the world. This is the first thing we confess in the very act of confessing our sin.

> Desist! and confess that I am God,
>> exalted among the nations, exalted upon the earth
>>> (Ps 46:11).

> Behold, his voice resounds, the voice of power:
>> "Confess the power of God!" (Ps 68:34–35)

>> . . . at the name of Jesus
>> every knee should bend,
>> of those in heaven and on earth and under the earth,

> and every tongue confess that
> Jesus Christ is Lord,
> to the glory of God the Father (Phil 2:10–11).

Furthermore, when we confess our guilt, we place ourselves in God's hands and acknowledge our dependence on his mercy. We show obedience to God's scriptural commandment that sins should be confessed.

> Whoever is guilty in any of these cases shall confess the sin he has incurred, and as his sin offering for the sin he has committed he shall bring to the LORD a female animal from the flock. . . . The priest shall then make atonement for his sin (Lv 5:5–6).

> Thus, they will have to confess that they and their fathers were guilty of having rebelled against me. . . . Then, when their uncircumcised hearts are humbled and they make amends for their guilt, I will remember my covenant . . . (Lv 26:40–41).

> I was still occupied with my prayer, confessing my sin and the sin of my people Israel . . . (Dn 9:20).

> Therefore, confess your sins to one another and pray for one another, that you may be healed (Jas 5:16).

Jesus adds something more to our confession. Because Christ revealed himself as the one true Passover lamb, we now understand that the source of God's mercy comes from the sacrifice of his only Son. This is why our confession of sin is also a confession of faith.

> For, if you confess with your mouth that Jesus is Lord and believe in your heart that God raised him from the dead, you will be saved (Rom 10:9).

> Lay hold of eternal life, to which you were called when you made the noble confession in the presence of many witnesses (1 Tim 6:12).

> Let us hold unwaveringly to our confession that gives us hope, for he who made the promise is trustworthy (Heb 10:23).

All of these passages point out a basic truth about confession. It is not a private matter. Confession suggests a courtroom scene. Our initial repentance may have occurred in the quiet of our conscience during a moment of private prayer, but a full confession means something more. Something must be done to show that our repentance is real. The question remains, what is to be done?

In the Old Testament, the answer was clear enough. Repentant sinners would make a confession to the one offended and then offer up something of value as a sin offering through the priest (Nm 5:7). In time, however, the prophets saw that God's people would never live up to the demands of the Law. God showed them how the sin offerings were often used as a way to conceal rather than confess the interior corruption in the hearts of his people.

What care I for the number of your sacrifices?
   says the LORD.
I have had enough of whole-burnt rams. . . .
In the blood of calves, lambs, and goats
   I find no pleasure.

When you come to visit me,
   who asks these things of you? (Is 1:11–12)

For you are not pleased with sacrifices;
   should I offer a holocaust, you would not accept it.
My sacrifice, O God, is a contrite spirit;
   a heart contrite and humbled, O God, you will not spurn
   (Ps 51:18–19).

From these Scripture passages, we can see that true sorrow for sin is what God desires from us. Nevertheless, if a contrite heart is all that matters to God, then why did he command Moses to perform animal sacrifice in the first place?

In the Old Testament, these sacrifices served as an exterior sign for inner repentance. They were God's way of preparing his people for the coming of Christ. God may have condemned rituals performed without reverence, but he did not condemn the rituals themselves. Likewise, in the New Testament, Jesus did not condemn ritual itself (after all, he established a few himself). Instead, he condemned *empty* rituals, or "human tradition" that were designed to get around God's real intent (Mk 7:8). When it comes to real traditions established by God, both the Old Testament and the New Testament insist on obedience.

For example, when God commanded Moses to keep the feast of the Passover, no one would have said to him, "I'd rather just pray on my own, because the Passover is an empty ritual." Similarly, when God spoke through John the Baptist and called the people to repentance, no one would have said to John, "I don't need to be baptized, because I can repent in my own way." Jesus insisted that the cleansed lepers go through the proper ritual. He sent them to the priests as the law prescribed (Mt 8:4). Participation in these rituals served as a sign that a person truly belonged to God. As such, the rituals fulfilled their purpose of expressing and preserving real contact between God and his people.

Nevertheless, the rituals of the Old Testament were limited in their capacity to bring about true forgiveness of sins.

> It is impossible that the blood of bulls and goats take away sins (Heb 10:4).

The old sacrifices were symbolic because the animals were being offered only as a sign of forgiveness. In the person of Christ, the signs were fulfilled. The rituals became real events of healing and cleansing. With the sacraments, we no longer sacrifice something of our own; it is Christ whom we offer up to God. Neither do we promise to live according to the law by the power of our own will. Instead, we promise to cooperate with the help of God's grace. This is why the faithful can be sure that their sins are forgiven when they go to Confession. Because this sacrament is derived from the sacrifice of Christ, those who participate can be sure that they are getting "the real deal."

If the priest were not present to hear the confession and grant forgiveness in Christ's name, then no one could ever know whether or not his repentance was truly "contrite" enough. In the sacrament of Penance, sinners are given a tangible and objective penance (in proportion to their sins) as their way to express true repentance. The purpose of Penance is twofold: it demonstrates both repentance and a turnaround; the sinner turns from sin in order to return to God. Because of the penance, there is no further need to speculate about whether or not a person's sins have been forgiven. More purification may need to take place (as will be discussed in the later chapter on purgatory), but forgiveness has been granted.

How can a sinner *know* that he has been forgiven? Jesus explained how his authority, knowledge, and teaching presence would be maintained in his Church always. He said to the disciples, "Where two or three are gathered together in my name, there am I in the midst of them" (Mt 18:20). Some people take this to mean that no one really is bound to a particular church. Since Christ seems to be promising that he will be present wherever two or more Christians gather together, it doesn't seem to matter whether or not they agree on various points of faith. The fact that Christians are "getting together" seems to be enough to invoke Christ's presence among them. The crucial point that is being missed here is that Christ is present in various ways in his Church. Surely, he is present in his people. But he is present in the shepherds of the Church in a different way. The apostles were seen by all the people as having an authority and a special power to bind and loose (Mt 18:18). They ordained other men in order to hand on the faith to us, bringing to us the presence of Christ as Shepherd, teacher, healer, and sanctifier. These are our bishops and the priests they ordain.

In fact, Jesus was carefully teaching the apostles to avoid conflicts and factions in the Church. Consider the passage in its entirety:

> If your brother sins [against you], go and tell him his fault between you and him alone. If he listens to you, you have won over your brother. If he does not listen, take one or two others along with you, so that "every fact may be established on the testimony of two or three witnesses." If he refuses to

listen to them, tell the church. If he refuses to listen even to the church, then treat him as you would a Gentile or a tax collector. Amen, I say to you, whatever you bind on earth shall be bound in heaven, and whatever you loose on earth shall be loosed in heaven. Again, [amen], I say to you, if two of you agree on earth about anything for which they are to pray, it shall be granted to them by my heavenly Father. For where two or three are gathered together in my name, there am I in the midst of them (Mt 18:15–20).

This passage obviously is dealing with Church authority. It tells how one can find out the truth and how to know right from wrong. When Jesus says that he is present wherever two or three are gathered, he is not saying that any two or three Christians can go off and start up their own church. Neither is he saying that any three Christians who happen to agree about something can define right and wrong. So, what is he saying, exactly?

To answer this question we must think about the difference between Christ's presence in our hearts *as individuals* and Christ's presence *in his Church as a whole.* We can all commune with God as individuals in private prayer, and we all must carry our personal crosses. None of us, however, should assume that we could naturally arrive at the complete truth in matters of faith and morality simply by looking into our hearts and interpreting the Bible for ourselves. Of course, we should pray, read the Scripture, and ask for guidance from the Holy Spirit, but history shows that even when all of this is done, people come up with different answers.

For us, Christ's promises mean that, for any dispute involving faith or morals, *we can rely on the united testimony of the Church.* This is the very thing Christ was talking about when he also said to the apostles, "The Advocate, the holy Spirit that the Father will send in my name—he will teach you everything . . ." (Jn 14:26). Again, Jesus was not promising that the Holy Spirit would guide every single individual Christian 100% of the time. Neither was he promising that Christians would never make a mistake with their interpretations or moral judgments. With his promise regarding the Holy Spirit, Jesus was saying that the Church as a whole would be guided; her testimony as a whole would be infallible.

Thus, when Christ said ". . . if two of you agree . . ." and "where two or three are gathered in my name . . ." etc., he was expressing the idea that the united testimony of the Church is authoritative and can be relied upon; the Holy Spirit guides the united Church into all truth.

This brings us back to Confession as a specific example of this reliability. When we take part in the sacrament of Penance, we can have the confidence that our repentance is real, and that God's forgiveness is truly offered to us. We have this confidence in our own confession because it is united to the "noble confession of faith" given by the entire Church.

As Christians, we are all called to an inward repentance, conversion of heart, and change of life direction that is manifested in an outward confession. This is what John the Baptist called the Jews to do while he preached beside the Jordan so many years ago. He came with the same spirit and austerity as Elijah in order to convince the people to repent of their sins and listen to God. St. Matthew believed that the Baptist fulfilled the prophecy from Isaiah concerning the one who would prepare the way for the Messiah: "A voice of one crying out in the desert, / 'Prepare the way of the Lord, / make straight his paths'" (Mt 3:3; Is 40:3). Whereas all the other prophets had written about Christ so that the people would be able to identify him when he came, St. John's role was unique. He called the people to repent and be baptized as a sign of their inward change of heart and so prepare *themselves* for the coming of the Holy One.

Many responded to St. John's effort to pull the Hebrews out of their indifference towards God. Nevertheless, St. John knew that no true repentance could come about without great suffering, and so he lived a life of personal austerity and suffering in order to give the people an example to live up to (just as modern-day saints do for us). He knew that not everyone was called to live on locusts and honey or to live in caves and wear camel-hair shirts, but he also made it clear that everyone was called to give up whatever prevented them from showing full obedience to God's will.

It was significant that St. John baptized the Hebrews in the River Jordan, because this was the very same river that the Hebrews had first passed through when they entered the Promised Land for the first time. By baptizing in the River Jordan, St. John was trying to convince the Hebrews that they would have to acknowledge and repent of their sins on an individual basis in order to be ready for the day when the Messiah would take them into the true Promised Land.

St. John's message remains relevant for every Christian who desires to live with Christ and participate fully in the life of his Church. The only way that God can ever be approached is with a repentant heart and a willingness to suffer for his sake. It is not enough to be a comfortable Catholic. If we cannot muster up heart-felt grief for our sins and make a serious commitment to suffer a true "death to ourselves," then we are in the same position as the Pharisees whom St. John the Baptist loudly condemned.

> When he saw many of the Pharisees and Sadducees coming to his baptism, he said to them, "You brood of vipers! Who warned you to flee from the coming wrath? Produce good fruit as evidence of your repentance. And do not presume to say to yourselves, 'We have Abraham as our father.' For I tell you God can raise up children to Abraham from these stones. Even now the ax lies to the root of the trees. Therefore every tree that does not bear good fruit will be cut down and thrown into the fire" (Mt 3:7–10).

It is because we need to repent on a daily basis that the sacrament of Confession is so important. It is the only means we have for truly preparing ourselves to receive Christ in the sacrament of Holy Communion. Every heart-felt confession to a priest accomplishes for our soul what an immersion from St. John in the River Jordan accomplished for the Hebrews. And just as the Hebrews did not try to baptize themselves in the River Jordan, but instead went to St. John, so Catholics do not go into an empty room to confess their sins. Instead, they meet with a true representative of Christ who has been given full authority either to forgive us or hold us bound to our sins.

Giving his apostles the authority to forgive sins was so important to Christ that it was the first mission he gave to them after the resurrection. The Gospel of John tells us how the risen Christ appeared to the disciples from behind locked doors, showed them his wounds, and told them that now they would fully share in his work and be given the power to forgive sins.

> [Jesus] said to them again, "Peace be with you. As the Father has sent me, so I send you." And when he had said this, he breathed on them and said to them, "Receive the holy Spirit. Whose sins you forgive are forgiven them, and whose sins you retain are retained" (Jn 20:21–23).

Not since God had formed Adam and "blew into his nostrils the breath of life" had such an event taken place (Gn 2:7). When God did this, he gave Adam authority over everything on earth. When Christ breathed on the apostles, he also made a clear delegation of authority. Therefore, Christ would not have given his disciples this authority if he had not intended them to make use of it, just as he had done throughout his three years of public ministry.

Going to a priest for the sacrament of reconciliation makes Christ's healing presence real for each of us—every time that we go. While it is true that Christ died so that the sins of the whole world could be forgiven, the merits of his sacrifice can only be applied on an individual basis. One by one, we must go before God with a repentant and obedient heart in order to receive the whole Christ, and his life-giving grace through the sacraments—including the sacrament of Confession.

The whole idea behind the sacramental life can be summarized in a simple way. Just as Christ became man by taking on a material body and a human soul so that he could be present to us in a very distinct and real way, so each of the sacraments offers us a visible, material, authentic, and particular expression of his continuing presence to us as individuals. The sacraments bring real, cleansing grace and the real presence of God in a visible way. And it is truly through the sacraments that Christ keeps his promise to each of us, "And behold, I am with you always, until the end of the age" (Mt 28:20). This is why we do not think of ourselves as going to Confession or Communion in order to get "paid" in grace, as some would suggest. Instead, we participate in the sacraments, because this is the kind of relationship that the Holy Trinity desires to share with us.

Christ came to forgive sins so that we could be joined with him in perfect unity, and he came to make this process one that is visible and reliable. When we go to a priest with true regret for our sins, we leave with positive assurance that Christ himself has forgiven us our sins through the priest.

We know from many stories in the Old Testament that it has always been important for God to have his children come before him (or else one of his prophets) to confess their sins with their own mouths. He asked Adam and Eve for a confession, even though their sin was already made known to him (Gn 3:12–13). God also pressed Cain to admit his guilt.

> Then the LORD asked Cain, "Where is your brother Abel?"
> He answered, "I do not know. Am I my brother's keeper?"
> The LORD then said: "What have you done!" (Gn 4:9–10)

Even with King David—whom God described as "a man after my own heart,"—nothing less than a full confession was expected from him after he had committed adultery and then arranged a murder (Acts 13:22; 2 Sm 11 and 12). God was even willing to have the prophet Nathan "trick" David with a parable of his misdeeds in order to hear David say before the prophet, "I have sinned against the LORD" (2 Sm 12:13).

In each of these Old Testament stories, the sinner's confession was to express a willingness to confront the suffering and grief caused by sin. In each case, God responded to the sinner with some kind of assurance that new life would be given to them for having admitted the truth. For Adam and Eve, God made clothes for them, settled them outside the garden, and blessed them with children after they departed from the Garden of Eden (Gn 3:21–24; 4:1–3). To Cain, God promised that no one would be allowed to take his life the way that he had taken the life of his brother (Gn 4:15–16). And finally, through the prophet Nathan, God assured David, "The LORD on his part has forgiven your sin: you shall not die" (2 Sm 12:13).

In the New Testament also, Christ does not shy away from exposing people to their sins. To the Samaritan woman at the well, he said in plain language, "You have had five husbands, and the one you have now is not your husband" (Jn 4:18). Peter was also rebuked in strong terms ("Get behind me, Satan!") after Peter had counseled him to avoid going up to Jerusalem (Mt 16:23). After the resurrection, Christ also put Peter through the pain of having to acknowledge (at least indirectly) that he had denied the Lord three times. The Gospel of John tells us that, "Peter was distressed that [Christ] had said to him a third time, 'Do you love me?'" (Jn 21:17). The matter of Peter's denial simply could not be overlooked and forgotten. It had to be dealt with, and Christ gave Peter the chance to say for a third time, "Lord, you know everything; you know that I love you" (Jn 21:17).

These examples show that we cannot enjoy an authentic and intimate union with God unless we are first willing to turn to Christ (sometime before our last breath) like the good thief, who died on the cross next to Jesus. He defended Christ and accused himself by reminding the other thief, "We have been condemned justly, for the sentence we received corresponds to our crimes" (Lk 23:41). Because the good thief first confessed his guilt and spoke the truth, Christ gave him enough hope and faith to ask for a favor: "Jesus, remember me when you come into your kingdom" (Lk 23:42). Likewise, when we admit our guilt before Christ through the priest, then we will also be given enough hope and faith to believe for ourselves Christ's promise to the dying man, "Amen, I say to you, today you will be with me in Paradise" (Lk 23:43).

Jesus gave us the sacrament of Confession in order to teach us to love the truth. When we finally accept the need for a confession, we can begin to understand the meaning behind Christ's conversation with Nicodemus, when Jesus said to him,

> And this is the verdict, that the light came into the world, but people preferred darkness to light, because their works were evil. For everyone who does wicked things hates the light and does not come toward the light, so that his works might not be exposed. But whoever lives the truth comes to the light, so that his works may be clearly seen as done in God (Jn 3:19–21).

What else could Christ's statements about darkness and light be referring to, if not Confession, where we meet Christ and allow our works to be exposed to his light? In what other way did God give us such an obvious and easy opportunity to turn away from darkness? To accept Christ's gift of the sacrament of reconciliation allows us truly to put on "the mind of Christ," in the words of St. Paul (1 Cor 2:16). Our conscience is a kind of spiritual organ or muscle that can become more efficient and powerful with every use. This means that exposing our conscience to the light of Christ will make it "sharper than any two-edged sword, penetrating even between soul and spirit, joints and marrow, and able to discern reflections and thoughts of the heart" (Heb 4:12). This is how the sacrament of Confession helps us become more aware of temptation and better able to withstand it as well. If we accept Christ's gift of Confession, our tears of sorrow and regret will one day be turned to joy when we stand at last before the throne of Christ with a clean conscience (Rv 21:4).

Getting to that point, however, is not easy. If we are going to make an effort in the confessional to admit all of our sins, it is helpful to have a definition of sin based on Church teaching. A sinful act is defined as a deliberate decision to go against God's will.[1] This decision is first made in a person's heart; outward actions express a sinful intention that was present before the act.

---

[1] CCC 1849, 1850.

Jesus emphasized this point when he was speaking to a group of Pharisees.

> You brood of vipers, how can you say good things when you are evil? For from the fullness of the heart the mouth speaks. A good person brings forth good out of a store of goodness, but an evil person brings forth evil out of a store of evil (Mt 12:34–35).

Christ also made it clear that many sins can be committed in one's heart. When the Pharisees were upset that Christ's disciples had not washed their hands as was prescribed by Jewish laws, Christ privately explained to the disciples the true source of sin.

> But the things that come out of the mouth come from the heart, and they defile. For from the heart come evil thoughts, murder, adultery, unchastity, theft, false witness, blasphemy. These are what defile a person, but to eat with unwashed hands does not defile (Mt 15:18–20).

Christ confirmed this teaching when he warned on another occasion that a man can commit adultery with a woman in his heart merely by looking at her with this intention (Mt 5:28). He also warned that, "Whoever is angry with his brother will be liable to judgment . . . and whoever says, 'You fool,' will be liable to fiery Gehenna" (Mt 5:22).

Although sinful behavior originates in the heart, it must not be confused with temptation, which could be defined as an urge to act against the law of love. It does not always take the form of an illicit pleasure. There are some sins such as pride, anger, envy, and jealousy that cause only grief and pain. Nevertheless, a person can either resist a temptation or give in to it with increasing degrees of complicity. Therefore, it is better to reject an idea sooner rather than later. This is why Christ warned us to pray at all times, so that by focusing our minds on God, we might be more quick to rely on him for help whenever temptation arises (Mk 14:38, 13:33). Temptation is therefore one of the forms of suffering that Christians are called to endure for Christ's sake.

But it is Christ's promise to us in the book of Revelation that, "To the victor, I will give the right to eat from the tree of life that is in the garden of God" (Rv 2:7).

In his letter to the Romans, St. Paul teaches that whenever we sin, we are slaves to sin (Rom 6:16). Less serious sins are sometimes called venial sins (from the Latin word *venia*, meaning "forgivable"), because God forgives them readily. They can still cause great harm if we allow them to weaken our resistance or dull our conscience to what is right or wrong. After all, it was Christ who said, "The person who is trustworthy in very small matters is also trustworthy in great ones; and the person who is dishonest in very small matters is also dishonest in great ones" (Lk 16:10).

There are three conditions that must be met in order for a sin to be considered very serious or "mortal," meaning "deadly." First of all, it must be a serious matter with grave consequences. Secondly, the sin must be committed with full knowledge and understanding that the matter is a serious sin. Finally, mortal sin requires serious forethought and a full consent of the will. In other words, the sin must be committed freely, without any form of coercion or compulsion involved. For example, the sin of detraction (otherwise known as gossip) occurs when a person reveals the hidden sins of another person without having a good reason for doing so (such as the prevention of further harm to someone). If my gossip amounts to small talk, then it would be considered sinful, but not serious. If what I say ruins a person's public reputation, then it would be a serious matter. If, by my gossip, however, I did not realize that I would be causing harm or that my actions were gravely sinful, then my sin would still be considered venial, because I acted without full knowledge. If, however, I knew it was a serious sin to ruin a person's public reputation and I hoped and planned that this would happen, then this sin would have to be considered mortal, because by my action I disobeyed God's laws, causing great harm to my neighbor, without any hesitation or remorse at the time.

When carried out under these three conditions, a mortal sin

constitutes a complete rejection of God. When a person dies without repenting of a mortal sin, then the sacrifice of Christ on the cross will not be applied to his sins. This means that the harm that has been done to the soul of the sinner will remain; the person will be damned. In his first epistle, St. John refers to this limit of intercession. He shows that God will not forgive a person who commits a mortal sin and refuses to repent for it.

> If anyone sees his brother sinning, if the sin is not deadly, he should pray to God and he will give him life. This is only for those whose sin is not deadly. There is such a thing as deadly sin, about which I do not say that you should pray. All wrongdoing is sin, but there is sin that is not deadly (1 Jn 5:16–17).

The Church teaches that mortal sins must be confessed and absolved by a priest through the sacrament of Reconciliation. The Church also teaches that it is gravely wrong for people to participate in Holy Communion without first being absolved of their mortal sins. St. Paul spoke strongly on this matter and warned the Corinthians that they would be bringing God's judgment on themselves if they were to partake "unworthily" of the body and the blood of the Lord (1 Cor 11:27–30). If we are truly sorry for the wrong we have done, then it is the least we can do to express our repentance by going to Confession. It was Christ who first commanded us to do so.

> Therefore, if you bring your gift to the altar, and there recall that your brother has anything against you, leave your gift there at the altar, go first and be reconciled with your brother, and then come and offer your gift (Mt 5:23–24).

For Catholics, sin is not merely a private matter between one's self and God. Sin rejects both the love for God and the love we have towards our neighbor; it therefore alienates us from the communal life we are supposed to live with one another. The sacrament of Reconciliation not only reconciles us to God but to the whole body of Christ. The Mass contains both a public expression of communal guilt and the Rite of Peace, signifying the restoring of love among the people. The private and public forms of reconciliation give us the grace and encouragement that we need to follow the law of the New Covenant, as described by St. Paul in his letter to the Corinthians.

> But I shall show you a still more excellent way. . . . Love is patient, love is kind. It is not jealous, [love] is not pompous, it is not inflated, it is not rude, it does not seek its own interests, it is not quick-tempered, it does not brood over injury, it does not rejoice over wrongdoing but rejoices with the truth. It bears all things, believes all things, hopes all things, endures all things (1 Cor 12:31, 13:4–7).

Even when we feel a great struggle occurring in our soul which cannot be easily repented or overcome, it can still be helpful for us to go to Confession and bring up the matter with a priest who can give us some advice. God is much more aware of the devil's power to tempt us than we are, and he looks with compassion on those who feel helpless in their struggle against the devil. Not once anywhere does Christ rebuke humble sinners who are willing to acknowledge their helplessness before him. Over and over again in the gospels, Christ declares that those who feel lost are the ones most dear to his heart. They are the lost sheep whom he has come to search out and rescue at all cost (Mt 18:12; Jn 10:14–17). In all of his teaching, Jesus upholds their dignity and defends them against the self-righteous. For example, he is forgiving with the woman caught in the act of adultery: "Has no one condemned you? . . . Neither do I condemn you. Go, [and] from now on do not sin any more" (Jn 8:10–11). He also teaches that the angels in heaven rejoice more over the repentance of a single sinner than they do over ninety-nine righteous people who have no need of repentance (Lk 15:7). He also brushes away the self-important by saying, "Those who are well do not need a physician, but the sick do. I did not come to call the righteous but sinners" (Mk 2:17). Finally, he teaches the parable of the prodigal son to show how much he and the Father rejoice when such a one returns home (Lk 15:11–32). In this parable, the Father runs out to meet the son, who is still quite a distance away. He puts a gold ring on his finger, clothes him with a new robe, and welcomes him with great joy.

> Take the fattened calf and slaughter it. Then let us celebrate with a feast, because this son of mine was dead, and has come to life again; he was lost, and has been found (Lk 15:23–24).

When speaking to Nicodemus, Christ explains very clearly that, "God did not send his Son into the world to condemn the world, but that the world might be saved through him" (Jn 3:17). In all of his teachings, Christ tries to reach out to the humble sinners and offer them hope for the future. In doing so, he truly fulfills the prophecy from Isaiah about the Messiah.

> A bruised reed he shall not break,
>   and a smoldering wick he shall not quench . . . (Is 42:3).

Jesus was indeed gentle and did not go out of his way to offend anyone. This did not stop certain people from taking offense at him, however. The Pharisees took offense at his claim to forgive sins. An example of this occurs with the healing of the paralytic.

One day Jesus performed a simultaneous healing for a paralyzed man who came to him on a stretcher. It was simultaneous in that both the man's soul and the man's body were restored to health. The Lord was in Capernaum at the time. When word got out of his arrival, the customary crowd pressed in on the house where he stayed (Mk 2:1–2).

> When Jesus returned to Capernaum after some days, it became known that he was at home. Many gathered together so that there was no longer room for them, not even around the door . . . (Mk 2:1–2).

> Unable to get near Jesus because of the crowd, they opened up the roof above him. After they had broken through, they let down the mat on which the paralytic was lying (Mk 2:4).

Our Lord, on seeing the faith of the men still up on the roof, declared to the crippled man that his sins were forgiven (Mk 2:5). Note that it was *faith* that initiated the miracle of forgiveness—not only the faith of the man on the stretcher, but of the men who carried the stretcher, as well. They had performed this favor for their brother because they were convinced that Jesus could heal him.

> When Jesus saw their faith, he said to the paralytic, "Child, your sins are forgiven" (Mk 2:5).

The motivation for this dramatic lowering of the stretcher had to have been obvious to our Lord; the men were looking for a physical healing. Why then, did Jesus first forgive the man's sins? Why didn't he begin by healing his paralysis? The reason was that Jesus intended to use the man's broken physical condition as a witness to the *validity of his power to forgive*. John the Baptist had said of Jesus, "Behold, the Lamb of God, who takes away the sin of the world" (Jn 1:29). But how was anyone to *know* the truth of those words? Jesus would offer them proof through miracles.

Our Lord's pronouncement of forgiveness was met with immediate condemnation by some of the scribes, who, due to their status, were no doubt seated very close to him (Mk 2:6). They had come to hear the teachings and to see the signs that Jesus always performed; yet, when it came to forgiving sins, they drew the line.

> Now some of the scribes were sitting there asking themselves, "Why does this man speak that way?" (Mk 2:6–7)

Puffed up with self-righteousness and justified by their knowledge of Scripture, they questioned in their hearts how Jesus could possibly presume to have God's authority to forgive sins. On this point, the Scriptures seemed incontrovertible: Jesus was stepping out of bounds.

> And if my people, upon whom my name has been pronounced, humble themselves and pray, and seek my presence and turn from their evil ways, I will hear them from heaven and pardon their sins . . . (2 Chr 7:14).

> For you, O LORD, are good and forgiving . . . (Ps 86:5).

O LORD, hear! O LORD, pardon! O LORD, be attentive and act without delay . . .! (Dn 9:19)

In Jesus they saw nothing more than a teacher and a miracle worker. They were willing to accept his teaching, so long as it was consistent with their preconceived notions of religion. Here, however, Jesus was acting as if he were God himself! Since they were unwilling to recognize Jesus as the Messiah, their only alternative was to accuse him of blasphemy.

Why does this man speak that way? He is blaspheming. Who but God alone can forgive sins? (Mk 2:7)

Blasphemy was a serious accusation. Recall that when Jesus was later brought before the council of the Jews, he was indicted for blasphemy and immediately sentenced to death (Mt 26:65–66). Such an accusation was not to be taken lightly. Nevertheless, our Lord was willing to risk this slander. He took the offensive and offered up a challenge for his critics to consider: "Which is easier, to say to the paralytic, 'Your sins are forgiven,' or to say, 'Rise, take up your mat and walk'?" (Mk 2:9).

At this point, the people must have been wondering what kind of forgiveness Jesus meant. Anyone in the crowd could have told the man on the stretcher that *they forgave him*. But such forgiveness would be merely superficial. Here, Jesus was obviously talking about a forgiveness that was so profound it would affect the very life of the soul. This was a forgiveness that people had longed for—but had never been assured of having. It was the forgiveness symbolized by the blood of countless sacrificial lambs.

To prove that he had the power to grant such forgiveness, Jesus said to the man, "I say to you, rise, pick up your mat, and go home" (Mk 2:11). The man did just that. To witness the man as he first stood up must have caused quite a stir; but even more dramatic was the healing of the man's soul that transformed the event into a historic moment. The age of reconciliation was at hand!

> "But that you may know that the Son of Man has authority to forgive sins on earth"—he said to the paralytic, "I say to you, rise, pick up your mat, and go home." He rose, picked up his mat at once, and went away in the sight of everyone. They were all astounded and glorified God . . . (Mk 2:10–12).

People were amazed at the healing, of course. But there was also simple amazement at the fact that God had given such authority to Jesus: "When the crowds saw this they were struck with awe and glorified God who had given such authority to human beings" (Mt 9:8). Jesus explicitly gave this type of authority to his apostles on several occasions.

After his resurrection, for example, Jesus told his apostles, "As the Father has sent me, so I send you. . . . Whose sins you forgive are forgiven them, and whose sins you retain are retained" (Jn 20:21, 23). The same forgiveness that Jesus bestowed on the paralytic was to be the Holy Spirit's free gift to everyone who came to the Lord, through his Church, for healing.

The Gospels show that Christ was merciful and kind to sinners, *except when they were in positions of power or leadership*. He could forgive those who felt compelled to disobey the law in order to avoid suffering or hardship. He was also lenient towards those who slipped into a state of degeneracy; but as for those who fell into the sin of pride—Jesus showed no mercy. After all, pride had been the sin by which Satan first took his hold on humanity. Consequently, in both the Old and New Testaments, God's wrath is most often directed towards those who use their gifts for the sake of personal gain or grandeur. The scribes and Pharisees offended Christ precisely because they knowingly refused to help the people beneath them.

Even with the apostles, Jesus warned them not to abuse their power. In his parable of the wayward servants who stopped working after the master had gone away, the lesser servants were let off with a slight punishment, but the overseers who had been given more responsibility were given a severe beating (Lk 12:47–48). In other words, those in power are called to a stricter account than the have-nots who misbehave. Therefore, those who are in power and tend to feel most self-satisfied about their lives are the ones who are in the greatest danger of having God's judgment fall against them (Lk 12:48).

The medicine of Confession is the perfect antidote to the wounds that our own pride can inflict on our souls. During our confession, we humble ourselves. In doing this, we disavow our personal sins. This disavowal is the way we "take our medicine" in order to be healed. For those who suffer from the consequences of personal sin, Christ offers himself as medicine, dispensing his grace through the Church and through the person of the priest who stands in his place.

We listen to the doctor and "take our medicine." This medicine is healing because it is real. As physical beings, we are made from matter and we relate to the world by means of our physical senses. We were put together as creatures of habit, and we learn best with the help of routine and ritual, as well as symbolic objects such as water, wine, bread, and oil. God made us this way! Christ did not come to do away with the many rituals from the Old Testament. Instead, he came to animate them so that we could experience a real encounter with the living God. This is exactly what happens at Confession. We may not necessarily *feel* the direct presence of the Holy Spirit, but he is there, giving us the grace necessary to be reconciled to God. We can know this because our faith is part of the united confession and testimony of his Church, and we accept our individual penance as God's way of reconciling us to himself.

St. Paul called upon everyone to humble themselves and be reconciled to God through Jesus Christ and the ambassadorship of his Church:

> God was reconciling the world to himself in Christ, not counting their trespasses against them and entrusting to us the message of reconciliation. So we are ambassadors for Christ, as if God were appealing through us. We implore you on behalf of Christ, be reconciled to God (2 Cor 5:19–20).

Let us heed Paul's advice and be reconciled to God.

The Early Church Fathers
on Confession

St. Clement of Rome (A.D. 92): *Letter to the Corinthians* (v. 1, 26a)

For whatever our transgressions, and whatever we have done through the attacks of the adversary, let us pray that we may be forgiven. . . . For it is good for a man to confess his failings rather than to harden his heart.

Didache or *Teaching of the Twelve Apostles* (A.D. 140): (v. 1, 3)

Confess your offenses in church, and do not go up to your prayer with an evil conscience. This is the way of life.

An Anonymous Homily: A.D. 150 *The So-called Second Letter of Clement of Rome to the Corinthians* (v. 1, 103)

Let us, then, so long as we are in this world, repent whatever evils we have done in the flesh, so that we may be saved by the Lord while yet we have time for repentance. For after we have departed from this world it will no longer be possible to confess, nor will there be then any opportunity to repent.

Tertullian (A.D. 155/160–240/250): *On Repentance* (v. 1, 315)

Confession is all of this, so that it may excite repentance; so that it may honor God by fear of danger; so that it may, by its own pronouncement against the sinner, stand in place of God's indignation; and so that it may by temporal mortification, I will not say frustrate, but rather expunge the eternal punishments. Therefore, while it abases a man, it raise him; while it covers him with squalor, the more does it cleanse him; while it condemns, it absolves. In so far as you do not spare yourself, the more, believe me, will God spare you!

(v. 1, 316)

I presume they are more mindful of modesty than of salvation, like those who contract a disease in the more shameful parts of the body and shun making themselves known to the physician; and thus they perish along with their own bashfulness. Why do you flee from the partners of your misfortunes as you would from those who deride? The body is not able to take pleasure in the trouble of one of its members. It must necessarily grieve as a whole and join in laboring for a remedy.

(v. 1, 317)

If you are inclined to draw back from confession, consider in your heart the hell which confession extinguishes for you, and imagine first the magnitude of the penalty, so that you will not hesitate about making use of the remedy. What do you think of that storehouse of eternal fire when certain of its smoke-holes rouse such a pressure of flames that nearby cities either already are no more, or are daily in expectation of destruction? The grandest mountains part asunder in the birth of their eternal fire. . . . Who will not regard these occasional punishments inflicted on the mountains as examples of the impending judgment? Who will not agree that such sparks are but a few missiles and random darts from some unimaginably great center? Therefore, when you know that after the initial support of the Lord's Baptism there is still in confession a second reserve against hell, why do you desert your salvation? Why do you hesitate to approach what you know will heal you?

Aphrahat the Persian Sage (A.D. 280–345): *Treatises* (v. 1, 685)

Anyone who has been wounded in a battle ought not be reluctant to put himself in the care of a wise physician, because he was overcome and lost the battle. . . . You physicians, then, who are the disciples of our illustrious Physician, you ought not deny a curative to those in need of healing. And if anyone uncovers his wound before you, give him the remedy of repentance. And he that is ashamed to make known his weakness, encourage him so that he will not hide it from you. And when he has revealed it to you, do not make it public, lest because of it the innocent might be reckoned as guilty by our enemies and by those who hate us.

St. Ambrose of Milan (A.D. 333–387): *Penance* (v. 2, 1297).

Things that are impossible with men are possible with God. God is able, whenever he wills, to forgive us our sins, even those we think cannot be forgiven. Thus it is possible for God to give us what to us seems impossible to obtain. . . . It seemed likewise impossible for sins to be forgiven through penance; yet Christ granted even this to his Apostles, and by his Apostles it has been transmitted to the offices of priests.

St. Augustine of Hippo (A.D. 354–430): *Sermons* (v. 3, 1494)

If you want God to forgive, you must confess. Sin cannot go unpunished. It was unseemly, improper, and unjust for sin to go unpunished. Since, therefore, sin must not go unpunished, let it be punished by you, lest you be punished for it. Let your sin have you for its judge, not its patron. Go up and take the bench against yourself, and put your guilt before yourself. Do not put it behind you, or God will put it in front of you.

St. Augustine of Hippo (A.D. 354–430): *Christian Combat* (v. 3, 1579)

Let us not listen to those who deny that the Church of God is able to forgive all sins. They are wretched indeed, because they do not recognize in Peter the rock and they refuse to believe that the keys of the kingdom of heaven, lost from their own hands, have been given to the Church.

The Early Church Fathers on
the Nature of Sin in General

Hermas (A.D. 140/155): *The Shepherd* (v. 1, 86a)

"Give me understanding for I am very foolish, and I comprehend absolutely nothing." He answered me and said: "I preside over repentance and I give understanding to all who repent. Indeed, do you not realize that this very repentance is understanding? To repent is great understanding. For the sinner understands that he has done wickedly before the Lord; and the deed which he has done comes into his heart, and he repents and does wickedly no longer; rather, he does good abundantly, and humbles his soul and puts it to the torture because it sinned. You see, then, that repentance is great understanding."

(v. 1, 90)

And the shepherd answered me and said: "As many as repent with their whole heart and purify themselves of all the wickedness mentioned before, and no longer add anything to their former sins—they shall receive from the Lord a healing for their former sins, provided they are not double-minded in regard to these commandments; and they shall live to God. But as many as add to their sins and live in the lusts of this world—they shall condemn themselves to death."

St. Justin Martyr (A.D. 100/110–165): *First Apology* (v. 1, 123)

If the human race does not have the power of a freely deliberated choice in fleeing evil and in choosing good, then men are not accountable for their actions, whatever they may be. That they do, however, by a free choice, either walk upright or stumble, we shall now prove. . . . God did not make man like the other beings, the trees and the four-legged beasts, for example, which cannot do anything by free choice. Neither would man deserve reward or praise if he did not of himself choose the good; nor, if he acted wickedly, would he deserve punishment, since he would not be evil by choice, and could not be other than that which he was born. The Holy Prophetic Spirit taught us this when he informed us through Moses that God spoke as follows to the first created man: "Behold, before your face, the good and the evil. Choose the good."

St. Theophilus of Antioch (A.D. 191): *To Autolycus* (v. 1, 184)

By nature, in fact [God] made [man] neither mortal nor immortal. For if God had made him immortal from the beginning, he would have made him God. Again, if he had made him mortal, it would seem as if God were the cause of his death. He made him then, neither mortal nor immortal, but, as we said above, capable of either. Thus, if he should incline to the ways of immortality, keeping the command of God, he should receive from God the reward of immortality, and become God. If, however, he turns aside to the ways of death, disobeying God, he should become for himself the cause of death. For God made man free and self-determining.

St. Irenaeus (A.D. 140–202): *Against Heresies* (v. 1, 224a–225)

But, this man [of whom I have been speaking] is Adam, if the truth be told, the first-formed man. . . . We, however, are all from him; and as we are from him, we have inherited his title. . . .

Resisting the wanton impulse of the flesh, for he had lost his natural disposition and childlike mind, and had come to a knowledge of evil, [Adam] girded both himself and his wife with a bridle of continence, fearing God and expecting His coming, and indicating something such as this: "Inasmuch," he said, "as I have lost by disobedience the mantle of holiness which I had from the Spirit, I do acknowledge that I am worthy of such a covering, which provides no comfort, but stings and irritates the body."

Minucius Felix (A.D. 135): *Octavius* (v. 1, 273)

You punish crimes when they have been committed. With us, it is a sin even to consider a crime. You fear witnesses. We fear even our own conscience, which we cannot escape. And finally, the jails are full of your people; but there is no Christian there, unless his crime is his religion.

St. Irenaeus (A.D. 140–202): *Against Heresies* (v. 1, 239)

As in the New Testament man's faith in God has been increased by the addition of the Son of God, whereby man becomes a partaker of God, so also is there an increase in diligence in our lives, since we are commanded to abstain not only from evil deeds, but even from the thoughts themselves and from wicked talk and empty language and scurrilous words. So also is the penalty increased of those who do not believe the Word of God and despise his coming and whose attention is directed to the past; for it is not merely temporal, but eternal.

Tertullian (A.D. 155/160–240/250): *The Testimony of the Soul* (v. 1, 286)

Finally, in every instance of vexation, contempt, and abhorrence, you pronounce the name of Satan. He it is whom we call the angel of wickedness, the author of every error, the corrupter of the whole world, through whom man was deceived in the very beginning so that he transgressed the command of God. On account of his transgression man was given over to death; and the whole human race, which was infected by his sin, was made the transmitter of condemnation.

Lactantius (A.D. 250–317): *Divine Institutions* (v. 1, 641)

For this, therefore, it is clear that the knowledge of good and evil is one thing, but virtue is another; for knowledge can exist without virtue. . . . Virtue is not the knowing of good and evil. Rather, virtue is the doing of good and not doing of evil. Knowledge, however, is in fact joined to virtue in such wise that knowledge precedes virtue and virtue follows knowledge. Cognition is of no value unless it is followed by action.

St. Peter Chrysologus (A.D. 405–450): *Sermons* **(v. 3, 2176)**

No need to despair, man. Look, there has still remained for you a means to satisfy your Most Pious Creditor. Do you want to be forgiven? Then love! "Love covers over a multitude of sins." What worse crime is there than denial? And yet Peter was able to wipe away even this by love alone, when the Lord, to test him, says: "Peter, do you love me?" Among all God's precepts, love takes the first place.

Confession Bible Study—
Scriptures Cited in the Chapter

Ps 46:11, Ps 68:34–35, and Phil 2:10–11—God as the judge of the world.

Lv 5:5–6, Lv 26:40–41, Dn 9:20, and Jas 5:16—We are all called to confess our sins.

Rom 10:9, 1 Tim 6:12, and Heb 10:23—To "confess" also means to witness to Christ; we are called to make "official" confessions of our faith.

Nm 5:7—Offering sacrifice is part of true repentance. Shown by a sin offering in the Old Testament.

Is 1:11–12, Ps 51:18–19, and Heb 10:4—Old sacrifices not good enough. They are powerless to remove sin.

Mk 7:8—Jesus condemned *empty* ritual, or "human tradition."

Mt 8:4—Jesus insisted that the cleansed lepers go through the proper ritual.

Mt 18:15–20—This entire passage emphasizes Church authority in dealing with disputes.

Is 40:3 and Mt 3:3—St. John the Baptist fulfills Elijah's role in calling everyone to repentance in order to prepare for Christ's coming.

Mt 3:7–10—"Therefore every tree that does not bear good fruit will be cut down and thrown into the fire."

Jn 20:19–23—"Receive the holy Spirit. Whose sins you forgive are forgiven them, and whose sins you retain are retained."

Mt 28:20—"And behold, I am with you always, until the end of the age."

Gn 3:12–13 and Gn 4:9–10—God demands confessions from Adam and from Cain.

2 Sm 12:13—God forces King David to confess.

Gn 3:21–24; 4:1–3—Though Adam and Eve had to leave the garden, after Adam's confession they were settled and were blessed with children.

Gn 4:15–16—After Cain's confession, God promised him that no one would take his life.

2 Sm 12:13—After King David's confession, God promised him that God had put away his sin.

Jn 4:18—Jesus tells the woman at the well of her sins: "You have had five husbands."

Mt 16:23—"Get behind me, Satan!" Jesus rebukes Peter.

Jn 21:17—Jesus gives Peter the chance to make up for his earlier betrayal.

Lk 23:41–43—Jesus rewards the good thief for his confession.

Jn 3:19–21—"Whoever lives the truth comes to the light, so that his works may be clearly seen as done in God."

1 Cor 2:16—We are given the "mind of Christ."

Heb 4:12—Christ's spirit of discernment is "sharper than any two-edged sword, penetrating even between soul and spirit, joints and marrow, and able to discern reflections and thoughts of the heart."

Rv 22:3–4—Our tears of sorrow and regret will one day be turned to joy when we stand at last before the throne of Christ with a clean conscience.

Mt 12:34–35—"A good person brings forth good out of a store of goodness, but an evil person brings forth evil out of a store of evil."

Mt 15: 18–20—Christ explains that rituals or lack of rituals cannot defile; rather, the actions and evil thoughts that come from within us are what defile us.

Mt 5:22—"Whoever is angry with his brother will be liable to judgment . . . and whoever says, 'You fool,' will be liable to fiery Gehenna."

Mk 13:33; 14:38—We should be on guard and pray at all times.

Rv 2:7—"To the victor I will give the right to eat from the tree of life that is in the garden of God."

Rom 6:16—St. Paul teaches that whenever we sin, we are slaves to sin.

Lk 16:10—"The person who is dishonest in very small matters is also dishonest in great ones."

1 Jn 5:16–17—Mortal and venial sin.

1 Cor 11:27–30—No one should approach communion with unrepented sin.

Mt 5:23–24—We should not approach God if we have not reconciled with our brother.

1 Cor 12:31; 13:4—Love is the new law and the new covenant.

Mt 18:12 and Jn 10:14–17—Christ declares that those who feel lost are the ones most dear to his heart. They are the "lost sheep" whom he has come to search out and rescue at all cost.

Jn 8:10–11—Christ forgives the woman caught in adultery; tells her "do not sin any more."

Lk 15:7—"There will be more joy in heaven over one sinner who repents than over ninety-nine righteous people who have no need of repentance."

Mk 2:17—"Those who are well do not need a physician, but the sick do. I did not come to call the righteous but the sinners."

Lk 15:11–32—Parable of the prodigal son.

Jn 3:17—"God did not send his Son into the world to condemn the world, but that the world might be saved through him."

Is 42:3—"A bruised reed he shall not break, / and a smoldering wick he shall not quench."

Mk 2:1–12—The story of the paralytic: Pharisees are offended at Jesus' claim to have authority to forgive sins.

Jn 1:29—"Behold, the Lamb of God, who takes away the sin of the world."

2 Chr 5:14, Ps 86:5, and Dn 9:19—God forgives the humble.

Mt 26:65–66—Jesus was brought before the council of the Jews, indicted for blasphemy, and given a sentence of death.

Mt 9:7—Crowds are awed that God gave human beings the authority to forgive sins.

Jn 20:21, 23—Through the Apostles, Jesus gives the Church authority to forgive sins. He said to them, "Whose sins you forgive are forgiven them, and whose sins you retain are retained."

Lk 12:47–48—Those with greater knowledge and authority will be held to a higher standard.

2 Cor 5:19–20—As God's ambassadors, we call everyone to reconciliation with God.

Purgatory: The Fire of God's Love

God plans for each of us to try to become perfect like him during our lifetime. He gives the grace we need to fulfill our duties and show true charity towards the people around us. Because of our weakness, however, and our lack of faith, we often need his forgiveness because of something that we have either done or else failed to do. If we were all to die today, most of us would not be ready to stand before God's throne with a perfectly clean conscience. The question for this chapter concerns what happens to the souls who die in this state of imperfection. In St. John's apocalyptic vision of heaven, we are told that, "Nothing unclean will enter it" (Rv 21:27). Since we understand heaven to be a state of perfect harmony, accord, and acceptance of God, no one can exist in heaven unless he is completely purified of all attachment to sin—including venial sin. There must therefore be an intermediary state of existence, where souls can be prepared to become perfectly obedient to God before entering heaven.

Some Christians do not accept the doctrine of purgatory. Instead, they teach that the souls of the saved go through an instantaneous and painless transformation that cleanses them of every sin on their soul. According to this teaching, the souls of the dead have no need of our prayers: they are already in heaven enjoying perfect peace or else they have been damned to spend eternity in hell. The Catholic Church, however, holds fast to the Jewish and early Christian tradition (of Jewish origin) that God has reserved a place or state of being for those who die with some residue of sin on their souls. The Old Testament refers to this place as *Sheol*.[1] Both the just and the sinful descended

---

[1] *Sheol* was a general term for the place of the dead; it did not have the

to it after death. Ideas about Sheol were not clear. The ancient biblical writers could not imagine that a Patriarch like Abraham or Jacob would be sent to hell, but neither could they imagine any of them as being perfect enough to coexist with God in heaven. Instead, a gray and more mysterious afterlife—like the Greek *hades*—seemed more reasonable.

The Hebrews therefore accepted that their sins made them unworthy of eternal life with God. They could nevertheless find comfort in the prophecy of King David,

> As far as the east is from the west,
> so far has he put our transgressions from us (Ps 103:12).

People might not have understood how (or when) God would so radically separate us from our sins. We now understand that the sacrifice of Christ fulfills this prophecy.

For the first Christians, the death and resurrection of Christ also clarified much of the mystery surrounding the Old Testament concept of Sheol. Christ must have revealed to the apostles that he descended to Sheol just after he died, because St. Peter recounts the event in one of his epistles. Peter explains that the purpose for Christ's descent was "to preach to the spirits in prison, who had once been disobedient . . ." (1 Pt 3:19–20). After many centuries of discussion, the Church began referring to this state of purification as "purgatory" (from the Latin word *purgatio*, which means "cleansing").

Some object to the doctrine of purgatory because there is no explicit mention of the word in Scripture. These same critics, however, readily accept the doctrine of the Trinity and the Incarnation even though these words also go unmentioned. It is true that neither Christ nor the apostles specifically said that, "Some who die will have to suffer in purgatory before they can go to heaven." But just as the Church has inferred the doctrine

---

connotation of being a place of purification, though 2 Mc 12 shows the idea of purgatory was present in an implicit way.

of the Trinity and the Incarnation from the sum of all the Scriptures and the living Tradition of the Church, so the doctrine of purgatory can also be inferred.

First of all, the doctrine of purgatory is founded on some basic Judeo-Christian beliefs, such as the immortality of the soul and the need to pray for the dead. Since Old Testament times, it has been considered "a holy and pious thought" to pray for the dead (2 Mc 12:45). Early Christians prayed for their dead, as is evident from the prayers written on Roman catacombs of the first centuries and also from the writings of early Church Fathers. In fact, finding scriptural proof for the existence of purgatory begins with this one fact—that Jews and Christians have always said intercessory prayers for one another and for those who have died. Abraham, for example, begged God not to destroy the cities of Sodom and Gomorrah for the sake of the righteous ones whom he thought might be living there (Gn 18:23–33). Moses also made intercessory prayers before God, and the people relied on him so much that Scripture describes them as begging before Moses, "You speak to us and we will listen; but let not God speak to us, or we shall die" (Ex 20:19). Later, when the people of Israel displeased God by demanding to have a king like other nations, they begged Samuel to intercede on their behalf (1 Sm 12:17, 19). Based on Samuel's response, we know that he considered praying for others to be a sacred obligation.

> As for me, far be it from me to sin against the LORD by ceasing to pray for you and to teach you the good and right way (1 Sm 12:23).

Scripture also tells how the prophet Job offered up intercessory prayers for the sake of his children. In assuming that his children had sinned, Job was merely operating with a good and practical understanding of human nature and its tendency to fall prey to sin.

His sons used to take turns giving feasts. . . . And when each feast had run its course, Job would send for them and sanctify them, rising early and offering holocausts for every one of them. For Job said, "It may be that my sons have sinned and blasphemed God in their hearts." This Job did habitually (Jb 1:4–5).

The Jewish practice of offering up intercessory prayers for one another also extends beyond the grave. In this tradition of praying for the dead, we find the strongest evidence that God has prepared a temporary place of existence for those who have been judged to be righteous but not yet ready for heaven. These are the souls who benefit most from the prayers and sacrifices offered up by those of us who are still alive. The book of Maccabees offers striking evidence that the Jews did in fact pray for their dead. The events recounted towards the end of the second book occurred about 150 years before Christ, when the Jews were attempting to free their nation from foreign control. After one of their battles, the Jews set out to bury the fallen soldiers. As the bodies were examined, it became apparent that God had allowed these soldiers to die in battle because they had been wearing the pagan amulets—"sacred to the idols of Jamnia"—beneath their tunics during the battle (2 Mc 12:40). Although it was forbidden for Jews to wear such amulets, this sin was not considered cause for damnation. Therefore, Maccabeus' men immediately turned to prayer and begged God to forgive the sins of their brothers who had died (2 Mc 12:42). Judas Maccabeus also pleaded on behalf of the dead by asking each soldier to offer up money as well as prayers.

He then took up a collection among all his soldiers, amounting to two thousand silver drachmas, which he sent to Jerusalem to provide for an expiatory sacrifice (2 Mc 12:43).

The author of this historical book then praises Maccabeus' act of atonement for the sake of the dead and affirms Jewish belief in an afterlife existence that is unmistakably akin to purgatory.

In doing this he acted in a very excellent and noble way, inasmuch as he had the resurrection of the dead in view; for if he were not expecting the fallen to rise again, it would have been useless and foolish to pray for them in death. But if he did this with a view to the splendid reward that awaits those who had gone to rest in godliness, it was a holy and pious thought. Thus he made atonement for the dead that they might be freed from this sin (2 Mc 12:43–46).

Even to this day, the Jews continue their traditional practice of praying for the dead. In this tradition (known as *Kaddish* in Hebrew), faithful Jews will make gift offerings to the synagogue and recite special prayers for the dead every day for one year's time.[2]

With such evidence of purgatory stated so clearly in the book of Maccabees, how could anyone who believes in the Scriptures continue to doubt in this doctrine? Often enough, the reason is that the entire book of Maccabees has been withheld from those who are searching. Although this book of the Bible can be found in all Catholic and Orthodox translations of the Bible, most Protestant versions omit it, along with six other books that are deemed "apocryphal" (meaning "uncanonical" or "of questionable authenticity").

In rejecting these books, Protestant scholars follow the Jewish canon of the Old Testament defined by the council at Jamnia in A.D. 90. The Jews decided to remove these books from the collection of what they considered to be "inspired writings." They were judged instead to be mere historical accounts. (Some have pointed out that the Jews of that council might have sought to delete the book of Maccabees from their canon because it contained lavish praise for the Romans, who had just destroyed Jerusalem in A.D. 70 [1 Mc 8]). It is important to note how-

---

[2] It is unclear if the Kaddish intends the same sort of intercession intended in Catholic prayers for the dead.

ever, that *during the time of Christ, these seven books were considered Scripture.*

This body of writings was called the "Septuagint" (meaning "seventy"), because of the traditional story associated with the original seventy Jewish scholars who are credited with translating the Hebrew Scriptures into Greek. The story tells how when each translator was locked in a room until he completed the entire translation by himself, each of the scholars ended up with the same exact translation, word for word.[3] The popular saying "seventy men in seventy days" came to describe their work, giving it the same prestige accorded the Hebrew version of the Scriptures.

It was this famous canon of writings that was rejected by Jewish leaders of the first century.[4] They rejected seven books from the Septuagint (including the book of Maccabees), ostensibly because they could not locate any original Hebrew manuscripts. (Several original Hebrew manuscripts have since been found with the discovery of the Dead Sea scrolls that date back to the time of Christ.) Part of the reason that the council of Jewish scholars at Jamnia decided to reject these books is that Christians were using certain passages from them to prove that Christ was the Messiah.[5] Regardless of the decision made by first century Jews, *the Catholic Church did not remove these books.* Jesus had never called any of the Scriptures into question, so the Church saw no need to doubt his judgment. After all, Jesus came as the fulfillment of all Scriptures, and if he accepted the Septuagint, then it made sense for his Church to follow his example.

The decision to remove the books of Maccabees as well as other "apocryphal books" from the Protestant version of the

---

[3] "Septuagint," *The International Standard Bible Encyclopedia,* ed. G. W. Bromily, vol. 4 (Grand Rapids, Mich.: W. B. Eerdman's, 1990), 400–408.

[4] *Canon* means "official list." In this case it refers to the official list of books that belong in the Bible.

[5] Please see appendix B.

Bible was made by Martin Luther. *He made that decision in the sixteenth century.* Luther tried to follow the same line of reasoning as the Jews of the first century, but his real purpose for excluding these books was to remove any evidence for the Catholic beliefs that he sought to oppose, including the Catholic doctrine of purgatory. Before Luther decided by himself that these "apocryphal" books should be deleted, they had been accepted as sacred Scripture for more than a thousand years.

Martin Luther made the first challenge to Catholic teaching on the subject of purgatory. He lived at a time when the Church had surrendered all too often to the demands of secular leaders who wanted their friends and kinsmen to rule over the Church. A great many of these religious leaders cared very little about the faith but instead concerned themselves primarily with controlling the property and wealth of the Church. During Martin Luther's time (1500–1600), the Holy See often granted certain bishops and priests the permission to sell an "indulgence" throughout a certain region, in exchange for a share in the profits.[6] But instead of encouraging the laity to pray and perform acts of charity for their deceased family members, certain charlatan priests would make "special offers" that would "guarantee" the release of loved ones in purgatory—in exchange for large sums of money.

Luther was rightly offended when he witnessed such corruption, but his response to the problem was to attack true Church teaching rather than the corrupt practice. Instead of pressing for the end of corrupt preaching, Luther argued that the Catholic doctrine on purgatory was altogether false. No one, he said, could lessen the sufferings of the dead. Our prayers could not help those destined for hell, and those chosen for heaven were taken there immediately upon death. Concerning the just who happened to die with venial sin on their souls, Luther argued that God simply declares them to be perfect and covers over

---

[6] The Holy See means the administrators of the Vatican in this context.

their sins with the blood of Jesus. Luther even compared the souls of the just in heaven with cow dung that has been covered over with snow.

Nowadays, almost no Protestant will accept the radical idea that sinners can enter heaven with sin on their souls. They do, nevertheless, continue to reject Church teaching on purgatory. As mentioned before, they teach that the souls of the just go through an instantaneous and painless transformation that renders their soul spotless and prepared for heaven. They object to the idea of purgatory, because they think this doctrine leads people to think they can earn their own way into heaven. The Catholic Church, however, does not teach this at all. Just as our initial acceptance of Christ during our lifetime is made possible by God's grace, so also our final cleansing in purgatory is an application of the grace that Christ won for us. Faithful to Christ, the Church teaches that we can do nothing without God's assistance. Even in the suffering that we endure for the sake of purification, God helps us.

Critics of purgatory will often cite Christ's promise to the good thief from the cross, "Amen, I say to you, today you will be with me in Paradise" (Lk 23:43). They consider this passage to be strong proof that purgatory does not exist, since Christ makes it clear that the thief will be going to paradise that very day. What needs to be acknowledged, however, is the context in which these words were spoken. Jesus was dying on the cross. It was not the time for him to be explaining details of doctrine. He wanted to provide strong reassurance to the dying man that his sins were forgiven and his soul was saved. Christ promised paradise to the sinner so that future generations would learn this lesson by heart: God will forgive us even when we are a few breaths away from our last breath.

Tradition holds that even when Jesus died, he did not immediately go to heaven. Instead, he went to the place known as "the bosom of Abraham" where the just were waiting for Christ's redemption before they could enter into heaven (cf. Lk 16:23). And since Christ promised the thief, "Today you will be with me," we can assume that the good thief went with him to this place of preparation for heaven. In the Apostles' Creed, we express this belief about Christ's journey to purgatory when we say, "He was crucified, died, and was buried. He descended into hell." We do not say that Christ descended to the hell of the damned, where the dead souls neither deserved nor desired to receive him. Instead, we refer to the place where he descended as "hell." This word originally had a wide sense, like the Hebrew word *Sheol*, or the Greek *hades*, referring to the world of the dead in general.

The first letter of St. Peter refers to this event, traditionally known as "the harrowing of hell."

> For Christ also suffered for sins once . . . that he might lead you to God. Put to death in the flesh, he was brought to life in the spirit. In it he also went to preach to the spirits in prison, who had once been disobedient . . . (1 Pt 3:18–20).

From this passage, it is clear that Jesus went to a place of detainment in the spiritual realm. Once there, like a shepherd seeking wayward sheep, he called to the souls waiting there and brought them home. We can suppose that Jesus was in purgatory, because the spirits are described as having changed and become more obedient to the Lord than they once were. St. Peter tells us that Christ "preached" to them, and this shows that the souls detained in this "prison" were not static, but rather dynamic. They could benefit from the hearing of the word, just as the people of Nineveh benefited from listening to Jonah, whose three-day experience in the belly of a whale prefigured Christ's three-day experience in purgatory (Jn 2:1–2; 3:5; Mt 12:41). Those who worry about the prospect of purgatory should take comfort in the fact that, before ascending to his Father in heaven, Christ chose to go to the abode of the dead to bring them the truth that could set them free.

St. Peter was not the only one in the New Testament Scriptures to refer to this spiritual place of detainment as a "prison." Christ also uses the same term "prison" to describe the place of punishment for those who do not make up for their sins before they die.

> Settle with your opponent quickly while on the way to court with him. Otherwise your opponent will hand you over to the judge, and the judge will hand you over to the guard, and you will be thrown into prison. Amen, I say to you, you will not be released until you have paid the last penny (Mt 5:25–26).

Unless one is willing to reduce this verse to simple advice regarding one's finances, the "accuser" in this warning is our conscience, and "the judge" is the Lord, who will bring us to judgment ("the court") when we die. The "prison" must be referring to purgatory and not hell, because if Christ had been referring to hell, then he would not have mentioned the prospect of being released (namely, by paying the last penny of suffering). There is also scriptural proof for the existence of purgatory in a different passage where Christ warns the disciples that anyone who speaks against the Holy Spirit will not be forgiven.

> And whoever speaks a word against the Son of Man will be forgiven; but whoever speaks against the holy Spirit will not be forgiven, either in this age or in the age to come (Mt 12:32).

Although Christ makes no explicit reference to purgatory in this passage, he does say that the sin against the Holy Spirit will not be forgiven in the next age. For Christ to make this statement implies that other sins can and will be forgiven in the next age. And this is what purgatory is all about.

One of the strongest scriptural proofs for the existence of purgatory comes from the letter of St. Paul to the Corinthians. Paul describes the souls of the saved as buildings that have been laid on the foundation of Christ (1 Cor 3:11). Some of these buildings, however, will not fully withstand the test of God's judgment.

> The work of each will come to light, for the Day will disclose it. It will be revealed with fire, and the fire [itself] will test the quality of each one's work. If the work stands that someone built upon the foundation, that person will receive a wage. But

if someone's work is burned up, that one will suffer loss; the person will be saved, but only as through fire (1 Cor 3:13–15).

The significant promise made by Paul is that some people will be saved "as through fire" (1 Cor 3:15). Because some will have accomplished very little for God, they will suffer the loss of everything they falsely valued. *But they will be saved.* How could such a passage be understood except as evidence for the doctrine of purgatory?

One further question that can be drawn from this passage is why purgatory has come to be associated with fire. Why does purification take place through fire? Why not water, or light or wind?

Throughout both the Old and the New Testament, the presence of God has been associated with fire that sometimes destroys and at other times discloses, illuminates, or expresses his presence. For example, God first appeared to Moses as an angel of fire from within a flaming bush that was burning without being consumed (Ex 3:2). As God pronounced his solemn promise to free the Hebrew slaves, the burning bush served to bring *a message of freedom.* Later, when God appeared as a pillar of fire in the desert at night, the fire served not only to encourage the people with a promise of protection, but it also directed their path to the Promised Land. ("Thus they could travel both day and night" [Ex 13:21].) In the New Testament, the Holy Spirit descended upon the apostles in the form of tongues of fire.

And suddenly there came from the sky a noise like a strong driving wind, and it filled the entire house in which they were. Then there appeared to them tongues as of fire, which parted and came to rest on each one of them. And they were all filled with the holy Spirit . . . (Acts 2:2–4).

The unconsuming flames of fire symbolize the truth, the power, and the presence of God that was imparted unto the disciples so that they could build up the Church and proclaim the gospel until the end of time. The fire rested upon their heads as a sacramental anointing by God himself—a visible sign of his presence within them.

When Jesus said in the Gospel of Luke, "I have come to set the earth on fire, and how I wish it were already blazing!" he was referring to the fire of purification (Lk 12:49). He knew that no one could be made pure enough for heaven until he completed his sacrifice on the cross, and so this is why the two ideas are so joined together in his spoken thoughts.

> I have come to set the earth on fire, and how I wish it were already blazing! There is a baptism with which I must be baptized, and how great is my anguish until it is accomplished! (Lk 12:49–50)

With his baptism on the cross, Christ's blood washed the curse of Satan from the human family once and for all. While almost all Christians will accept this last point, there are many who go one step further and say that since Christ won our salvation, there is no more work to be done. This is not true. If all the work had been done, then Paul would never have urged us to do our part, saying, "Work out your salvation with fear and trembling" (Phil 2:12). Furthermore, our own experience of carrying the cross in our daily lives makes it clear that Christ is not finished with us yet. Therefore, considering how many of us die with "unfinished business" to deal with, it makes perfect sense to think of purgatory as a kind of finishing school for those who need it. Purgatory completes the work of applying to each soul the grace that Christ won for us. And that work is best described as a fiery experience.

The process of purification is described as experiencing a fire. People can experience the fire of divine presence in different ways, depending on the state of their soul. For those who reject and hate God and who are concentrated on their own selfishness, God's presence is a bitter pain. This is why the fire of hell has been likened to the beatific vision as experienced through the eyes of Satan.

For those who accept God, God's presence causes a mixed experience. There is, of course, recognition of God's purity, love, and beauty. Yet there is also a pain that is caused by recognizing the degree to which we are still caught up in selfish desires.[7] These insights cause a certain amount of humiliation and shame. Our pain in purgatory is a pain born of our humility—and our horror—at the vision of our sinfulness as seen from God's perspective.

When we have finally become purified and have accomplished the full expiation for all of our sins, then God's presence will no longer bring us the slightest pain. At this time, we will experience his fire in a different way—as an intense and passionate love—a kind of rampant purity. The fire of God's love will be of tremendous beauty, expressed in myriad ways, and we will have a share in them.

Freedom Is Not Free

One need not rely solely on the imagery of fire in order to understand why purgatory is a perfect remedy for the soul tainted by sin. Purgatory can also be understood as the purification of our free will. Throughout the Scriptures, we can see the force of free will at work. Free will was humanity's first gift, and God has preserved this gift in each of us throughout the ages. When Moses spoke to his people on God's behalf, he affirmed the primacy of our free will in choosing or refusing to serve God.

> Here, then, I have today set before you life and prosperity, death and doom. If you obey the commandments of the LORD, your God . . . you will live and grow numerous, and the LORD, your God, will bless you in the land you are entering to occupy. If, however, you turn away your hearts and will not listen, but are led astray and adore and serve other gods, I tell you now that you will certainly perish . . . (Dt 30:15–18).

---

[7] The suffering of purgatory has always been presented as different from the suffering of hell; the CCC speaks of it only in terms of being a purification (nos. 1030–32).

God's gift of free will makes us accountable for everything we do. Paul explains this point when he writes that those who seek "glory, honor, and immortality through perseverance in good works" will receive eternal life (Rom 2:7). For those who are faithless, however, there will be "wrath and fury" (Rom 2:8).

The reason why this warning makes sense is because when we sin, we are actually delivering up our will and handing it over to the devil on a silver platter. The more we sin, the less freedom we have. Just as all addicts eventually lose their capacity for self-control, we also lose control when we allow ourselves to be overcome by temptation. From this perspective, the reality of hell is perhaps best understood as the complete loss of free will. When Christ warned that, "Whoever wishes to save his life will lose it," he was referring to the phenomenon of sin that leads to slavery (Lk 9:24).

The depth of God's love for us is made all the more manifest in these situations. For instead of leaving us to perish, as we deserve, God gives us all the extra graces that we need to return once more to a state of freedom. This is what Paul meant when he wrote, "Where sin increased, grace overflowed all the more . . ." (Rom 5:20).

Purgatory, then, is one further expression of God's love and mercy. Knowing our general weakness and the fact that many of us would need more than a lifetime in which to complete our sanctification, God provided a place where our free will could be restored to us. When we accept the suffering that is required in order to secure for ourselves once more God's original gift of free will, then we will be able to love and serve him with perfect joy.

For many reasons, then, the Catholic Church rejects the idea that a person's sins can simply be "erased" at death—as if God would go against his own law of cause and effect. To believe that a person's sins can be wiped out in a painless instant reveals a shallow understanding of the nature of sin and the effect that sin has on our souls. Every sin that we commit constitutes a rejection of God and a rejection of God's authority. By our sinful thoughts and actions, we are declaring that God's law and his plan for us is not good enough—and that we have our own law and our own plan that we think is better. How can such a sinful attitude be changed instantly without any work or pain involved on our part?

As we have seen, sin is an ugly and false abuse of our free will. Therefore, every sinful person who seeks entrance into heaven has to confront the fact that his will is still clouded by some kind of attraction to sin. In the same way that persons who practice a strict diet can still feel a powerful urge for certain foods they should not eat, most of us at death will still be attached or drawn to certain sins, whether they be sins of commission or omission. We should therefore think of purgatory as an act of the most profound mercy on God's part. Knowing that most of us are still attached to our sins when we die, God purifies our wills, so that we no longer have any desire whatsoever to do anything or have anything that is harmful or selfish.

The reason why the experience of purgatory must involve suffering is so that our decision to choose God is really our own. By handing to us the burden of suffering that we ourselves have brought about by our selfish behavior, God gives us the chance to show him that we are truly sorry for the things that we have done or failed to do during our lifetime. And so, although it is Christ who does the cleansing, still the pain teaches us the real effect of sin. It clarifies for us what sin really is, so that sin loses all attraction. The pain of purgatory, then, is like the pain of withdrawal for a recovering addict or alcoholic. We may experience grief and sorrow for our sins, but we are thankful for being set free. We feel hope even as we suffer for the consequences for our sins. The result is that we not only grow in grace but also in character. St. Paul describes this other purpose for suffering in his letter to the Romans.

> Not only that, but we even boast of our afflictions, knowing that affliction produces endurance, and endurance, proven character, and proven character, hope, and hope does not disappoint, because the love of God has been poured out into our

hearts through the holy Spirit that has been given to us (Rom 5:3–5).

The purification that souls endure in purgatory is not so much assigned by God, as it is asked for by each soul. St. John writes that those who wish to stand in God's presence know that they must purify themselves first.

> Beloved, we are God's children now; what we shall be has not yet been revealed. We do know that when it is revealed we shall be like him, for we shall see him as he is. Everyone who has this hope based on him makes himself pure, as he is pure (1 Jn 3:2–3).

Our Desire to be Made Pure Again

King David once begged for his purgatory on earth. Despite the closeness he had once enjoyed with God, David fell into grievous sin when he committed adultery with Bathsheba and then caused her husband Uriah to die (2 Sm 11:4, 15). Even when David finally did confess and repent of his sin, he did not experience the return of God's favor until after he had endured great suffering. Bathsheba's infant son became ill, and David understood that their child was dying because of the sin he had committed.

> David besought God for the child. He kept a fast, retiring for the night to lie on the ground clothed in sackcloth. The elders of his house stood beside him urging him to rise from the ground; but he would not, nor would he take food with them (2 Sm 12:16–17).

From David's Psalm, we know that he willingly accepted God's punishment in order to be restored once again to his grace.

> Thoroughly wash me from my guilt
> and of my sin cleanse me.

> Cleanse me of sin with hyssop, that I may be purified;
> wash me, and I shall be whiter than snow.

A clean heart create for me, O God,
  and a steadfast spirit renew within me.
Cast me not out from your presence,
  and your holy spirit take not from me
    (Ps 51:4, 9, 12–13).

We cannot comprehend the bliss of the souls in heaven, but we do in this life experience at least a shadow of these joys to come. We should therefore be willing to face God's judgment and punishment with the same attitude as David. Even in this life, we can pray on a daily basis, "Do whatever it takes, Lord, so that my soul can be united to you, for no pain is too great in comparison to the glory of your presence."

"Today salvation has come to this house" (Lk 19:9).

Such a conversion of heart and submission to correction is also recorded in the story of Zaccheus, the chief tax collector. Although most people knew Zaccheus to be dishonest, greedy, and self-serving, Jesus was impressed when he saw that Zaccheus had climbed a tree in order to catch a glimpse of the Lord as he passed through Jericho. That very day Jesus went to his house and heard from Zaccheus a magnanimous confession of guilt and repentance.

Zaccheus stood there and said to the Lord, "Behold, half of my possessions, Lord, I shall give to the poor, and if I have extorted anything from anyone I shall repay it four times over" (Lk 19:8).

Zaccheus must have seen in Jesus the hope of salvation, for why else would he have submitted so graciously to those whom he had offended? Like David, Zaccheus accepted his punishment with honor and gratitude. He knew that receiving favor from the Lord was worth any price. This is exactly what Zaccheus received when Jesus said to him, "Today salvation has come to this house . . ." (Lk 19:9).

In so many stories of the saints, we find the same enthusiasm shown by Zaccheus, who was willing to pay any cost in order to enter heaven. Many early Christian martyrs, for example, would sing songs of praise and thanksgiving, even as they were led to the lions, because they were convinced of the glory waiting for them at the end of their trial.

A similar trial awaits each soul destined to suffer for a time in purgatory. Nevertheless, it would be better to go through such trials while we are alive and to accept our portion of suffering in this life without complaining. St. Paul taught that the sufferings in this life should be embraced in light of all the good they can accomplish.

> Therefore, we are not discouraged; rather, although our outer self is wasting away, our inner self is being renewed day by day. For this momentary light affliction is producing for us an eternal weight of glory beyond all comparison (2 Cor 4:16–17).

Apart from accepting the joys and sorrows of this life with equal gratitude, we can make up for our sins by showing mercy and forgiveness whenever possible. When Peter asked Christ how many times a person should be expected to show forgiveness to his brother, Christ responded that we should be ready to forgive "seventy-seven" times, and then he explained why (Mt 18:21–22). He told the parable of the king who wanted to settle accounts with all of his servants (Mt 18:23–35). One servant who owed a large sum threw himself before the king and begged for mercy.

The king felt so sorry for the man that, instead of giving him more time to pay, he forgave him the entire debt. Later, that same servant came upon a fellow servant who owed him a tiny sum. Unlike the king who had compassion and canceled the debt, the servant ranted and raved, insisting on payment. When the other servant begged for a little time to collect the money, he refused to hear it and had him thrown into jail.

Hearing of this injustice, the other servants went to the king to protest the outrageous behavior of the servant whose debt had been forgiven. The king called him back and asked for an explanation. The servant had no explanation. The king then reprimanded him for his lack of compassion.

> You wicked servant! I forgave you your entire debt because you begged me to. Should you not have had pity on your fellow servant, as I had pity on you? Then in anger his master handed him over to the torturers until he should pay back the whole debt (Mt 18:32-34).

That God would require a person to suffer "until he should pay back the whole debt" suggests once again a place of confinement after death but before entrance into heaven. (Recall how St. Peter used this idea when he described our Lord going to teach the souls in "prison" [1 Pt 3:19].) These passages all show that if we have no mercy on others, then God will demand full justice for every sin we commit. This is why Jesus ended his parable of the wicked servant with the severe admonition,

> So will my heavenly Father do to you, unless each of you forgives his brother from his heart (Mt 18:35).

The mercy that we hope to have from God, we must first practice ourselves. St. James reiterated this point when he said "Mercy triumphs over judgment" (Jas 2:13). This should be a great solace for those who feel overwhelmed by their sins; for the compassion and mercy they show to others can mitigate some of the judgment against themselves.

> For the judgment is merciless to one who has not shown mercy; mercy triumphs over judgment (Jas 2:13).

In the prayer of the Our Father, Jesus promised that God will show mercy if we do the same.

> And forgive us our debts,
> as we forgive our debtors . . . (Mt 6:12).

If you forgive others their transgressions, your heavenly Father will forgive you. But if you do not forgive others, neither will your Father forgive your transgressions (Mt 6:14-15).

Love is the ultimate virtue that satisfies justice and calls down mercy. St. Peter wrote "Love covers a multitude of sins" (1 Pt 4:8). It is the universal remedy for sin. When he was visiting the home of a certain tax collector, Jesus looked tenderly upon the woman who was washing his feet with her tears, and he expressed the same idea with equal eloquence: "Her many sins have been forgiven; hence, she has shown great love" (Lk 7:47). So it is that the sword of justice can be sheathed by forgiveness, and the love we show to others can heal our own brokenness.

> Above all, let your love for one another be intense, because love covers a multitude of sins (1 Pt 4:8).

Judgment in the Mirror

It is clear that the system of justice we adopt will be the same one that God will adopt towards us (Lk 6:38). None of us is Jesus Christ, and none of us can pronounce judgment on another; yet, in practicing forgiveness and mercy, we show that we are sons and daughters of the Father and that we wish to be perfect just as he is perfect.

> Give and gifts will be given to you; a good measure packed together, shaken down, and overflowing, will be poured into your lap. For the measure with which you measure will in return be measured out to you (Lk 6:38).

In imitation of Christ then, we forgive; and in the process, prepare to receive forgiveness ourselves.

> Stop judging, that you may not be judged. For as you judge, so will you be judged, and the measure with which you measure will be measured out to you (Mt 7:1–2; cf. Rom 2:1, 3).

The severity of our trial in purgatory will depend on the quality of charity and mercy that we demonstrated during our lifetime. God metes out perfect justice.

In his teachings on forgiveness, Jesus demonstrated that it was the healing of the sinner he desired, not the "payback" for damages. The demands of retribution serve only to coax the hearts of those who are still hardened against his perfect law of love. God wants our hearts to be like his, and this is why he wants us to love our neighbors as we love ourselves. Achieving true selflessness requires nothing less than a true and complete conversion of heart.

Gradually, through the struggles of our daily lives, we eventually conform ourselves to the image of Christ. And like our Savior who died on the cross to secure our redemption, we too must "die to self" in order to reap the fruits of salvation. Nevertheless, for those of us who die before we finish "dying to self," God does not abandon us to the dark corners of the universe. In his compassion, he takes us through purgatory, where our soiled baptismal robes may be purified, and on into heaven.

Early Church Fathers
on Purgatory

Tertullian (A.D. 211): *The Crown* (v. 1, 367)

We offer sacrifices for the dead on their birthday anniversaries.

Tertullian (A.D. 213): *Monogamy* (v. 1, 382)

Indeed, she prays for his soul and asks that he may, while waiting, find rest; and that he may share in the first resurrection. And each year, on the anniversary of his death, she offers the sacrifice.

St. Cyril of Jerusalem (A.D. 315–386): *Catechetical Lectures* (v. 1, 852, 853)

We make mention also of the holy fathers and bishops who have already fallen asleep, and, to put it simply, of all among us who have already fallen asleep; for we believe that it will be of very great benefit to the souls of those for whom the petition is carried up . . . and I wish to persuade you by an illustration. For I know that there are many who are saying this: "If a soul departs from this world with sins, what does it profit it to be remembered in the prayer?" Well, if a king were to banish certain persons who had offended him, and those intervening for them were to plait a crown and offer it to him on behalf of the ones who were being punished, would he not grant a remission of their penalties? In the same way we too offer prayers to Him from those who have fallen asleep, though they be sinners. We do not plait a crown, but offer up Christ who has been sacrificed for our sins; and we thereby propitiate the benevolent God from them as well as for ourselves.

St. Gregory of Nyssa (A.D. 383): *Sermon on the Dead* (v. 2, 1061)

After his departure out of the body, he . . . finds that he is not able to partake of divinity until he has been purged of the filthy contagion in his soul by the purifying fire.

St. Epiphanius of Salamis (A.D. 315–403): *Panacea Against All Heresies* (v. 2, 1109)

Furthermore, as to mentioning the names of the dead, how is there anything very useful in that? What is more timely or more excellent than that those who are still here should believe that the departed do live, and that they have not retreated into nothingness, but that they exist and are alive with the Master? . . . useful too is the prayer fashioned on their behalf, even if it does not force back the whole of guilty charges laid to them. And it is useful also, because in this world we often stumble either voluntarily or involuntarily, and thus it is a reminder to do better.

St. John Chrysostom (A.D. 334/354–407): *Homilies on the Epistle to the Philippians* (v. 2, 1206)

Weep for the unbelievers! Weep for those who differ not a whit from them, those who go hence without illumination, without the seal! These truly deserve our lamentation, our tears . . . weep for those who die in their wealth, and who with all their wealth prepared no consolation for their own souls . . . let us weep for them, let us assist them to the extant of our ability, let us think of some assistance for them . . . by praying for them and by entreating others to pray for them, by constantly giving alms to the poor on their behalf.

St. Augustine of Hippo (A.D. 354–430): *Explanations of the Psalms* (v. 3, 1467)

Lord . . . in this life may You cleanse me and make me such that I have no need of the corrective fire, which is for those who are saved, but as if by fire . . . for it is said: "He shall be saved, but as if by fire." And because it is said that he shall be saved, little is thought of that fire. Yet plainly, though we be saved by fire, that fire will be more severe than anything a man can suffer in this life.

Sermons (v. 3, 1513)

The names of the martyrs are read aloud in that place at the altar of God, where prayer is not offered for them. Prayer, however, is offered for other dead who are remembered. For it is wrong to pray for a martyr, to whose prayers we ought to ourselves be commended.

(v. 3, 1516)

But by the prayers of the Holy Church, and by the salvific sacrifice, and by the alms which are given for their spirits, there is no doubt that the dead are aided, that the Lord might deal more mercifully with them than their sins would deserve. For the whole Church observes this practice which was handed down by the Fathers: that it prays for those who have died in the communion of the Body and Blood of Christ, when they are commemorated in their own place in the sacrifice itself; and the sacrifice is offered also in memory of them, on their behalf.

Genesis Defended Against the Manicheans (v. 3, 1544)

The man who has not cultivated the land and has allowed it to be overrun with brambles has in this life the curse of his land on all his works, and after this life he will have either purgatorial fire or eternal punishment.

Purgatory Bible Study—
Scriptures Cited in the Chapter

Rv 21:27—Nothing unclean will enter heaven.

Ps 103:12—"As far as the east is from the west, / so far has he put our transgressions from us."

1 Pt 3:19–20—Christ went "to preach to the spirits in prison, who had once been disobedient. . . ."

Gn 18:23–33—Abraham intercedes on behalf of any holy people that might be living in Sodom and Gomorrah.

Ex 20:19—The Hebrews tell Moses, "You speak to us and we will listen; but let not God speak to us, or we shall die."

1 Sm 12:17, 19—Israel displeased God by demanding to have a king like other nations, they begged Samuel to intercede on their behalf.

1 Sm 12:23—Samuel considered praying for others to be a sacred obligation.

Jb 1:4–5—Job offers sacrifices on behalf of his children.

2 Mc 12:42–45—Maccabeus' men pray on behalf of their fallen comrades. Judas takes up a collection to send to Jerusalem for a sacrifice on their behalf. It is considered "a holy and pious thought" to pray for the dead.

Lk 23:43—Christ promises paradise for the good thief.

Jon 2:1–2; 3:5 and Mt 12:41—Jonah's three-day experience in the belly of a whale prefigured Christ's three-day experience in purgatory.

Mt 5:25–26—Christ warns us to settle accounts in this life because, in the next life, we will not be let out of prison until the last penny has been paid.

Mt 12:31–32—Christ says that whoever blasphemes against the Holy Spirit will not be forgiven in this age or the one to come.

1 Cor 3:11—Paul says that Christ is the foundation we build upon.

1 Cor 3:13–15—"The person will be saved, but only as through fire."

Ex 3:2 and Ex 13:21–22—God's presence depicted as fire.

Acts 2:2–4—The Holy Spirit, on Pentecost, appears as tongues of fire.

Lk 12:49—"I have come to set the earth on fire, and how I wish it were already blazing!"

Dt 30:15–18—God sets the Law of Life and Law of Death before the Israelites and asks them to choose life.

Rom 2:7–8—Paul promises eternal life for those who persevere in doing good works. For those who are faithless, however, there will be "wrath and fury."

Lk 9:24—"Whoever wishes to save his life will lose it. . . ."

Rom 5:20—Paul wrote "Where sin increased, grace overflowed all the more. . . ."

Rom 5:3–5—The pain of purifying suffering is good for us and conforms us to Christ.

1 Jn 3:2–3—"We shall be like him, for we shall see him as he is."

2 Sm 11:4, 15 and 2 Sm 12:16–17—David endured great suffering because of his sin.

Ps 51:4, 9, 12–13—"Cleanse me of sin with hyssop . . . / wash me, and I shall be whiter than snow." David trusts God to purify him.

Lk 19:8—Zaccheus commits to restitution: "Behold, half of my possessions, Lord, I shall give to the poor, and if I have extorted anything from anyone I shall repay it four times over."

Lk 19:9—Jesus responds to Zaccheus by saying: "Today salvation has come to this house. . . ."

2 Cor 4:17—"This momentary light affliction is producing for us an eternal weight of glory beyond all comparison."

Mt 18:21–22 and Mt 18:23–35—Jesus explains that we are forgiven as we forgive others. He tells the parable of the master and his servant who owed him a large sum of money.

Mt 18:32–34—The servant was handed over to the torturers until he should pay back the whole debt.

Mt 18:35—"So will my heavenly Father do to you, unless each of you forgives his brother from his heart."

Jas 2:13—"Mercy triumphs over judgment."

Mt 6:12, 14–15—We are forgiven as we forgive others.

1 Pt 4:8—"Love covers a multitude of sins."

Lk 7:47—"Her many sins have been forgiven; hence she has shown great love."

Mt 7:1–2, Rom 2:1, 3 and Lk 6:38—The system of justice we adopt will be the same one that God will adopt towards us. The measure with which we measure will be measured out to us.

The Blessed Virgin Mary

Mary is the Mother of Jesus and the Mother of all of us (Martin Luther, Sermon, Christmas, 1529).

The veneration of Mary is inscribed in the very depths of the human heart (Martin Luther: Sermon, September 1, 1522).

But the other conception, namely the infusion of the soul, it is piously and suitably believed, was without any sin, so that while the soul was being infused, she would at the same time be cleansed from original sin and adorned with the gifts of God to receive the holy soul thus infused. And thus, in the very moment in which she began to live, she was without all sin (Martin Luther).[1]

Martin Luther believed what the Catholic Church taught him about Mary. These beliefs represented 1,500 years of Christian reflection on Mary through the Scriptures. Luther did not see that abandoning mother Church must also ultimately lead to abandoning mother Mary by reducing her role to that of a simple "container" that God once used. Such a reduced role reflects badly on God and damages our relationship with Jesus. How can we call his Father "our Father" if we cannot call his mother "our mother?" Her presence nurtures an intimate relationship within the family of the Church, enabling us to love the Infinite God.

Is it possible that any one of us could understand anything if brought face to face with the Almighty and Infinite God? Would not any one person be completely overwhelmed? A Hindu might deal with this problem by saying that a person's individuality becomes lost in God. They might say that just as a drop of rain-

---

[1] Martin Luther, *Luther's Works, Weimar Edition*, trans. J. Pelikan (Concordia: St. Louis, 1957) vol. 4, 694.

water is lost in the ocean, an individual person dissolves in God when they get to "heaven."[2] As Christians, we cannot express union with God in this way. We believe that the individual human spirit remains distinct from God. So, how can an individual be in contact with God and yet still keep some sense of self? God answers this with motherhood.

In the act of creating, God brought motherhood, the essence of femininity, into existence. He created motherhood to host our contact with him, but because of the fall, it cannot host God perfectly. Through Mary, God restored motherhood and brought it to an even higher perfection than it had before the fall. How so? Before trying to answer this question, we must first see how God intended motherhood to connect us to him in nature, in humanity, and in our families.

A child fascinated by the beautiful black and orange pattern on the wings of a Monarch butterfly learns something from nature about God's beauty in details. Mother Nature presents this tiny portion of God's beauty without overwhelming the child with the Total Beauty that is God.[3] If the butterfly sips nectar from a flower, the child's mind will see something of the way that all living things are connected to one another in a community. From this, the child can be led to understand that he or she has a special place and a role in God's creation.

Mother Nature alone, however, is incomplete because water, rocks, trees, and animals cannot knowingly respond to God. Nature was made complete when God introduced in her an image of himself that could know him and respond to him. He created human beings. The assembly of a united humanity was meant to respond to God's beauty in a conscious way. The presence

---

[2] Hindus call heaven "nirvana," but it bears no resemblance at all to the Christian idea of heaven.

[3] For examples of a female creation being personified, see the quote from Hermas that begins the chapter on the Church. Also, see chapter 24 of Sirach.

of humanity, the conscious part of nature, elevates nature into a mother that is aware of her spouse and able to return his love. Our government, laws, and language should show communion with God and each other. Our homes, workplaces, and parks should direct God's beauty in nature back to him in worship. Art, literature, and music should celebrate loving communion with the Trinity.

Humanity thus makes possible a loving relationship between God and creation, but God also took care to provide for each individual human being. He gave us each a human father and a human mother, whose marriage should reflect the love between God and creation in a personal way to us as individuals.[4]

In this relationship, mother represents our home. This is literal, since an unborn baby actually lives inside the mother and takes its flesh and life from her. After birth, however, mother as home continues. Mother gives us a special role, a part to play, or a place to be. A mother is God to a child before a child is old enough to realize that anything more exists. In her being, a mother bears God and presents him to her child in a way that the child can understand. Mother teaches and nurtures us. She makes us part of a family by teaching our family's rules and ways of doing things. She represents the family's distinctive character with certain foods, a certain language and manner of speaking, certain types of clothes, habits, and songs, etc. She does all of this in the context of obedience, love, and devotion to our father, who is her husband. She thus directs all of her detailed work in making a home for her family and children toward the ultimate goal of union with God through her husband. Our family life should thus bear God to us in a *personal* way.

True motherhood teaches each of us three things: it teaches

---

[4] This representation is made possible by God becoming man in Jesus Christ. Jesus Christ is God, and the Church is the new and restored creation, his bride (Eph 5:25–27, 32; Rv 21:2, 9). Each Christian marriage therefore gives testimony to the love between Christ and the Church.

us about who God is, it tells each of us who and what we are, and it tells us how to relate rightly to God. But since motherhood is our connection to God, the fall means that our connection to God has been damaged. It is damaged in nature, because amidst the beauty we see terror—just as when a baby deer is unable to escape a lion. It is damaged when human society is torn by conflicts and war. It is damaged when mothers abandon their children for "more important matters."

Sin in all of these forms damaged the ability of human beings to have a personal relationship with God. Human beings began to worship creation itself as God (Pantheism) or even their own perverted desires in the form of various goddesses and gods. Christianity restores true religion and teaches that fallen creation is to be renewed and reconstructed without blemish as the body of Christ, the home and spouse of God.

God has made this new and perfect connection to him through Mary by manifesting his grace in her sinlessness, total dedication, and motherhood. God joined both Creation and Humanity when the Holy Spirit overshadowed Mary. Her person thus affirms the dignity of both. Through her and in her, a new creation comes forth as the body of Christ, a new society is formed in the heavenly community (which the Church on earth tries to imitate), and each of us is given a common mother within that family of God.

Mary has become the human face of Creation, just as Christ has become the human face of God. Just as motherhood makes knowledge of God possible, so Mary makes possible our personal relationship with Jesus Christ. What is this personal relationship and how does Mary make it possible?

Many consider that a personal relationship with Christ means not needing to be a part of the Church, but this is like a finger wanting to be connected directly to the head without any connection through the hand, arm, shoulder, and neck. A finger alone, however, has no purpose apart from the rest of the body, and it cannot have any sort of relationship to the Head while it is separated from the body. Each part is borne by (or has a home in) the body and draws its lifeblood (the Holy Spirit) from the body. Because "bearer" means "mother," the body is mother to each part. A perfect personal relationship can only be completed in a perfect body.

In her immaculate body and by her perfect devotion and love, Mary provides the pattern of perfection for the body of Christ, the Church as the New Creation. The water of baptism, the bread of communion, the oil of confirmation, the sanctity of human marriage, all restore each one of us personally. We are restored by being connected to Christ in a new human society (the Church) that is itself connected to Christ in a new Creation (the flesh from Mary that Christ offered to his Father on the cross). "Being saved" means perfect unity to Christ in the Church. Because of sin, however, the union and perfection of his body is made possible on earth only through the cross.

The Church therefore points us to the Cross of Christ in order to achieve this perfect unity. Just as our earthly mothers wash our infant bodies with water, so also our heavenly mother washes away our sins with the blood of Christ and with her tears. There, at the cross, we are each joined to him as members of a family in a bond of love.

Love consummated within marriage between husband and wife generates a family. Similarly, the family of God is based on the strong bond of love Christ expressed on the cross. The cross is Christ's wedding bed, and he consummated our marriage to him there.

It is easy to say, "I believe in Christ," but many contradict this by seeking a relationship with God apart from the body of Christ. They do this to escape the difficulties that arise whenever people try to do things together. Enduring and even forgiving others' shortcomings, as well as obeying those in authority over us (even when we would rather not), are all part of relating to God as a family while we are here on earth. Our relationship with one another tells whether God is present among us. When we communicate to Christ through each other and intercede for each other by ministering Christ to one another, *we are not covering up or losing sight of Christ.* On the contrary, we are becoming more deeply unified with him and with each other by the Holy Spirit. Our effort at unity is helped when we remember that Jesus gave us a common mother in Mary just before he died on the Cross.

Fallen creation gives us a glimpse of motherhood through nature, society, and in our own earthly mothers. Jesus restored and perfected true motherhood through Mary. He restored nature by taking material flesh from the immaculate body of Mary and making it into his New Creation. He restored and perfected human society by giving all human beings a common mother in Mary. We are all one family once again. He restored and perfected personal motherhood by giving her as a mother to every individual believer.

Now, we ask the reader to get ready to do some work, as we explore Mary's role according to the Bible. We will begin with five biblical themes. These themes show that motherhood is brought to completion in Mary and that the Church's motherhood derives from Mary as our mother.

1. Mary as "Daughter Zion" and the image of the Church
2. Mary as the New Eve
3. Mary as the Ark of the Covenant
4. Mary's faith and love
5. Mary as mother of the Church

Then, we will examine the Church's reasoning from Scripture regarding:

1. The perpetual virginity of Mary
2. Mary's conception without original sin
3. Mary's assumption into heaven

These three doctrines make clear how motherhood, according to the new creation, is brought to perfection in Mary.

1. Mary as "Daughter Zion"
and the Image of the Church

Luke purposely alludes to Mary as the New Zion. "Zion" in the Old Testament personifies the people of God as a bride. Originally, Zion was the fortress that King David had to conquer in order to capture Jerusalem (2 Sm 5:7). It became the site where King Solomon (King David's son) built the Temple. The word "Zion" later came to mean not only the temple, but also Jerusalem and Israel as the people of God. For Christians, Zion means the New Israel, the Church (Heb 12:22).

The Old Testament uses the titles "Zion" or "Daughter Zion" to depict the people of Israel personified as a virgin bride who belongs to the Lord. The prophet Isaiah often used this imagery.

> For Zion's sake I will not be silent,
>   for Jerusalem's sake I will not be quiet,
> Until her vindication shines forth like the dawn
>   and her victory like a burning torch.
>
> As a young man marries a virgin,
>   your Builder shall marry you;
> And as a bridegroom rejoices in his bride
>   so shall your God rejoice in you (Is 62:1, 5).

The gospel of Luke portrays Mary as the fulfillment of the ideal Zion, who has been looking for the coming of the Messiah and who now has received him in her midst. The Archangel Gabriel's announcement to Mary echoes an Old Testament text from the prophet Zephaniah. This was familiar to everyone as a prophecy regarding the coming of the Messiah. Luke includes details meant to remind listeners of the Old Testament prophecy in Zephaniah.[5]

---

[5] René Laurentin, *The Truth of Christmas Beyond the Myths*, trans. Michael Wrenn et al. (Petersham, Mass.: St. Bede's, 1986) 20–21. The * symbol indicates where Laurentin's own translation of biblical verse is being used.

Zephaniah 3:14–17 *	**Luke 1:28–33** *
Sing aloud,	
O daughter of Zion,	
shout, O Israel!	
Rejoice O daughter	Rejoice,
of Jerusalem	full of grace
The king of Israel,	
the LORD is with you. . . .	the Lord is with you!
Do not fear,	Do not fear,
O Zion . . .	Mary . . .
The LORD your God,	and behold
	you will conceive
is in your midst	in your womb
a warrior	and bear a son,
	and you shall call him
who saves . . .	Lord-savior [Ye-shu]
the King of Israel,	and he will reign
the LORD is with you	

Keep in mind that the name "Jesus" (In Hebrew pronounced Ye-shu, meaning Lord-savior) recalls the phrase "who saves." In addition, note how Luke's phrase "in your womb" recalls Zephaniah's phrase "in your midst." These parallels are not found when the angel announced the coming birth of John the Baptist to his father Zachariah:

---

* Asterisk indicates translation of R. Laurentin. See p. 215, n. 5.

Luke 1:13 *	**Luke 1:31** *
Your wife Elizabeth	You will conceive
	in your womb
shall bear	and shall bring forth
a son	a son
and you	and you
shall call	shall call
his name	his name
John	Jesus [Ye-shu]

Why was the phrase "in your womb" included in the annunciation to Mary, but not in the announcement to Zachariah? Luke put it there to call attention to Zephaniah's prophecy, "The King of Israel, the LORD, is *in your midst*" (Zep 3:15, emphasis added).

Luke's allusion to Zephaniah affirms that Mary is not only the mother of the Savior, but also the mother of God's people. His depiction of her fulfills Isaiah's final vision of Mother Zion and her children.

> Who ever heard such a thing,
>   or saw the like?
> Can a country be brought forth in one day,
>   or a nation be born in a single moment?
> Yet Zion is scarcely in labor
>   when she gives birth to her children (Isaiah 66:8).

2. Mary as the New Eve

This connection is not hard to make: if Christ is the New Adam, as St. Paul says in Romans 5, then Mary is the New Eve. Just as Eve cooperated with Adam in the fall, Mary cooperated with Christ in our redemption. Just as Eve is the mother of all according to the flesh, Mary is mother of all in the new creation.

God perfected Eve and she was given a name that means "Mother of all the living." Eve was unable to live up to the honor of her name, so God's grace provided another mother who would. The following are some comparisons between Eve and Mary: Eve was created without sin.

> Then God said: "Let us make man in our image, after our likeness" (Gn 1:26).

Mary was conceived without sin.

> And he came to her and said, "Hail, full of grace" (Lk 1:28).[6]

Eve was our mother according to the flesh.

> The man called his wife Eve [life], because she became the mother of all the living (Gn 3:20).

> So, too, it is written, "The first man, Adam, became a living being," . . . The first man was from the earth, earthly . . . (1 Cor 15:45–47).

Mary is our mother through Christ.

> But to those who did accept him he gave power to become children of God, to those who believed in his name, who were born not by natural generation nor by human choice nor by a man's decision but of God (Jn 1:12–13).

> Then he said to the disciple, "Behold, your mother" (John 19:27).

> "The first man, Adam, became a living being," the last Adam a life-giving spirit. . . . The first man was from the earth, earthly; the second man, from heaven (1 Cor 15:45–47).

Eve disobeyed God and, not believing him, ate the fruit.

> The woman saw that the tree was good for food, pleasing to the eyes, and desirable for gaining wisdom. So she took some of its fruit and ate it . . . (Gn 3:6).

Mary obeyed God and, believing him, bore great fruit.

---

[6] *Revised Standard Version, Catholic Edition*, ed. Luther Weigle (Nashville, Tenn.: Thomas Nelson Publishers, 1966). The *Revised Standard* translation of this verse will be used throughout the chapter. Please see appendix B.

Mary said, "Behold, I am the handmaid of the Lord. May it be done to me according to your word" (Lk 1:38).

Blessed is the fruit of your womb (Lk 1:42).

Sin (death) entered the world through Eve.

Gn 3:6–24 (This tells of the fall of Adam and Eve.)

Salvation (life) entered the world through Mary.

He will be great and will be called the Son of the Most High, and the Lord God will give him the throne of David his father, and he will rule over the house of Jacob forever, and of his kingdom there will be no end (Lk 1:32–33).

Whereas Eve allowed her body to become the source of death and corruption for her children, Mary allowed her body to serve as God's special home, so that grace and life enters into the souls of her children. Mary gave birth to one son, and then became mother for the whole world through him. In the second century, St. Irenaeus, bishop of Lyon, described these contrasts between Mary and Eve with striking clarity.

The knot of disobedience was loosed by the obedience of Mary. What the Virgin Eve had bound in unbelief, the Virgin Mary loosed through faith (Jurgens, v. 1, 224).

From the time of the apostles until now, the Church has continued to meditate on the mystery of Mary's role as the "New Eve."

The Gospel of John also draws parallels showing Christ as the New Adam and Mary as the New Eve. This masterpiece of literature arranges layers of meaning and symbolisms. Mary appears in two sections of the Gospel. First, she appears in the episode of the wedding at Cana. This event happens at the very beginning of Jesus' ministry. Secondly, she appears at the crucifixion, where his ministry on earth is finished. Let us examine the relationship between these two scenes.[7]

---

[7] For a good review of this subject see André Feuillet, *Jesus and His Mother*, trans. Leonard Maluf (Still River, Mass.: St. Bede's, 1984).

The Wedding Feast and the Cross

John 2:1–5, 11	John 19:25–28
On the third day there was a wedding at Cana in Galilee, and the mother of Jesus was there. Jesus and his disciples were also invited to the wedding. When the wine ran short, the mother of Jesus said to him, "they have no more wine." [And] Jesus said to her, "Woman, how does your concern affect me? My hour has not yet come." His mother said to the servers, "Do whatever he tells you" (Jn 2:1–5).	Standing by the cross of Jesus were his mother and his mother's sister, Mary the wife of Clopas, and Mary of Magdala. When Jesus saw his mother and the disciple there whom he loved, he said to his mother, "Woman, behold, your son." Then he said to the disciple, "Behold, your mother." And from that hour the disciple took her into his home.
Jesus did this as the beginning of his signs . . . and so revealed his glory, and his disciples began to believe in him (Jn 2:11).	After this, aware that everything was now finished, . . . Jesus said, "I thirst."

These two passages connect Genesis with the Crucifixion and the Resurrection. The Gospel of John connects to Genesis immediately by opening with the words, "In the beginning." John 1:1 through 2:1 explains about a series of six days.[8] These six days remind us of the six days of creation that ended with the

---

[8] The first chapters of John's Gospel cover this series of six days as follows: (Day One 1:1); (Day Two 1:29); (Day Three 1:35); (Day Four 1:43); (Days Four, Five, and Six 2:1). The phrase "on the third day" from 2:1 starts its counting including day four from 1:43. This same counting is used to say that Christ rose on the "third day," Sunday, even though he was Crucified on a Friday, which was the sixth day of the week. Note that 1:39 does not count as a "next day."

fall of Adam and Eve. It also foreshadows Christ's crucifixion on the sixth day of the week. John says that the wedding of Cana took place on the "third day," which foreshadows his resurrection from the dead "after three days."

When Mary says to Jesus, "They have no more wine," Jesus replies in a most unusual way, "Woman, how does your concern affect me? My hour has not yet come." He did not mean to show disrespect to Mary, because Jesus would not have broken the commandment: "Honor your father and your mother." It is true that Jesus makes use of this phrase when speaking to other women (Jn 4:21). The difference, of course, is that Mary is his mother. Why did he use the word "woman" in this way?

Jesus refers to his mother in this unusual way because he *intended* that everyone be reminded of other passages in the Bible that use the word "woman." One of them occurs later on in the Gospel of John. He called Mary "woman" again just before he died on the cross, and the "hour" that Jesus mentions refers to the time of his crucifixion as well: "The hour has come for the Son of Man to be glorified. . . . Yet what should I say? . . . 'Father save me from this hour?' I Father, the hour has come" (Jn 12:23, 27; 17:1). At Cana, Jesus calls Mary "woman" and says his hour had not come. At the crucifixion, his hour had come, and he calls her "woman" again. Jesus did this to recall the prophecy given to Eve when God called her "woman" and said that her offspring would strike the serpents head,

> I will put enmity between you and the woman,
>   and between your offspring and hers;
> He will strike at your head,
>   while you strike at his heel (Gn 3:15).

Jesus called Mary "woman" because he was the offspring who would crush the serpent's head. By saying this, he emphasized her cooperative role in redeeming us. Since the word "hour" refers to the cross, Jesus implied that Mary, the new Eve, would cooperate with him in redemption.

Mary as the new Eve does not mean that Mary relates to Christ as a spouse. The New Adam/New Eve parallel is limited to her role as his cooperative mother. We become her spiritual children when we become brothers and sisters to Christ; we do not call Christ our "Father." Jesus made this clear for all of us when he said to the beloved disciple, "Behold, your mother," and to his mother, "Woman, behold, your son." (Jn 19:26, 27) Jesus was not simply concerned about how his mother would be cared for. The only reason why John wrote the Gospel was so that we may come to believe and be saved (Jn 20:30–31). John therefore would not have included this detail in the Gospel unless it concerned all believers. It is clear from the context that the beloved disciple has become a son of Mary and she, his spiritual mother. The beloved disciple, then, typifies all disciples of Christ. The "woman" of Genesis, and Christ's using the word "woman" at Cana and at the Crucifixion thus definitively present Mary as cooperating with Christ's mission.[9] What follows is a summary of the Adam-Eve parallels in the Gospel of John.

Comparing the Wedding of Cana and the Crucifixion

Similarities

"Jesus is present"
"Mother of Jesus is present"
"Disciple(s) are present"
"Woman" used as a title
An abundance of Grace
"They have no wine" / "I thirst" (see Jn 2:3, 19:28)
Wedding on 6th day / Crucifixion is also on 6th day (Friday)
New Adam/New Eve gives spiritual birth to new children:
At Cana, disciples believe; at Cross, John becomes Mary's son.

---

[9] Just as in the Trinity, the Son resembles the Father, so in creation the Church resembles Mary. The Church is the body of Christ. His body came from Mary alone. Yet, the Church is a new reality. This mystery can be likened to the Trinity. There is a union and yet there is a distinction.

Contrasts

The Wedding at Cana	*At the Crucifixion*
Beginning of Ministry	End of Ministry
First Sign	Last Sign
Best wine in abundance	Sour wine in a meager quantity
"Hour" has not yet come	"Hour" is here
[Wedding Crowns of glory][10]	Crowns of pain
Water and Wine as symbol	Water and Blood as fulfillment
Joy	Sorrow
Jesus manifests his glory by miracle	Jesus manifests his glory by crucifixion

3. Mary as the Ark of the Covenant

The Hebrew people carried sacred objects with them when they wandered in the desert after the exodus. The holiest of these was the Ark of the Covenant (Ex 25:10; Nm 14:44). The Ark was a large wooden box, plated with pure gold that could be carried about by several priests. God commanded Moses to make it. In the Ark, Moses placed the three most precious items in their possession: the stone tablets containing the commandments of the Law that God gave Moses, some manna as a reminder of the heavenly food they ate in the desert, and the rod of Aaron that symbolized the true priesthood. These were the very life of the people. Most precious of all was the presence of God overshadowing the Ark and dwelling within. The Ark was placed in the tent of meeting, and above the Ark, God manifested his presence as a mysterious cloud that overshadowed and filled the place with his glory.

---

[10] The groom and the bride were crowned during Jewish wedding ceremonies before the destruction of the temple in A.D. 70. (See Sg 3:11, Is 61:10). (See also Rv 12:1 for the crowning of the Church and Mary.)

Then the cloud covered the meeting tent, and the glory of the LORD filled the Dwelling. Moses could not enter the meeting tent, because the cloud settled down upon it and the glory of the LORD filled the Dwelling (Ex 40:34–35; cf. Ex 25:22; Ex 30:6; Lv 16:2).

The Ark was so holy that there were strict prohibitions against touching it (Nm 4:15–20). Many miracles accompanied it (Jos 3, 4, 6). The Hebrews carried the Ark with them in battle and received special protection from God against their enemies (Nm 10:35). It was eventually placed in the Holy of Holies of the temple, but it was lost during the time of the Babylonian captivity (587 B.C.). The book of Maccabees has a prophecy that says it would be found when God "gathers his people together again and shows them mercy" (2 Mac 2:7).

Luke's Gospel shows that Mary fulfills the Ark of the Old Testament. Every precious thing about the Ark—the law, the manna, and the rod—was only a shadow of the reality of God present inside of Mary. Jesus within her fulfills the Law and becomes the true bread from heaven and the true high priest.[11] Jesus is conceived within Mary when the Holy Spirit overshadows her.

The Angel Gabriel says to Mary, "The holy Spirit will come upon you, and the power of the Most High will overshadow you. Therefore the child to be born will be called holy, the Son of God" (Lk 1:35). Notice that the Divine presence both overshadows and fills her so that the fruit of her womb is the Lord, the Holy One, the Son of God who will become manifest. In the same way, Exodus 40:34–35 speaks of the holy cloud as overshadowing the place of the Ark, encompassing it and filling it with the Divine presence so that the glory of the Lord becomes manifest.[12] The mother of the Lord thus begins to be identi-

---

[11] Jesus was born in Bethlehem, which means "house of bread." He gives himself as food for the life of the world.

[12] Luke uses the exact same Greek word for "overshadow" that the Sep-

fied with the new and perfect Ark of the Covenant, the living tabernacle of the Divine presence. The lost Ark of the Covenant has now reappeared. Mary becomes the living Ark carrying the Lord who will give life and salvation to all people.

Luke confirms the connection between the Ark and Mary by alluding to 2 Samuel 6:2, where the Ark of God is being transferred to Jerusalem by King David. The following comparison shows some of the parallel details of both narratives.[13]

---

tuagint uses to describe God's presence over the Ark of the Covenant. The Septuagint was a Greek version of the Hebrew Scriptures that was popular in the centuries before and after the birth of Christ. See appendix B.

[13] R. Laurentin, 56–59. The * symbol indicates where Laurentin's own translation of biblical verse is used.

2 Samuel 6:2 *	**Luke 1:39 ***
David	Mary
Arose	Arose
and went	and went
from	into the hill country
	to a city of
Baal- Judah	Judah
to bring up from there the	
Ark of God	

6:9	**1:43 ***
How can the	and why is this granted me,
	that the
ark of the LORD	mother of my Lord should
come to me?	come to me?

6:14	**1:44**
David came dancing	St. John the Baptist
before the LORD with	"leaped for joy" at the sound
abandon.	of Mary's voice.

6:11	**1:56**
The ark of the LORD	Mary
remained	remained
in the house of Obededom	with her [Elizabeth] about
. . . for three months.	three months.

St. Luke's depiction of Mary as the New Ark would have been both interesting and exciting to the Jews of Christ's time. This is because Judaism longed for the return of God's presence that the Ark represented. The book of Maccabees expresses this longing when it recounts how Jeremiah hid the Ark and prophesied that, "The place is to remain unknown until God gathers his people together again and shows them mercy" (2 Mac 2:7).

The Revelation of St. John continues the Mary/Ark parallel even more explicitly. Here, St. John's vision captures attention by showing that the Ark hidden by Jeremiah has been found!

> Then God's temple in heaven was opened, and the ark of his covenant could be seen in the temple. . . . A great sign appeared in the sky, a woman clothed with the sun, with the moon under her feet, and on her head a crown of twelve stars[14] (Rv 11:19; 12:1).

This verse begins John's retelling of the Genesis narrative concerning the woman and the serpent. He links the re-appearance of the Ark to "the woman," because he wants us to understand that the prophecy from Maccabees has been fulfilled in "the woman," who is the true ark of God's covenant (2 Mac 2:7).

4. Mary's Faith and Love

Who would have thought that God would choose a young teenage girl to cooperate with his plan of salvation? Living in Nazareth on the margins of Hebrew culture, she had no wealth, position, or power—nothing to attract the praise or attention of the world. Yet, all of heaven held its breath at the annunciation, awaiting her consent. She was the "most blessed of all women" because of God's grace, but God still left her free to believe the angel and to express her love for God by her acceptance of what the angel said.

Luke connects Mary's act of faith to Abraham, the man of faith. He does this once again by parallel references to Abraham and Mary in Scripture. First, Gabriel tells her that she has found favor with God:

---

[14] Note that being "clothed by the sun" makes the Woman golden, just as the Ark was a shining golden object. Secondly, none of the Scriptures were originally divided into chapters. This occurred in the middle ages. Apparently the connection between the ark and the woman was missed when chapter 11 and 12 were delineated.

Genesis 18:3 [15]	**Luke 1:30**
If I find favor with you	You have found favor with God

Second, there is a similar question of wonderment:

Genesis 18:12–13	**Luke 1:34**
Can a child be born to a man who is a hundred years old? Or can Sarah give birth at ninety?	How can this be since I have no relations with a man?

Third, there is an affirmation of God's might.

Genesis 18:14	**Luke 1:37**
Is anything too marvelous for the LORD to do?	For nothing will be impossible for God.

Like Abraham, Mary received the promise. She accepts God's word fully and conceives. At this point, she becomes the first believer of the New Testament, as well as the mother and example of all believers in the Church, even as Abraham was the father and example of the believers of the old Israel. The last two verses of the Magnificat reflect the same idea:

> He has helped Israel his servant,
>   remembering his mercy,
> according to his promise to our fathers,
>   to Abraham and to his descendants forever (Lk 1:54–55).

Just as Israel is the servant, Mary is the handmaid. What God has promised Abraham, the patriarchs, and all past generations has been fulfilled in Mary. Abraham was our father in faith, because it was through him that God gave us a promise. Mary be-

---

[15] Genesis 18:3 is taken from *The New Jerusalem Bible*, Gen. ed. Henry Wansbrough (Garden City, N.Y.: Doubleday, 1985).

came our mother in faith, because it was through her faith that the promise was fulfilled: Jesus became man. For this reason, the faith of every Christian is dependant upon Mary's faith. We can only "accept" Christ because Mary, through faith, first accepted Christ. Elizabeth, inspired by the Holy Spirit, paid tribute to Mary's faith when she said,

> Most blessed are you among women, and blessed is the fruit of your womb. And how does this happen to me, that the mother of my Lord should come to me? For at the moment the sound of your greeting reached my ears, the infant in my womb leaped for joy. Blessed are you who believed that what was spoken to you by the Lord would be fulfilled (Lk 1:42–45).

Here Luke contrasts Mary's faith with that of Zachariah, who was made mute by the angel when he expressed doubt about what the angel said to him (Lk 1:5–20). Shortly after Elizabeth's greeting, Mary expressed her own faith in a prayer that we call the "Magnificat."

> My soul proclaims the greatness of the Lord;
>   my spirit rejoices in God my savior.
> For he has looked upon his handmaid's lowliness;
>   behold, from now on will all ages call me blessed.
> The Mighty One has done great things for me,
>   and holy is his name (Lk 1:46–49).

Mary's "Magnificat" resounds with many allusions to Old Testament events, especially the prayers uttered by Judith and Hannah (Jdt 16:13–17; 1 Sm 2:1–10). Her prayer summed up everything that God had done for her people. God's grace perfected and brought Judaism to completion in Mary. Judaism, in her immaculate sinlessness, finally had a temple fit for God to dwell in. Although Mary celebrated what God had done for her, life did not go easy for her afterwards. She was an unwed pregnant teenager. If Joseph had not married her, she could possibly have been stoned.

Her marriage to Joseph did not end their troubles, however. They had to flee to Egypt. While there, they lived as refugees in a foreign land. When they finally returned, Mary had to endure the gossip about her. Even Jesus had to endure veiled references about "illegitimacy" (Jn 8:41). Such talk continued in non–Christian circles even after the resurrection. Still, Mary raised her son and did all that was prescribed according to the law (Lk 2:39,41). They made a long four-day pilgrimage to Jerusalem every year. Under her motherly care, Jesus advanced in "wisdom and age and favor before God and man" (Lk 2:52).

Mary followed Jesus during his ministry. She was there when it began at Cana and even caused Jesus to begin to manifest his glory. Her attitude and response during the wedding showed her complete trust and confidence (Jn 2). Mary told the servants at Cana, "Do whatever he tells you" (Jn 2:5). This corresponds perfectly to what she said to the angel Gabriel: "May it be done to me according to your word" (Lk 1:38). Her statement at Cana deserves great honor, because by it she shows her great faith. She disposes the servants to trust in Jesus. Her words prove that she is not only his mother on the physical level, but also a believer, a woman of profound faith.

Mary's faith is made manifest. When she requests a special favor of Jesus, he grants her wish and performs his first public miracle. The amount of wine created is astounding—between one hundred and two hundred gallons, much more than they needed, especially since the guests had already been "drinking a while." The miracle signifies the image of wine used by the prophets Amos and Joel, who both write about the superabundance of the messianic times: "On that day, / the mountains shall drip new wine" (Jl 4:18 cf. 2:23–24; Am 9:13–14). As was mentioned in the chapter on the Trinity, the wine symbolizes the gift of the spirit—the new life in God—and images redemption through the blood of Christ. The abundance and quality of the wine reflect the fullness of grace and the goodness of God's blessing. John tells us that the sign given by Christ at Cana "revealed his glory," which he also describes as "the glory as of the Father's only son" (Jn 2:11; 1:14). Finally, John also points out that this miracle (done through Mary's intercession) caused Jesus' disciples to believe in him for the first time (Jn 2:11).

During Christ's ministry, Mary was concerned about him, but unlike his "brothers," she believed (Mk 3:32). Jesus in turn presents Mary's faith as an example to us. When a woman from the crowd declares to Jesus, "Blessed is the womb that carried you and the breasts at which you nursed," Jesus says, "Rather blessed are those who hear the word of God and observe it" (Lk 11:27–28). Saying this, Jesus echoes Elizabeth: "Blessed are you who believed that what was spoken to you by the Lord would be fulfilled" (Lk 1:45).

5. Mary, Mother of the Church

When a woman is in labor, she is in anguish because her hour has arrived; but when she has given birth to a child, she no longer remembers the pain because of her joy that a child has been born into the world (Jn 16:21).

Jesus said this to his disciples when he saw them distressed over his pending crucifixion, but the idea also applies to the anguish that Mary endured at the Crucifixion. The cross was her hour of giving birth to us. Luke tells us this by mentioning a prophecy given by Simeon when Jesus was a baby. When Mary was in the temple with the baby Jesus, Simeon turned to Mary with a solemn prophecy:

This child is destined for the fall and rise of many in Israel, and to be a sign that will be contradicted (and you yourself a sword will pierce) so that the thoughts of many hearts may be revealed (Lk 2:34–35).

His words echo the piercing of Christ on the cross and the prophecy of Zechariah:

I will pour on the house of David and on the inhabitants of Jerusalem a spirit of grace and petition; and they shall look on

> him whom they have thrust through, and they shall mourn for him as one mourns for an only son, and they shall grieve over him as one grieves over a firstborn (Zec 12:10).

The opened side of Christ brings grace and petition (Zec 12:10). Those who look upon him without faith will be condemned when he comes as the glorious judge whom they have pierced (Rv 1:7). Mary's heart was also pierced when she witnessed the death of her son—and her pierced heart either gives life or is contradicted. Mary had suffered before, but at the Cross she received the fatal blow. From the depth of her faithful sorrow and compassion comes life. Mary and Christ shared intimately and inseparably in begetting the Church. Her birth pangs are depicted in the vision of John when he writes,

> She was with child and wailed aloud in pain as she labored to give birth (Rv 12:2).

That Mary's birth pangs are associated with the cross and not with Christ's birth at Bethlehem is clear from the context. The child is immediately taken up to God. The following verse shows that Jesus was not the only spiritual offspring of Mary. Rather, all those who keep God's commandments and bear witness to Jesus are her children:

> Then the dragon became angry with the woman and went off to wage war on the rest of her offspring, those who keep God's commandments and bear witness to Jesus (Rv 12:17).[16]

---

[16] There is some controversy regarding the identity of the woman of Revelation chapter 12. Modern biblical scholars say she represents the Church and not Mary. This position lacks solid ground. It is inconceivable that a first century writer, who was alive at the same time as the mother of Jesus, could speak about a woman giving birth to Christ without thinking of Jesus' mother in some way. The birth could also be a reference to the resurrection of Jesus. John (or a member of his community) wrote about Mary's presence at the cross in the Gospel. This, and the fact that she lived with John, would make it very hard to believe that Mary was not to be regarded as the woman of Revelation 12.

Jesus affirms that Mary is the mother of all these at the cross when he says to her, "Behold, your son" and to the beloved disciple, "Behold, your mother" (Jn 19:26–27). Therefore, Mary is the mother of the Church.

Mary is not our mother in Spirit only, but also in the sanctified flesh of Christ. We become part of Christ's body through the sacrament of Baptism. We continue to grow within it through the spiritual food that is the Eucharist. Since these things make us one body with him, his mother should become our mother also. Since we share in the same flesh, we are united in the same mother. Mary's role as our mother denies any way of thinking that presents her as only a tool used by God.

Mary, our mother, is the Ark of Yahweh. The New Zion bears the new people of God as the fulfillment of the old type. Mary, the virgin Jewess, links the old and the new. She is the renewed young image of the old Israel, belonging to a new order of creation—the order of grace.

God's grace completed Mary, and she believed and trusted him, so that she became our mother in faith and the first witness to Christ in the world. She consented to what the angel told her. She became the first witness to Christ when she visited Elizabeth. The Holy Spirit went forth from her to inspire both Elizabeth and John the Baptist (Lk 1:41). Mary preached the gospel for the first time when she spoke the Magnificat to Elizabeth. She continued in this faith ever after. Cana demonstrated how much she believed in Christ before his ministry ever began, and at the Cross, she remained faithful when even most of his disciples had been scattered.

She is our mother in the Spirit since she is the Temple of the Holy Spirit. The Holy Spirit comes to us through this Temple, our Mother. Gabriel told her that she would conceive in her womb. The Holy Spirit then overshadowed her, filling her with God's presence. In chapter one of Acts, the Holy Spirit overshadows her offspring while she is in the midst of the new Church.

Pentecost was a fitting time for the Spirit to descend on the community because it was the festival celebrating the first fruits of the harvest. At Pentecost, the apostles, her children in the faith, surrounded Mary. The Holy Spirit descending upon them made them into the first fruits among her children. Satan wars against these children, but Mary has been given a safe place in the desert (Rv 12:14). This recalls the desert of Sinai where God first formed the Israelites into a community by giving them the Ten Commandments (Ex 40).

The Perpetual Virginity of Mary

The first question people ask about this Catholic teaching is this:

If Mary did not have other children, why does the Bible mention that Jesus had "brothers" (or sisters)? (Mt 13:55 and Mk 6:3)

Surprisingly for some, Martin Luther answered this question by pointing out that Jesus' "brothers" were actually his cousins:

> Christ . . . was the only Son of Mary, and the Virgin Mary bore no children besides Him . . . "brothers" really means "cousins" here, for Holy Writ and the Jews always call cousins brothers (Martin Luther, *Sermons on John*).[17]

Why did Martin Luther, who took his authority from "The Bible Alone," believe that Mary was a perpetual virgin when the Bible *seems* to say otherwise? The words "brother" or "sister" in the Aramaic language spoken at the time of Christ have a wider meaning than they have in English. Aramaic has no single word for "cousin."[18] The word "brother" (or "sister") is used

---

[17] Martin Luther, *Luther's Works*, *Weimar Edition*, trans. J. Pelikan (Concordia: St. Louis, 1957) vol. 22, 214–215.

[18] Aramaic is a Semitic language similar to Hebrew. It was spoken in Palestine after the Aramaens conquered this area in the sixth century B.C. Jesus and the apostles spoke this language. It is the language that Jesus used to address the crowds when he taught them.

for any kind of relative, from a close to a distant cousin, brother in law, uncle, or nephew. Hebrew is the same. The Bible shows this in reference to Abraham and his nephew Lot. In 12:5 and 14:12 of the book of Genesis, we read clearly that Lot is Abraham's brother's son. Yet in Genesis 13:8 and 14:14 we again see clear examples of how Lot was referred to as Abraham's brother: "Abraham heard that his brother [Lot] was taken captive. . . ."[19] This proves that the Bible uses the word "brother" in the wider sense.[20] Let us go from here to consider further evidence that the "brothers" of Christ were actually his cousins.

The table below shows how two of these "brothers of the Lord" reappear as either "James and Joses" or else "James and Joseph," depending on whether one is reading from the Gospel of Mark or Matthew. Both Mark and Matthew later identify these brothers as the sons of a *different* Mary; their mother is *not* Mary the mother of Jesus.

Mark 6:3	Mark 15:40
Is he not the carpenter, the son of Mary, and the brother of *James and Joses* and Judas and Simon? And are not his sisters here with us?	There were also women looking on from a distance. Among them were Mary Magdalene, Mary the mother of the *younger James and of Joses*, and Salome.

Matthew 13:55	Matthew 27:56
Is he not the carpenter's son? Is not his mother named Mary and his brothers *James, Joseph, Simon,* and Judas? Are not his sisters all with us?	Among them were Mary Magdalene and Mary the mother of *James and Joseph*, and the mother of the sons of Zebedee.

---

[19] For this section, The King James version is best for illustrating the literal use of the word "brother."

[20] Though Christ's words were later written in Greek, the Gospel writers followed the Semitic practice of calling *anyone* related to Christ a brother or a sister. He became the "eldest of many brothers." Christians continue this Semitic usage even to this day.

How do we know for sure that "James and Joseph" did not have Jesus' mother Mary as their own mother? First, in Semitic culture, a woman is commonly identified as the mother of her first-born son. Therefore, if Jesus really did have James and Joseph as younger brothers, neither Mark nor Matthew would have insulted Jesus by referring to their common mother as the "mother of James and Joseph." Instead, they would have referred to her as "Mary, the mother of Jesus, James, and Joseph." Therefore, we must conclude that the persons mentioned as the brothers of Jesus were sons of a Mary who was not the mother of Jesus.

The Gospel of John provides even stronger evidence that the mother of "James and Joseph" was actually a "sister" (or cousin) to Mary the mother of Jesus. John identifies three different Marys at the cross, and since we know from Mark and Matthew that the mother of James and Joseph was named Mary (and that this Mary was present at the crucifixion), we must therefore conclude that the mother of James and Joseph is the same person whom John refers to as "Mary the wife of Clopas."

> Standing by the cross of Jesus were his mother and his mother's sister, Mary the wife of Clopas, and Mary of Magdala (Jn 19:25).

Two further points lead us to the same conclusion that Jesus was the only son of Mary: first, no mention is ever made of other sons or daughters of Mary, only the "brothers" and "sisters" of Jesus. Second, at the cross, Jesus gives Mary to John as his mother (John 19:26). This would have been insulting to his blood brothers if Jesus had any. Besides, John 19:27 says that, "From that hour the disciple took her into his home." If Mary had other sons, she would have stayed with them; John would never have taken her into his home.

What about the Gospel of Matthew? Did not Matthew point out that Joseph had relations with Mary after Jesus was born? How else can you explain Matthew 1:25 where it says "He had

no relations with her until she bore a son, and he named him Jesus"?

This passage offers no such proof at all, but it does cause confusion because of Matthew's use of the word "until." The word "until" does not necessarily indicate what took place afterwards. For example, in Matthew 28:20 Jesus says to his apostles, "I am with you always, *until* the end of the age" (emphasis added). This does not imply that Jesus will not be with them *after* the end of the age! Matthew used the word "until" to stress the fact that Jesus was conceived by the Holy Spirit and not by Joseph's seed, since he had no relations with Mary at any time before she bore a son. Matthew was not trying to give any indication of what took place *after* she gave birth.

A last point must be made. Mary is the fulfillment of the Ark of the Covenant and is therefore more sacred than the old Ark was. God made the Ark's holiness clear through what happened to Uzzah:

> Uzzah reached out his hand to the ark of God and steadied it, for the oxen were making it tip. But the LORD was angry with Uzzah; God struck him on that spot, and he died there before God (2 Sm 6:6–7).

Joseph knew this story about the Ark. He also knew who and what Mary represented, because he knew who Jesus' father was. Can any reasonable person propose that, Joseph knowing all of this, would ever consider reaching out his hand in a carnal fashion to Mary?

In Luke 2:7 it says, "She gave birth to her *firstborn* son" [emphasis added]. Doesn't this mean that Jesus was the first son and Mary had other children afterwards?

No. In the Hebrew culture, "Firstborn" does not imply other children. It is an honorary title given to the first son, even if he was the only child. A "firstborn" had special privileges of authority, responsibility, inheritance, and succession according to tradition and the law.

Consecrate to me every first-born that opens the womb among the Israelites, both of man and beast, for it belongs to me (Ex 13:2).

Is it very important if Mary had other children or not?

Yes. Consecrated virginity is a sign of total dedication, purity, and devotion for the sake of the kingdom (Mt 19:12). Most important of all, it fosters the begetting of spiritual children. Those who have children according to the flesh can also have spiritual children, but these are born in proportion to one's devotion. Mary's total loving consecration allowed her to bear spiritual children proportionally. By giving all she received all. We refer to her as our mother precisely because she became the spiritual mother of all Christians at the cross. Furthermore, Mary is the image of the Church, which is "without spot or wrinkle or any such thing" (Eph 5:27). Just as the heavenly Jerusalem (the Church) is our mother (Gal 4:26), Mary too is our mother (Jn 19:27, Rv 12:2, 17). In Genesis, we see that Eve became the mother of all the living according to the flesh. The order of the flesh is passing away. Nothing of Mary is passing away. Mary is the New Eve who became mother of all the living within the new creation. To say that Mary had other children according to the flesh not only diminishes her total devotion to Jesus, but more importantly, it denies her vital role in giving birth to God's children by her association in Christ's saving sacrifice on the cross. It is fitting that the mother of God should be his alone.

The Immaculate Conception

Many people confuse the doctrine of the Immaculate Conception with the conception of Jesus by the Holy Spirit. They are not the same thing. The doctrine of the Immaculate Conception has to do with Mary's conception in the womb of her mother, Anna. While Anna conceived her in the normal way, God preserved Mary from being affected in any way by the original sin of Adam and Eve.

Some object to this by saying it would mean that Mary had no need of a savior. The answer to this objection is that God graced Mary because he could *see* Christ's redemption *coming in the future.* God's grace was already active in the world before Christ's redemption. The fact that Christ came after her does not matter to God, because God is outside of time. If Jesus was not our savior until his death on the cross, then why would John the Baptist, as a six-month-old pre-born, be touched by the Holy Spirit and leap for joy in the womb of Elizabeth? Likewise, how could Elias and Moses have appeared with Christ on Mount Tabor, if the merits of Christ's redemption had not enabled them to appear before the crucifixion?

God would not have a mother who was touched by Satan in any way. She was completely pure. Her free will was always in complete harmony with God's will. She had a special relationship with God from the beginning. All of God's creation was affected by sin, and all of it was marred in some way; Mary is the sole exception. She became the connection between God and his creation.

The words spoken by Gabriel, *"Chaire kecharitomenē"* are revealing (Lk 1:28). St. Jerome translated this Greek phrase as "Hail Mary, full of grace."[21] As the original Greek indicates, however, the Angel Gabriel did not actually make use of her given name. Instead, he addressed her as, " Hail, Full of Grace,"

---

[21] Gabriel here uses the word "Grace" twice. In English, it might have been "Grace, Oh Completed in Grace!" He was thus giving Mary a special title. In doing this, he was referring to Zechariah 4:7. There, an angel relates how Zerubabel will place the finishing stone, the capstone that completes the Temple. The cheer of "Grace, Grace!" accompanies the arrival of the capstone to finish the Temple. (The *New American Bible* translates the cheer as "Hail, Hail") The prophet Zechariah certainly was making a connection to Jacob's act in Genesis 28:22, where Jacob sets up a memorial stone at the very spot where the Temple was eventually built, and Jacob gives it the title "The House of God." In the New Testament, the angel Gabriel uses "Grace, Grace" as a title for Mary because she makes possible the arrival of the capstone of Judaism, Jesus Christ. The flesh she gives is the "Temple" that God's Word will now inhabit to form Christ's body.

giving her a title. The meaning behind her new title is clear: Mary was without sin. She was perfected by grace at her conception and she remained full of God's grace throughout her life. The Bible does not have to say explicitly, "Mary was conceived without original sin," anymore than a beautiful woman has to carry a sign that says "I am beautiful."

The Assumption of Mary

There are no relics of Mary. The Church possesses and venerates the bones of many apostles and early martyrs and saints. No one ever saved the bones of Mary, because there were no bones here on earth to save.

The Scriptures show that some people other than Jesus were taken up to heaven bodily. The general resurrection of everyone's bodies will happen at Jesus' second coming, but some people experienced being raised in glory immediately:

> But Jesus cried out again in a loud voice, and gave up his spirit. And behold, the veil of the sanctuary was torn in two from top to bottom. The earth quaked, rocks were split, tombs were opened, and the bodies of many saints who had fallen asleep were raised. And coming forth from their tombs after his resurrection, they entered the holy city and appeared to many (Mt 27:50–53).[22]

In the Old Testament, we find clear evidence of other assumptions into heaven. The book of Genesis, for example, tells the story of a righteous man named Enoch, the father of Methuselah.

> Then Enoch walked with God, and he was no longer here, for God took him (Gn 5:24).

The same story from Genesis is recounted in the Old Testament books of Sirach and Wisdom, where we are told that, "Few on

---

[22] The word "appeared" here means to be manifested to people as in a heavenly vision. This means that people saw the risen saints in glorified form.

earth have been made the equal of Enoch / for he was taken up bodily" (Sir 49:14; 44:16; Wis 4:10). In the New Testament also, Paul refers to Enoch's assumption as his reward for having pleased God (Heb 11:5–6). These citations show that the Hebrews believed in the possibility of a bodily assumption for those whom God loved in a special way.

An even more dramatic assumption from the Old Testament occurs in the second book of Kings (2 Kgs 2:10–12). Here, the prophet Elisha is present when his master and teacher Elijah is taken up.

> As they walked on conversing, a flaming chariot and flaming horses came between them, and Elijah went up to heaven in a whirlwind. When Elisha saw it happen he cried out, "My father! my father! Israel's chariots and drivers!" (2 Kgs 2:11–12)

Our Blessed Mother was worthy to receive this honor as well. She was the first and perfect disciple of Jesus, and her merits surpassed even those of the patriarchs and prophets. Nevertheless, like every other privilege granted to Mary, the assumption was not meant for her alone. Mary was *one of us*, and her assumption is celebrated as a victory for all believers—and a signpost for the future.

> And when this which is corruptible clothes itself with incorruptibility and this which is mortal clothes itself with immortality, then the word that is written shall come about:
>
> "Death is swallowed up in victory.
> Where, O death, is your victory?
> Where, O death, is your sting?"
>
> The sting of death is sin, and the power of sin is the law. But thanks be to God who gives us the victory through our Lord Jesus Christ (1 Cor 15:54–57).

The Resurrection of the Dead will mark the final and perfect restoration of the grace and dignity that was our heritage from the beginning. In fact, we will receive even more grace, because Christ came to establish a new creation far greater than anything

Adam and Eve could have imagined. By Christ's sacrifice and Resurrection, there is a New Man in heaven. By Mary's cooperation and Assumption, the New Woman assures us that the new heaven and new earth will be a human place. It will not be alien to us. We will not be disembodied spirits—instead, our lives will have a relationship to what we were and who we were on earth. God will take our sinful identities and remove all stains of sin and suffering from them. Once we are purified, we will receive new and glorified bodies, fit for heaven. This heavenly glory awaits those who love Christ. His mother and ours will be there to welcome us home.

Devotion to the Virgin Mary

Native Americans have always viewed the earth as their mother. Catholics know exactly how they feel, because we view Mary in the same way. What is more, we know that when Christ reunited the human family together through her common motherhood, he also began to restore all of the material creation to bear his bodily presence as well. This is why the Church is able to use water for Baptism, oil for Confirmation, stone and wood for her altars, and bread and wine for Communion: through the motherhood of creation, Christ makes himself physically present to us, restoring the cosmos to its original calling.

Mary protects us from worshiping creation as God, however. In fact, she shelters us from worshipping *all* false Gods, because she is the consecrated temple of the one true God. Facing her while we worship God ensures that we are joined to the real Christ.

We need this, because false concepts of motherhood and false concepts about God speedily lead us astray. Peoples' corrupted versions of motherhood are often appalling. A man could be inspired by the wonderful heritage of his country and be willing to die for it. Such passion for one's own nation is actually a form of reverence for motherhood. This is a good thing. This same man, however, might spoil the purity of his loyalty by talking about setting up fences and machine-gunning illegal aliens. People who think this way deny that they and the "aliens" have a common mother in Mary.

A young man on a championship team might really appreciate the sacrifice, dedication, and teamwork that it took to win. He might feel deep respect for the ceremony where his team receives their winning trophy. Yet, this same young man might never think to make a similar sacrifice for his future wife—the one who is supposed to be his crowning glory. He might not even honor his wedding ceremony. Instead, he might always look at women (even his own wife) with disrespect, as if having relations with a woman were simply another form of fun.

Similarly, a young woman who can clearly see that it is wrong to needlessly cut down forests, kill whales, or pull the wings off a butterfly, might have no problem at all with an abortionist dismembering the unborn. She recognizes that nature is sacred, but she does not allow herself to see the sacred in humanity. Ironically, modern-day support for abortion often masquerades under the banner of "feminism," even though it is a complete denial of everything feminine. Consider what the following early feminists had to say about abortion:

> When we consider that women are treated as property, it is degrading to women that we should treat our children as property to be disposed of as we see fit.
>
> —Elizabeth Cady Stanton in a letter to Julia Ward Howe, Oct. 16, 1873, recorded in Howe's diary at Harvard University Library

> Guilty? Yes. No matter what the motive, love of ease, or a desire to save from suffering the unborn innocent, the woman is awfully guilty who commits the deed. It will burden her conscience in life, it will burden her soul in death; But oh, thrice guilty is he who drove her to the desperation which impelled her to the crime!
>
> —Susan B. Anthony in her publication *The Revolution*, July 8, 1869

Compare what the early feminists taught about abortion with what Mother Teresa has said about it in our own time:

> If we accept that a mother can kill even her own child, how can we tell other people not to kill each other? . . . Any country that accepts abortion is not teaching its people to love, but to use any violence to get what they want.[23]
>
> —Mother Teresa

The early feminists, unlike some modern feminists, were still devoted to motherhood. Mother Teresa learned about motherhood from her Catholic mother who was also devoted to the Virgin Mary. Devotion to Mary teaches motherhood and femininity, and her message can cure what ails us. Respect for Mary restores our respect for nature and for our own bodies. She teaches us to recognize the presence of Jesus Christ in our fellow man. We cannot be devoted to Mary and the saints in heaven and still believe that our relationship to God is only a private matter.[24]

An invisible, private relationship with God is a good thing. But if it does not grow into something more, then we can easily become separated from God. Mary and the saints teach us that God is present in his creation. Once we understand this, we cannot destroy beauty in nature for no good reason or kill an unborn child. We cannot look at sex as simply a way of having fun, and we cannot ignore a hungry stranger whom we pass in the street. Because Mary shows us the personal presence of Christ in all of these, we can surely say that a "personal relationship with Jesus Christ" begins with devotion to our Mother Mary.

---

[23] Mother Teresa of Calcutta, "Whatsoever You Do," National Prayer Breakfast (Washington, D.C., 3 Feb 1994). See also Peggy Noonan, "Still, Small, Voice," *Crisis* 16, no. 2 (Feb. 1998): 12–17.

[24] Please see appendix G for an explanation of prayer to the saints.

The Early Church Fathers
on the Mother of God

St. Ignatius of Antioch (A.D. 110): *Letter to the Ephesians* (v. 1, 42)

For our God, Jesus Christ, was conceived by Mary in accord with God's plan: of the seed of David, it is true, but also of the Holy Spirit. He was born and was baptized so that by His submission He might purify the water. The virginity of Mary, her giving birth, and even the death of the Lord, were hidden from the prince of this world: three mysteries loudly proclaimed, but wrought in the silence of God.

St. Justin Martyr (A.D. 100/110–165): *Dialogue with Trypho the Jew* v. 1, 141)

For Eve, a virgin and undefiled, conceived the word of the serpent, and bore disobedience and death. But the Virgin Mary received faith and joy when the angel Gabriel announced to her the glad tidings that the Spirit of the Lord would come upon her and the power of the Most High would overshadow her, for which reason the Holy One being born of her is the Son of God. And she replied: "Be it done unto me according to thy word."

St. Irenaeus (A.D. 140–202): *Against Heresies* (v. 1, 224)

Consequently, then, Mary the Virgin is found to be obedient, saying: "Behold, O Lord, your handmaid; be it done to me according to your word." Eve, however, was disobedient; and when yet a virgin, she did not obey. Just as she, who was then still a virgin although she had Adam for a husband, . . . having become disobedient, was made the cause of death for herself and for the whole human race; so also Mary, betrothed to a man but nevertheless still a virgin, being obedient, was made the cause of salvation for herself and for the whole human race. . . . Thus, the knot of Eve's disobedience was loosed by the obedience of

Mary. What the virgin Eve had bound in unbelief, the Virgin Mary loosed through faith.

St. Irenaeus (A.D. 140–202): *Against Heresies* (Liturgy of the Hours, Friday, 2nd week of Advent)

The enemy would not have been defeated fairly if his vanquisher had not been born of a woman, because it was through a woman that he had gained mastery over man in the beginning, and set himself up as man's adversary. That is why the Lord proclaims himself the Son of Man, the one who renews in himself that first man from whom the race born of woman was formed; as by a man's defeat our race fell into the bondage of death, so by a man's victory we were to rise again to life.

Tertullian (A.D. 155/160–240/250): *The Flesh of Christ* (v. 1, 358)

Likewise, through a Virgin, the Word of God was introduced to set up a structure of life. Thus, what had been laid waste in ruin by this sex was by the same sex re-established in salvation. Eve had believed the serpent; Mary believed Gabriel. That which the one destroyed by believing, the other, by believing, set straight.

Tertullian (A.D. 155/160–240/250): *Monogamy* (v. 1, 380)

It was a virgin who gave birth to Christ: and she would marry once only, after she brought Him forth. The reason for this was that both titles to sanctity might be exhibited in Christ's parentage, born as He was of a Mother who was both a virgin and a wife to one husband.

St. Ephrem (A.D. 306–373): *Songs of Praise* (v. 1, 711)

This Virgin became a Mother while preserving her virginity; And though still a Virgin she carried a Child in her womb; And the handmaid and work of His Wisdom became the Mother of God.

St. Ephrem (A.D. 306–373): *The Nisibene Hymns* **(v. 1, 719)**

> You alone and your Mother
> Are more beautiful than any others;
> For there is no blemish in you,
> Nor any stains upon your Mother,
> Who of my children
> Can compare in beauty to these?

St. Athanasius (A.D. 295–373): *The Incarnation of the Word of God* **(v. 1, 788)**

The Son of God became Son of Man, so that the sons of man, that is, of Adam, might become sons of God. The Word begotten of the Father from on high, inexpressibly, inexplicably, incomprehensibly and eternally, is He that is born in time here below, of the Virgin Mary, the Mother of God,—so that those who are in the first place born here below might have a second birth from on high, that is, of God.

St. Ambrose of Milan (A.D. 333–397): *Commentary on Psalm 118* **(v. 2, 1314)**

Come, then, and search out Your sheep, not through Your servants or hired men, but do it Yourself. Lift me up bodily and in the flesh, which is fallen in Adam. Lift me up not from Sara but from Mary, a Virgin not only undefiled but a Virgin whom grace has made inviolate, free of every stain of sin.

St. Augustine of Hippo (A.D. 354–430): *Holy Virginity* **(v. 3, 1643–1644)**

In being born of a Virgin who chose to remain a Virgin even before she knew who was to be born of her, Christ wanted to approve virginity rather than to impose it. And He wanted virginity to be of free choice even in that woman in whom He took upon Himself the form of a slave.

That one woman is both Mother and Virgin, not in spirit only but even in body. In spirit she is Mother, not of our Head, who is our Savior Himself, —of whom, rather, it was she who was born spiritually, since all who believe in Him, including even herself, are rightly called children of the bridegroom, —but plainly she is in spirit Mother of us who are His members, because by love she has cooperated so that the faithful, who are the members of that Head, might be born in the Church. In body, indeed, she is Mother of that very Head.

St. Augustine of Hippo (A.D. 354–430): *Nature and Grace* **(v. 3, 1794)**

How do we know what abundance of grace for the total overcoming of sin was conferred upon her, who merited to conceive and bear Him in whom there was no sin.

St. Gregory of Tours (A.D. 538–594): *Eight Books of Miracles* **(v. 3, 2288a)**

The course of this life having been completed by Blessed Mary, when she would be called from the world, all the Apostles came together from their various regions to her house. And when they had heard that she was about to be taken from the world, they kept watch together with her. And behold, the Lord Jesus came with His angels, and taking her soul, He gave it over to the Angel Michael and withdrew. At daybreak, however, the Apostles took up her body on a bier and placed it in a tomb; and they guarded it, expecting the Lord to come. And behold, again the Lord stood by them; and the holy body having been received, He commanded that it be taken in a cloud into paradise: where now, rejoined to the soul, [Mary] rejoices with the Lord's chosen ones, and is in the enjoyment of the good of an eternity that will never end.

The Teachings of
Early Protestant Reformers

Martin Luther: 1483–1546 (Leader of the Protestant Reformation) *Luther's Works*
Christ our savior was the real and natural fruit of Mary's virginal womb. . . . This was without the cooperation of a man, and she remained a virgin after that.

Martin Luther: Jaroslav Pelikan's 21-volume "Luther's Works" (St. Louis: Concordia).
[In a 1527 sermon, he spoke about Mary's sinlessness in a way that approaches the Catholic doctrine of the Immaculate Conception, which was finally formulated three hundred years later in the nineteenth century:] "But the other conception, namely the infusion of the soul, it is piously and suitably believed, was without any sin, so that while the soul was being infused, she would be at the same time cleansed from original sin and adorned with the gifts of God to receive the holy soul thus infused. And thus, in the very moment in which she began to live, she was without all sin." [At that time, virtually all of Saxony was Protestant.]

Zwingli: 1484–1531 ("Father of Protestantism") *Augustine Bea, Mary and the Protestants*
I firmly believe according to the words of the Gospel that a pure virgin brought forth for us the Son of God and remained a virgin pure and intact in childbirth and also after the birth, for all eternity.

Mary Bible Study—
Scriptures Cited in the Chapter

2 Sm 5:7—Zion was the fortress that King David had to conquer in order to capture Jerusalem.

Is 52:1–5—The prophet Isaiah uses the titles "Zion" or "Daughter Zion" to depict the people of Israel personified as a virgin bride who belongs to the Lord.

Zep 3:15 and Lk 1:31—When the angel says to Mary, "You will conceive in your womb...," she fulfills the prophecy of Zephaniah to Zion: "The King of Israel, the LORD, is in your midst."

Lk 1:13 and Lk 1:31—Announcements to Elizabeth and Mary are compared. "In your womb" [or "in your midst"] is missing in Elizabeth's case.

Is 66:8—"Can a country be brought forth in one day, / or a nation be born in a single moment? / Yet Zion is scarcely in labor / when she gives birth to her children."

Gn 1:26 and Lk 1:28—Eve is created and Mary is conceived without sin.

Gn 3:20 and 1 Cor 15:45–47—Adam and Eve are said to be our parents according to the flesh. Eve is "the mother of all the living."

Jn 1:12–13, Jn 19:27, and 1 Corinthians 15:45–47—Mary becomes mother of all of us through Christ.

Gn 3:6—Eve disobeyed God and, not believing him, ate the fruit.

Lk 1:38–42—Mary obeyed God and, believing him, bore great fruit.

Gn 3:6–24—Sin (death) entered the world through Eve.

Lk 1:32–33—Salvation (life) entered the world through Mary.

Jn 2 and Jn 19:25–28—A comparison between Mary's cooperation with Christ at Cana and her cooperation with him at the Cross.

Jn 1:1 through 2:1—The series of six days in the gospel is meant to recall the six days of creation.

Jn 4:21—Jesus refers to other women as "woman," but they are not his mother.

Jn 12:23, 27; 17:1—Jesus refers to his "hour" as the time of the Crucifixion.

Gn 3:15—"I will put enmity between you and the woman."

Jn 20:30–31—John chose what he wrote carefully, so that we "may [come to] believe" and be saved. He did not include unnecessary details.

Sg 3:11 and Is 61:10—Hebrew bride and groom were crowned during their wedding ceremony when the Temple stood.

Rv 12:1—Mary crowned in heaven.

Ex 25:10 and Nm 14:44—Ark of the Covenant was holy and consecrated to God.

Ex 40:34, Ex 25:22, Ex 30:6, and Lv 16:2—God depicted as a cloud that overshadows the Ark.

Nm 4:15–20 and Jos chapters 3, 4, and 6—The Ark was so holy that there were strict prohibitions against touching it, and many miracles accompanied it.

Ex 16:33, Nm 17:25, and Heb 9:3–4—The Hebrews carried the Ark with them in battle and received special protection from God against their enemies.

2 Mac 2:7—Lost Ark will be found when "God gathers his people together and shows them mercy."

2 Sm 6:2–14 and Lk 1:39–56—A comparison between the Ark's trip to Judea and Mary's trip to Judea, showing that Luke presents Mary as the fulfillment of the Ark.

Rv 11:19–12:1—Mary replaces the vision of the ark in heaven.

Gn 17:17 through 18:14 and Lk 1:30–37—Mary's faith is presented as the fulfillment of Abraham's faith.

Lk 1:46–55—In the Magnificat, Mary expresses her joy at receiving the promise made to Abraham.

Lk 1:45—"Blessed are you who believed that what was spoken to you by the Lord would be fulfilled."

Lk 1:5–20—Luke contrasts Mary's faith with the doubt of Zechariah.

Jdt 16:13–17 and 1 Sm 22:1–10—Mary's Magnificat sums up the prayers made in the past.

Jn 8:41—Jesus had to endure veiled references about "illegitimacy."

Lk 2:39,41—Mary raised him and did all that was prescribed according to the law.

Lk 2:52—Jesus advanced in "wisdom and age and favor before God and man."

Jn 2:5—"Do whatever he tells you."

Lk 1:38—"May it be done to me according to your word."

Am 9:13–14 and Jl 2:23–24; 4:18—The superabundance of the wine Jesus made at Cana recalls the prophecies about the superabundance of the messianic times.

Jn 2:11 and Jn 1:14—This sign "revealed his glory," which is elsewhere in John described as "the glory as of the Father's only Son," and which caused his disciples to believe in him.

Mk 3:32—Jesus' mother and "brothers" come looking for him.

Lk 11:27; cf. Lk 1:45—Jesus makes clear it was Mary's faith rather than her body that made her holy and blessed.

Jn 16:21—Jesus expresses the suffering endured by Mary and the Church because of his crucifixion.

Lk 2:34–35—Simeon prophesies to Mary that she will be pierced as well.

Zec 12:10—"They shall look on him whom they have thrust through, and they shall mourn for him as one mourns for an only son, and they shall grieve over him as one grieves over a firstborn."

Rv 1:17—Jesus will be seen in heaven as an awesome judge, inspiring fear.

Rv 12:2—"She was with child and wailed aloud in pain as she labored to give birth." Here, Mary is depicted in her suffering at the cross.

Rv 12:17—The dragon, angry with the woman, chases after her spiritual offspring.

Lk 1:41—The Holy Spirit went forth from Mary to inspire Elizabeth and St. John the Baptist.

Acts 1—The Holy Spirit goes forth into the apostles while Mary is in the midst of them at Pentecost.

Ex 40 and Rv 12:14—Mary, as the "tent of God" (the Tabernacle) is given a safe place in "the desert," recalling the theophany on Mount Sinai.

Mt 13:55 and Mk 6:3—Brothers and sisters of Christ.

Gn 12:5 and 14:12—Shows that Lot is Abraham's brother's son.

Gn 13:8 and 14:14—Lot is called Abraham's "brother" (King James Version).

Mk 15:40 and Mt 27:56—These passages show that the "brothers" of Christ are sons of a different mother. This means that they are in fact his cousins.

Jn 19:25—Their mother is shown to be another Mary who is the cousin of the Virgin Mary. She is called a "sister" of the Virgin Mary. This means that she was her cousin.

Jn 19:26–27—Jesus gives Mary to John to be his mother, showing that Christ had no other brothers who were sons of Mary.

Mt 1:25—"He had no relations with her until she bore a son, and he named him Jesus." This does not mean that there were relations after Jesus was born. (See the following note.)

Mt 28:20—"I am with you always, *until* the end of the age" (emphasis added). This does not imply that Jesus will not be with them *after* the end of the age!

2 Sm 6:23—"Michal was childless *until* she died" (according to some Bible translations). This does not mean she had children after she died.

2 Sm 6:6–7—God strikes Uzzah dead for touching the Ark.

Lk 2:7—"She gave birth to her *firstborn* son" (emphasis added). This does not mean other children. (Consider the following cite, where the firstborn are given a special, consecrated status.)

Ex 13:2—"Consecrate to me every first-born that opens the womb among the Israelites . . . for it belongs to me." To be firstborn is an honorary title that does not imply other children.

Mt 19:12—Consecrated virginity is a sign of total dedication, purity, and devotion for the sake of the kingdom

Eph 5:27—Mary is image of the Church, having no "spot or wrinkle."

Gal 4:26, Jn 19:27, and Rv 12:2, 17—Both Mary and Church portrayed as our Mother.

Lk 1:28—"Hail Mary, Full of Grace!" is a title given to Mary by the angel (*Revised Standard Version, Catholic Edition*).

Mt 27:50–53—After Christ's death on the cross, many were raised from the dead and appeared to people.

Gn 5:24, Sir 44:16, and Wis 4:10—"Then Enoch walked with God, and he was no longer here, for God took him up." This shows that assumption is a biblical idea.

Heb 11:5–6—Paul says Enoch received this reward for pleasing God.

2 Kgs 2:10–12—Elijah goes to heaven in a flaming chariot. Again, this shows that the idea of assumption is biblical.

1 Cor 15:54–57—"Where, O death, is your victory? / Where, O death, is your sting?"

Epilogue

History serves a purpose. God did not draw the Hebrew people to himself for nothing, and he does not fill our hearts and minds with deep longing for no reason. God creates us with both a body and a soul. Both body and soul are to be sanctified. In the modern world, both are under attack. At one extreme are those (such as Hindu ascetics) for whom the material world is a worthless illusion. They present their discipline as a means of escaping from the "trap" of material existence. Subscribing to this belief enables some to deal with their suffering by treating suffering itself as an illusion. Unfortunately, to subscribe to this attitude also encourages an ultimately selfish effort to ignore the suffering and problems of other people. It also causes a general lack of concern about human society and institutions.

At the other extreme, pop culture and the media treat the material world as everything. This world is all-important and an end in itself. When a singer glorifies the fact that she is "a material girl . . . living in a material world," people are encouraged to reduce the meaning of life to a simple digging through the muck to satisfy animal appetites. The only thing that matters is having fun and feeling good. Jesus rejected both of these worldviews. In becoming man and in offering himself to us through the Eucharist, Christ elevated the material world to its proper end so that it can attain perfect union with God. Those united with God experience a new birth:

> The wind blows where it wills, and you can hear the sound it makes, but you do not know where it comes from or where it goes; so it is with everyone who is born of the Spirit (Jn 3:8).

Those born of the spirit are children of the Church (the New Jerusalem). When we participate in the life of the Church, we are training our bodies and souls to be obedient to the will of

God. When this goal has been achieved (with the help of God's grace through the sacraments), then his work in us will have been brought to completion.

This book was meant to help you understand and appreciate the role of the Church as the body of Christ and the source of salvation for the whole world. We are all invited to his holy banquet, to drink from the cup of his passion and receive the gift of eternal life. Those who accept this invitation are being formed into a "new creation" (2 Cor 5:17). For those who choose to live in Christ, "the old things have passed away" and "new things have come" (2 Cor 5:17; Rv 21:1).

APPENDIX A

The Fathers of the Church

The Fathers of the Church were bishops or other respected writers in the early Church whose writings are revered today as a witness to sacred Tradition. How does the Church decide who, among the ancients, is a "Father," and who isn't? The Nicene Creed teaches four marks by which the true Church can be known: it is one, holy, catholic, and apostolic. Deciding who is an authentic "Church Father" involves a similar test.

The writings of a Church Father must be consistent with the one Church, meaning that they must not contradict Church witness and teaching. This does not mean that no Church Father ever made a mistake. It means that the essence of his work is consistent with that of the other Church Fathers. We accept as valid what the Church Fathers say with a united voice, even if we might reject a specific statement or position held by a Church Father, whenever it contradicts what is held generally.

A Church Father is holy in the sense that his life was lived as an expression of the Gospel; he practiced what he preached, and his writings express the Gospel in an especially clear or inspiring way.

A Church Father is catholic. Catholic is the Greek word for "universal." The Fathers represent the universality of the Church in two ways. First, they represent diverse backgrounds (and time periods), and each one says things in his own way. Secondly, though they may have written in Greek, Syriac, or Latin, their message is universally applicable to all men at all times.[1]

Finally, the writings of a Church Father must be apostolic.

---

[1] Syriac is the language that Christ spoke; the older form in his day was called Aramaic.

This means that what they teach must derive from the teachings of the apostles. Some of the Church Fathers (like Clement of Rome) knew the apostles personally and so have special insight into what authentic Christianity is. They also pass along important teachings that were not written in Scripture:

> There are also many other things that Jesus did, but if these were to be described individually, I do not think the whole world would contain the books that would be written (Jn 21:25).

> Therefore, brothers, stand firm and hold fast to the traditions that you were taught, either by an oral statement or by a letter of ours (2 Thes 2:15).

Thus, it is through the Church Fathers that the apostolic Tradition has been passed on to us. The Church Fathers were familiar with the apostles themselves or they at least were close enough in time to the apostles to be handing on some of the original deposit of faith given by Christ and the Holy Spirit. It is conventional to say that the time of the "Fathers" ended in the West after the death of St. Isidore of Seville in A.D. 636 and in the East with the death of St. John Damascene in A.D. 749.

It should also be mentioned that not all the ancient writings that are revered are ascribed to a specific Father of the Church. For example, the author of the Didache remains unknown. It was said to be the teaching of the twelve apostles, hence the name (*Didache* meaning "The Teaching" in Greek).[2] The Didache is very ancient, written between A.D. 140 and 160. Parts of it may even go back to the first century. We cite it in this book because of its sound doctrine and the fact that many early Christian writers quote from it.

Although this book reprints certain quotes from Tertullian, he is not, strictly speaking, a Church Father. Because Tertullian left the Catholic Church later in his life, he is called an "Eccle-

---

[2] The *Didache* was held by some to be an inspired book and part of the canon up until the Third Council of Carthage in A.D. 397.

siastical Writer." The quotes we have included are both moving and instructive and were written when he was still a member of the Church. What follows are brief biographies of some of the Church Fathers who were quoted at the end of each chapter. Here we chose seven of the best known, but there are many more.

Selected Biographies of the Church Fathers

St. Clement of Rome, Pope (A.D. 80):

St. Clement was the bishop of Rome around A.D. 80; he was the third successor of Peter at Rome. His *Letter to the Corinthians* is the only one of his writings to survive, and the letter is often cited as a proof for papal authority. In writing this letter, Pope Clement invoked his authority to restore the offices of church leaders whom the Corinthians had deposed. This was a case where he intervened in the internal matters of a church outside his diocese even while the Apostle John was still alive. A portion of the early church even considered this letter to be Scripture for a few hundred years.[3]

St. Ignatius of Antioch (d. A.D. 110):

St. Ignatius was Bishop of Antioch, succeeding St. Evodius, who succeeded St. Peter before St. Peter went to Rome. He knew the apostle John. During the reign of the Emperor Trajan he was sentenced to die in the arena. On the way to Rome from Antioch, he was allowed to write and to send letters to the various Christian churches. Seven of these have survived; it is from

---

[3] It took six centuries before the whole Church throughout the world used the same list of New Testament writings. Although the four Gospels were never a point of contention, churches in various parts of the world had disputes over whether a handful of letters were inspired or not (including the book of Revelation). By the seventh century disputes were settled and everyone used the same list we have today. But it was not until the Council of Trent in the sixteenth century that the canon of Scripture was formally codified.

them that the quotes used in this book are drawn. This bishop of Antioch looked forward to his martyrdom, anticipating that he would become as "wheat ground by the teeth of lions." His letters also make the first known use of the word "catholic" to describe the one true apostolic church. It is an interesting historical note that the Church of Antioch is the place that the word "Christian" was first used to describe the followers of Christ (cf. Acts 11:26). It was also in Antioch that the word "Trinity" first appears in writing, coined by St. Theophilus of Antioch in A.D. 181.

St. Justin the Martyr (A.D. 110–165):

St. Justin Martyr was born a pagan in Palestine. As a young man, he tried many different philosophical schools of thought, including Stoicism, Pythagorism, Platonism, etc. After much experimentation, he became a Christian. He went to Rome and established a school for teaching Christianity. He, along with six of his companions, was beheaded in A.D. 165

St. Irenaeus (A.D. 140–202):

He was the second bishop of Lyons. In his youth, he was a follower of St. Polycarp, who was in turn a disciple of St. John the Apostle. Known as the Peacemaker, he advised Pope Victor of Rome against excommunicating Eastern clergy for failing to accept the Western formula for the calculation of the date of Easter. He is most famous for his treatise, *Against all Heresies*, wherein he refutes the Gnostic sects.

St. Ephrem (A.D. 306–373):

He was called the "Lyre of the Holy Spirit" because of his talent for expressing the faith and liturgy in poetic song. He popularized this genre, and won over many converts from sects who had been using popular music to lure people away from their faith. He was the first to employ popular melodies for religious hymns and the first to compose an all-women's choir. His voluminous compositions represent not only the best of religious poetry but also the best of Syriac theology. His work continues to be studied for its Semitic character and biblical orientation.

St. John Chrysostom (A.D. 344–407):

He was a contemporary of St. Augustine. Just as Augustine was considered the best preacher in the West, Chrysostom (meaning "gold-mouth") was the best in the East. Like Augustine, he was a prolific writer, and many of his works are preserved today. As an outspoken critic of the decadence of the Byzantine Imperial court, Chrysostom was sent into exile many times. At last, he was banished to Pityus, on the eastern shore of the Black Sea, and he died en route.

St. Augustine of Hippo (A.D. 354–430):

Like St. Justin Martyr, he experimented freely with different schools of philosophical thought before becoming Christian. Many believe that the prayers of his long-suffering mother (St. Monica) brought about the grace of Augustine's conversion. (She happily witnessed his baptism before she died.) He became a bishop in North Africa during a very tumultuous time, when barbarian hordes were invading many parts of the Roman Empire. He is considered the best writer and the best theologian among the Western Fathers, as well as the most prolific. His most famous works are the *City of God* and the *Confessions*.

APPENDIX B

Versions of the Bible That Were Used/Bible Versions

For most Scripture quotes in this book, we have used the *New American Bible with Revised New Testament (NAB)*, because it is widely known, very readable and precise, and contains excellent historical and linguistic notes. When quoting from the Psalms, however, we made use of the original New American Version from 1970. We consider this original to be far superior to the revised version which makes heavy use of "inclusive language" even when referring to God. Consider, for example, the changes made to Psalm 23:

1970 Version	**Revised Version**
The LORD is my shepherd, I shall not want. / In verdant pastures he gives me repose; / . . . he leads me; / he refreshes my soul. / He guides me . . . / for his name's sake.	The LORD is my shepherd; / there is nothing I lack. / In green pastures you let me graze; / . . . you lead me; / you restore. . . . / You guide me . . . / for the sake of your name.

Now, decent people with the best of intentions can debate whether or not God should be presented as having a gender, and whether it is male, female, neuter, or other. But the fact of the matter is that such questions are not for the translator to answer. A Hebrew or Greek text that says "He guides me" does not say "You guide me," and no amount of wishful thinking can make it so. We feel that readers in general, and our readers in particular are entitled to a faithful translation of these biblical passages. For this reason, we have decided to use the original 1970 version of the *New American Bible* whenever quoting from the Psalms.

The *New American* version also has some obscurity regarding certain important connections between the Old Testament and the New. Christians have always believed that the New Testament is the fulfillment of the Old. Jesus quoted the Old Testament frequently, and the Gospel writers often point out connections between the life and ministry of Jesus and relevant passages in the Old Testament. For example, when Jesus says, "Before Abraham came to be, I AM," the reader is supposed to recall that Moses was told that God's name is "I AM" (Jn 8:58; Ex 3:14).

Keep this example and suppose for a moment that a modern translator decides that he does not like the implication that Jesus is claiming to be God. He might translate according to his own fancy and quote Jesus as saying: "I was there before Abraham existed." A person reading such a translation would miss an important connection to the Old Testament and might even believe that Jesus was an angel or some sort of reincarnated being. Jesus' definite statement that he was the God of the burning bush would be conveniently gone.

Our point is this: the New Testament writers expected readers to recognize when the New Testament was referring to the Old. To accomplish this, they often presented a word or phrase in the New Testament that *exactly* matched the relevant Old Testament word or phrase in context. Where it is obvious that the New Testament writers intended to create such a parallel, the modern translator should be obligated to preserve the original parallel as much as possible.

Some might object that such "perfect matches" cannot possibly exist since the Old and New Testaments were not even written in the same language. While it is true that the Old Testament was originally written in Hebrew, the writers of the New Testament were not relying on the Hebrew version when they quoted from the Old Testament. Instead, they were quoting from the

Greek version of the Old Testament called the Septuagint. As mentioned previously in the chapter on purgatory, the Septuagint was translated into Greek before the time of Christ in the city of Alexandria. At that time, the Greek language was spoken throughout the entire eastern Mediterranean. Jewish scholars produced this Greek version of the Old Testament because they wanted to make the Scriptures available to all Jews throughout the Diaspora, many of whom were no longer familiar with the ancient Hebrew.

It is obvious that the writers of the New Testament were relying on this Greek version of the Old Testament because so many of their Old Testament quotes consistently match up with the Greek of the Septuagint. For example, the previous chapter on Mary already discussed how St. Luke understood Jesus' mother to be the fulfillment of the Ark. This is why so many of his references to Mary draw upon Old Testament descriptions of the Ark. The most striking "match-up" occurs when the angel assures Mary that, "The power of the Most High will overshadow you" (Lk 1:35). St. Luke intentionally chose to use the word "overshadow" in order to match exactly with the Old Testament where God "overshadows" the Ark of the Covenant (Ex 40:35).[1]

St. Luke chose his words carefully and deliberately, so we find it extremely disappointing that not one modern English translation preserves this parallel. None of them preserve the Septuagint use of the verb "overshadow" when describing God's presence over the Ark. The *New American Bible* undoes the parallel and translates the Old Testament by saying, "the cloud settled down upon" the Ark (Ex 40:35).

The Septuagint has even more to recommend it. Besides the question of parallel passages, there is the question of the canon (the official list of the books in the Bible). The Septuagint con-

---

[1] "Overshadow" (επισκιαζω), *Theological Dictionary of the New Testament*, vol. 7, ed. Gerhard Kittel and Gerhard Friedrich, trans. Geoffrey Bromiley (Grand Rapids, Mich.: Eerdmans, 1988) 399.

tains all the Old Testament books found in Catholic Bibles but not in Protestant or Jewish ones. After the time of Christ, the Jewish council at Jamnia in about A.D. 90 removed these books from the Judaic canon. We feel that there were two motives for doing so. First, there was the question of Christianity. Some of these seven books contain very explicit prophecies regarding the Messiah that point to Christ. Here is one example referred to in Matthew:

He calls blest the destiny of the just
and boasts that God is his Father.

For if the just one be the son of God, he will defend him and deliver him. . . .

Let us condemn him to a shameful death;
for according to his own words, God will take care of him (Wis 2:16–20).

The chief priests with the scribes and elders mocked him and said, "He saved others; he cannot save himself. . . . Let him come down from the cross now, and we will believe in him. He trusted in God; let him deliver him now if he wants him. For he said, 'I am the Son of God'" (Mt 27:41–43).

The second reason that the council of Jamnia rejected these books is that one of them contained elaborate praise for the Romans, who had just destroyed Jerusalem and the Temple:

Judas had heard of the reputation of the Romans. They were valiant fighters and acted amicably to all who took their side. They established a friendly alliance with all who applied to them . . . none of them put on a crown. . . . They had made for themselves a senate house . . . deliberating on all that concerned the people and their well being . . . and there was no envy or jealousy among them (1 Mc 8:1, 14–16).

The Jewish council justified its removal of these books by stating that there were no extant versions of these books in Hebrew.

Martin Luther and the Protestant Reformers justified their removal of these books from the Protestant canon by following the decision made at Jamnia.[2] In the sixteenth century, Luther advocated removing these books because one of them contained a passage explicitly contradicting his position against praying for the dead:

> He then took up a collection . . . which he sent to Jerusalem to provide for an expiatory sacrifice . . . he acted in a very excellent and noble way. . . . Thus he made atonement for the dead that they might be freed from this sin (2 Mc 12:43–46).

It is a fact that the New Testament writers used the Septuagint to draw clear parallels between the Old and New Testaments. It is also a fact that the Septuagint sets forth a canonical list *before* Jewish-Christian or Catholic-Protestant disputes could possibly have prejudiced scholars' judgment. It is also a fact that the early Christians (including the apostles) and all of the Church Fathers considered the Septuagint to be a faithful translation of Scripture. For all of these reasons, we have on occasion in this book used versions of the Bible other than the *New American* where we felt that, in context, they better represented the parallels between the Greek New Testament and the Septuagint (Greek Old Testament).

Bible Versions

Why are there so many Bible versions? Which one do I use?

Words in any language have many nuances depending on how they are used in the culture. For example, the word "country" in English can be used to refer to a political geographic area or to "open country" or even "country music." It is a challenge to capture nuances that one word has in one language that it may not in another. In some cases, there are no matching words at all. The translator has to also consider how the meaning of words can change, how there is different syntax, and a host of

---

[2] The original King James Bible contained the seven so-called "apocryphal" books.

other factors that make translation a very challenging profession. There is no "best" translation. Where in one area one version may be strong, the other may be weak, and vice versa. For intensive study purposes, it is best to compare many versions at a time. But for general reading and spiritual reflection, it is best to choose one.

Below we describe a few from among the many English version that exist today.

Catholic Bibles

New American Bible (1970; NT revised 1986; Psalms revised 1992):

This is the first complete American Catholic Bible translated from the original languages. Its style is more direct than that of the Jerusalem Bible.

New Jerusalem Bible (1985):

An update of the Jerusalem Bible, with revised footnotes and less colloquial language. Its expressions are at times a bit extravagant in order to bring out nuances that may be relevant.

Jerusalem Bible (1966):

Inspired by the French *La Bible de Jerusalem*, it is intended as a study Bible in modern English in contrast to the English of the older Douay-Rheims.

Douay-Rheims

In 1752, Bishop Richard Challoner revised the older Rheims edition that went back to 1582. These translations into English are from the Latin Vulgate (translated by St. Jerome from the original languages). To the modern reader, the English seems similar to the King James.

Protestant Bibles [3]

New Revised Standard Version (1990):

The updated Revised Standard Version incorporates changes resulting from archaeological and textual discoveries made in recent decades. There is also a Catholic version.

New King James Version (1982):

This Bible is intended to update the language of the King James Version, while preserving its exalted tone.

New International Version (NT, 1973; OT, 1978):

An international group of scholars from several different denominations cooperated to publish this version in modern English.

King James (1611):

Commissioned by King James, it uses an exalted and inspiring Shakespearean English. It has many minor errors but it is useful for its literal sense.

---

[3] Protestant bibles are either missing seven books from the Old Testament, or else they are mistakenly relegated to status as "Apocrypha."

APPENDIX C

The Tale of Years: B.C.

2000	Pre-History: Adam, Tower of Babel, The Flood, Noah
1900	The Time of the Patriarchs: Abraham, Isaac, and Jacob
1800	
1700	
1600	
1500	
1400	
1300	
1200	The Exodus: Moses leads the Hebrews out of Egypt
1100	Judges
1000	Establishing the Kingdom: Saul, David, Solomon Temple completed
900	Kingdom Split in Two
800	Israel in the North; Judah in the South
700	Defeat and Captivity
600	Fall of the northern kingdom to Assyria "Lost Tribes of Israel" Fall of the southern kingdom to Babylon; first Temple destroyed
500	"The Babylonian Captivity"
400	The Return from captivity
300	Under the Greeks: Alexander the Great
200	Maccabean Revolt
100	Under the Roman Empire: Pompey conquers Palestine
0	Birth of Christ*

---

* (Actual year is estimated to be around 4 B.C.)

A.D.

0   Ca. A.D. 30 Crucifixion, Resurrection of Christ; Romans destroy
  Temple, A.D. 70; A.D. 90 Jewish council defines Jewish canon;
  Letter of Clement, Ignatius of Antioch uses word "catholic"

100   132–135 Final Jewish revolt fails; Judea is renamed "Palestine"

200

  313 Edict of Milan: Constantine establishes tolerance of Christianity;

300   325 First Great Ecumenical Council—The Council of Nicea;
  380 Christianity declared official state religion

400   410 Rome is sacked. The Western Roman Empire declines; 431 Council
  of Ephesus affirms that Mary may be called the Mother of God;

500   451 Council of Chalcedon: Declares that Christ has two natures

600   637 Muslims capture Jerusalem

700

800

900

  1054 Official split formalized between the Eastern (Orthodox) and

1000   Western Church;
  1095–1291 the time of the Crusades

1100

1200   1225–1274 St. Thomas Aquinas

1300

1400   1453 Constantinople falls to the Turks; the Eastern Roman Empire ends.
  1492 Columbus discovers the new land

1500   1517 Martin Luther begins Protestant Reformation; 1531 Apparition of
  the Virgin Mary at Guadalupe, Mexico; 1534 Henry VIII establishes

1600   Anglican Church; 1545–1563 Council of Trent responds to Protestants
  1609 Baptist Church founded by John Smyth

1700

1800   1827 Joseph Smith founds Mormon church. 1870 Russell founds Jehovah's
  Witnesses 1869–1870 First Vatican Council declares doctrine of papal in-

1900   fallibility
  1917 Apparition of Mary at Fatima; 1962–1965 Second Vatican Council—

2000   permits the use of vernacular, institutes various reforms

APPENDIX D

Old Testament Types and Prophecies Fulfilled

Prophecies about Jesus Christ

OLD TESTAMENT

NEW TESTAMENT

The Word as God

Ps 119—Each verse of this Psalm praises God's Law, using many different words to describe it

Is 55:11—So shall my word be / that goes forth from my mouth; / It shall not return to me void, / but shall do my will, / achieving the end for which I sent it.

Jn 1:1–3, 14—In the beginning was the Word, / and the Word was with God, / and the Word was God. / He was in the beginning with God. / All things came to be through him, / and without him nothing came to be. / . . . And the Word became flesh / and made his dwelling among us. . . .

Messiah born in Bethlehem to a Virgin

Mi 5:1—But you, Bethlehem-Ephrathah, / too small to be among the clans of Judah, / From you shall come forth for me / one who is to be ruler in Israel; / Whose origin is from of old, / from ancient times.

Mt 2:1–5—Jesus was born in Bethlehem of Judea, in the days of King Herod . . . he inquired of them where the Messiah was to be born. They said to him, "In Bethlehem of Judea, for thus it has been written through the prophet. . . ."

OLD TESTAMENT	NEW TESTAMENT
Is 7:14—Therefore the Lord himself will give you a sign: the virgin shall be with child, and bear a son, and shall name him Immanuel.	Lk 1:31–36—"Behold, you will conceive in your womb and bear a son, and you shall name him Jesus." . . . But Mary said to the angel, "How can this be, since I have no relations with a man?" And the angel said to her in reply, "The holy Spirit will come upon you, and the power of the Most High will over-shadow you. Therefore the child to be born will be called holy, the Son of God."

Herod sought to kill the Messiah

Jer 31:15—Thus says the LORD: / In Ramah is heard the sound of moaning, / of bitter weeping! / Rachel mourns her children, / she refuses to be consoled / because her children are no more.	Mt 2:16–17—Herod . . . ordered the massacre of all the boys in Bethlehem and its vicinity two years old and under. . . . Then was fulfilled what had been said through Jeremiah the prophet. . . .

Return from Egypt

Hos 11:1—When Israel was a child I loved him, / out of Egypt I called my son.	Mt 2:14–15—Joseph rose and took the child and his mother by night and departed for Egypt. He stayed there until the death of Herod, that what the Lord had said through the prophet might be fulfilled, "Out of Egypt I called my son."

OLD TESTAMENT   NEW TESTAMENT

John the Baptist, in the spirit of Elijah,
would prepare for the arrival of the Messiah

Is 40:3–4—A voice cries out: /
In the desert prepare the way
of the LORD! / Make straight
in the wasteland a highway for
our God! / Every valley shall
be filled in, / every mountain
and hill shall be made low. . . .

Mt 3:1–3—John the Baptist
appeared, preaching in the
desert . . . saying, . . . "Prepare the way of the Lord, /
make straight his paths."

Mal 3:1, 23—Lo, I am sending
my messenger, / to prepare the
way before me . . . / Lo, I will
send you / Elijah, the prophet,
/ Before the day of the LORD
comes. . . .

Mt 11:13–15—"All the
prophets and the law prophesied up to the time of John.
And if you are willing to
accept it, he is Elijah, the one
who is to come. Whoever has
ears ought to hear."

Messiah, riding on an ass, enters into
Jerusalem in triumph, amid rejoicing

Zec 9:9—Shout for joy, O
daughter Jerusalem! / See, your
king shall come to you; / a just
savior is he, / Meek, and riding
on an ass, / on a colt, the foal
of an ass.

Mt 21:7–9—They brought
the ass and the colt and laid
their cloaks over them, and
he sat upon them. . . . The
crowds preceding him and
those following kept crying
out and saying: / "Hosanna to
the Son of David; / blessed is
he who comes in the name of
the Lord; / hosanna in the
highest."

OLD TESTAMENT **NEW TESTAMENT**

Silence of the Messiah before his accusers

Is 53:7—Though he was harshly treated, he submitted / and opened not his mouth; / Like a lamb led to the slaughter / or a sheep before the shearers, / he was silent and opened not his mouth.

Mt 27:12–14—When he was accused by the chief priests and elders, he made no answer. Then Pilate said to him, "Do you not hear how many things they are testifying against you?" But he did not answer him one word, so that the governor was greatly amazed.

Messiah beaten, spat upon, mocked

Is 50:6—I gave my back to those who beat me, / my cheeks to those who plucked my beard; / My face I did not shield / from buffets and spitting.

Mt 26:67—Then they spat in his face and struck him, while some slapped him, saying, "Prophesy for us, Messiah: who is it that struck you?"

Wis 2:12–18—Let us beset the just one, because he is obnoxious to us; / he . . . styles himself a child of the LORD. / . . . / He judges us debased; / he holds aloof from our paths as from things impure. / He . . . boasts that God is his Father. / . . . / let us find out what will happen to him. / For if the just one be the son of God, he will defend him / and deliver him from the hand of his foes.

Mt 27:41–43—Likewise the chief priests with the scribes and elders mocked him and said, "He saved others; he cannot save himself. . . . He trusted in God; let him deliver him now if he wants him. For he said, 'I am the Son of God.'"

OLD TESTAMENT

NEW TESTAMENT

*Messiah to be crucified with
the wicked and pray for his enemies*

Ps 22:15–19—I am like water poured out; / all my bones are racked. / . . . / Indeed, many dogs surround me, / a pack of evildoers closes in upon me; / They have pierced my hands and my feet; / I can count all my bones. / . . . / they divide my garments among them, / and for my vesture they cast lots.

Mt 27:31, 34–35—And when they had mocked him, they stripped him of the cloak, dressed him in his own clothes, and led him off to crucify him. . . . they gave Jesus wine to drink mixed with gall. But when he had tasted it, he refused to drink. . . . After they had crucified him, they divided his garments by casting lots. . . .

Ps 69:21–22—I looked for sympathy, but there was none; / for comforters, and I found none. / Rather they put gall in my food, / and in my thirst they gave me vinegar to drink

Lk 23:32–34—Now two others, both criminals, were led away with him to be executed. . . . they crucified him and the criminals there. . . . [Then Jesus said, "Father, forgive them, they know not what they do."]

Is 53:12—He surrendered himself to death / and was counted among the wicked; / And he shall take away the sins of many, / and win pardon for their offenses.

OLD TESTAMENT	NEW TESTAMENT

Messiah, as the Passover Lamb of God,
would not have legs broken

Nm 9:12—. . . and not leaving any of it over till morning, nor breaking any of its bones, but observing all the rules of the Passover.	Jn 19:32–33—So the soldiers came and broke the legs of the first and then of the other one. . . . But when they came to Jesus and saw that he was already dead, they did not break his legs.

Messiah to die as a sacrifice for sin

Is 53:5–11—But he was pierced for our offenses, / crushed for our sins, / Upon him was the chastisement that makes us whole, / by his stripes we were healed. / We had all gone astray like sheep, / each following his own way; / But the LORD laid upon him / the guilt of us all. / . . . / If he gives his life as an offering for sin, / he shall see his descendants in a long life, / and the will of the LORD shall be accomplished through him. / Because of his affliction / he shall see the light in fullness of days; / Through his suffering, my servant shall justify many, / and their guilt he shall bear.	Jn 1:29—The next day he saw Jesus coming toward him and said, "Behold, the Lamb of God, who takes away the sin of the world." Jn 11:49–52—But one of them, Caiaphas, who was high priest that year, said to them, "You know nothing, nor do you consider that it is better for you that one man should die instead of the people, so that the whole nation may not perish." He did not say this on his own, but since he was high priest for that year, he prophesied that Jesus was going to die for the nation, and not only for the nation, but also to gather into one the dispersed children of God."

OLD TESTAMENT	NEW TESTAMENT

*Messiah to be raised from the dead
and sit at God's right hand*

Ps 16:10—Because you will not abandon my soul to the nether world, / nor will you suffer your faithful one to undergo corruption.	Mt 28:5–6—"I know that you are seeking Jesus the crucified. He is not here, for he has been raised just as he said. Come and see the place where he lay."
Ps 110:1—The LORD said to my Lord: "Sit at my right hand / till I make your enemies your footstool."	Mk 16:19—So then the Lord Jesus, after he spoke to them, was taken up into heaven and took his seat at the right hand of God.

Prophecies about the Holy Spirit Forming the Church

OLD TESTAMENT	NEW TESTAMENT

Spirit anoints a New Creation in Christ

Gn 1:1–2—In the beginning, when God created the heavens and the earth, the earth was a formless wasteland, and darkness covered the abyss, while a mighty wind swept over the waters.

Then God said, "Let there be light," and there was light. God saw how good the light was.

Lk 3:21–22—After all the people had been baptized and Jesus also had been baptized and was praying, heaven was opened and the holy Spirit descended upon him in bodily form like a dove. And a voice came from heaven, "You are my beloved Son; with you I am well pleased."

Jesus gives the Spirit of life to his apostles

Gn 2:7—The LORD God formed man out of the clay of the ground and blew into his nostrils the breath of life, and so man became a living being.

Jn 20:22—And when he had said this, he breathed on them and said to them, "Receive the holy Spirit."

Jesus' disciples share in this spirit and power

Nm 11:16–17—Then the LORD said to Moses, "Assemble for me seventy of the elders of Israel, men you know for true elders and authorities among the people, and bring them to the meeting tent. When they are in place beside you, I will come down and speak with you there. I will also take some of the spirit that is on you and will bestow it on them,

Lk 10:1, 17–19—After this the Lord appointed seventy [-two] others whom he sent ahead of him in pairs to every town and place he intended to visit. . . .

The seventy [-two] returned rejoicing, and said, "Lord, even the demons are subject to us because of your name." Jesus said, "I have observed Satan fall like lightning from the sky. Behold, I have given

OLD TESTAMENT	NEW TESTAMENT

that they may share the burden of the people with you. You will then not have to bear it by yourself.

you the power 'to tread on serpents' . . . and upon the full force of the enemy and nothing will harm you."

The Spirit will guide the Church

Wis 9:17—Or who ever knew your counsel, except you had given Wisdom / and sent your holy spirit from on high?

Jn 14:26—The Advocate, the holy Spirit that the Father will send in my name—he will teach you everything and remind you of all that [I] told you.

Neh 9:20—Your good spirit you bestowed on them, to give them understanding. . . .

Jn 16:13—But when he comes, the Spirit of truth, he will guide you to all truth.

Is 59:21—This is the covenant with them / which I myself have made, says the Lord: / My spirit which is upon you / and my words that I have put into your mouth / Shall never leave your mouth, / nor the mouths of your children / Nor the mouths of your children's children / from now on and forever, says the Lord.

Jn 14:16–17—I will ask the Father, and he will give you another Advocate to be with you always, the Spirit of truth. . . .

The Spirit gives us new life

Ps 104:30—When you send forth your spirit, they are created, / and you renew the face of the earth.

Jn 3:5—Amen, amen, I say to you, no one can enter the kingdom of God without being born of water and Spirit.

OLD TESTAMENT	NEW TESTAMENT

Jdt 16:14—Let your every creature serve you; / for you spoke, and they were made, / You sent forth your spirit, and they were created; / no one can resist your word.

Acts 8:17—Then they laid hands on them and they received the holy Spirit.

Is 32:14–15—Yes, the castle will be forsaken, / the noisy city deserted; / . . . / Until the spirit from on high / is poured out on us.

Rom 8:11—If the Spirit of the one who raised Jesus from the dead dwells in you, the one who raised Christ from the dead will give life to your mortal bodies also, through his Spirit that dwells in you.

Eph 2:22—In him you also are being built together into a dwelling place of God in the Spirit.

Spirit forms and gives life to the Church

Is 4:4–6—When the Lord washes away / . . . / And purges Jerusalem's blood from her midst / with a blast of searing judgment, / Then will the LORD create, / over the whole site of Mount Zion / and over her place of assembly, / A smoking cloud by day / and a light of flaming fire by night.

Acts 1:8–9—"But you will receive power when the holy Spirit comes upon you, and you will be my witnesses in Jerusalem, throughout Judea and Samaria, and to the ends of the earth." When he had said this, as they were looking on, he was lifted up, and a cloud took him from their sight.

Is 42:1—Here is my servant whom I uphold, / my chosen one with whom I am pleased, / Upon whom I have put my spirit; / he shall bring forth justice to the nations.

Acts 2:2–4—And suddenly there came from the sky a noise like a strong driving wind, and it filled the entire house in which they were. Then there appeared to them

OLD TESTAMENT	NEW TESTAMENT

Jl 3:1–2—Then afterward I will pour out / my spirit upon all mankind. / Your sons and daughters shall prophesy, / your old men shall dream dreams, / your young men shall see visions; / Even upon the servants and the handmaids, / in those days, I will pour out my spirit.

tongues as of fire, which parted and came to rest on each one of them. And they were all filled with the holy Spirit and began to speak in different tongues. . . . Now there were devout Jews from every nation under heaven staying in Jerusalem. At this sound, they gathered in a large crowd. . . .

Spirit will guide us to a mature love

Wis 8:19—I was a well-favored child, / and I came by a noble nature. . . .

1 Cor 13:11—When I was a child, I used to talk as a child, think as a child, reason as a child; when I became a man, I put aside childish things.

Wis 7:22–30 and 8:1[1]—Wisdom . . . / . . . / [is] not baneful, loving the good, keen, / unhampered, beneficent, kindly, / Firm, secure, tranquil, / all-powerful, all-seeing, / And pervading all spirits . . . / . . . / For she is the refulgence of eternal light, / the spotless mirror of the power of God, / the image of his goodness. / And she, who is one, can do all things, / and renews everything while herself perduring; / . . . / Indeed, she reaches from end

1 Cor 13:4–13—Love is patient, love is kind. It is not jealous, [love] is not pompous, it is not inflated, it is not rude, it does not seek its own interests, it is not quick-tempered, it does not brood over injury, it does not rejoice over wrong-doing but rejoices with the truth. It bears all things, believes all things, hopes all things, endures all things. . . . At present we see indistinctly, as in a mirror, but then face to face. . . . So faith, hope, love

---

[1] Brackets in Wis 7:22ff. are ours.

OLD TESTAMENT

to end mightily / and
governs all things well.

Ez 36:26–27—I will give you
a new heart and place a new
spirit within you, taking from
your bodies your stony hearts
and giving you natural hearts.

NEW TESTAMENT

remain, these three; but the
greatest of these is love.

2 Cor 3:2–3—You are . . . a
letter of Christ administered
by us, written not in ink but
by the Spirit of the living God,
not on tablets of stone but on
tablets that are hearts of flesh.

APPENDIX E

Genesis and Evolution

This essay is not about whether or not the book of Genesis should be interpreted literally. It is about the original meaning of the book when it was first written. Until recent archeological discoveries were made, the history and writings of this period were not clearly understood. Today we are privileged enough to know what the experience of reading the book of Genesis must have been like in ancient times.

For many people, the story of creation is confusing. We believe in the Bible as the word of God, but we cannot help but respect the power and truth of modern science, and modern scientific discoveries seem to contradict the biblical story of creation. People wrestle with these seeming contradictions and arrive at all sorts of conclusions. Some say that Genesis is purely myth. Others reject scientific conclusions and insist that Genesis is a literal description of events. In other words, if there had been a video recording of creation, we would see exactly what Genesis describes. Fortunately, the either-or approach and everything else in-between is the wrong place to begin. Why? Because it forces an interpretation of Genesis based on modern concerns rather than the ancient ones for which it was written. Knowing these ancient concerns will awaken our minds to the urgent truths of the book of Genesis that must still be proclaimed even more insistently in today's world.

John Paul's 1996 message to the Pontifical Academy of Science on evolution explains those things that must be accepted and/or rejected by Catholics in regards to evolution. In this message, the Holy Father referenced Pope Pius XII's *Humani generis*.

To understand the meaning of Genesis and uncover its treasures, we must go back to the time in which it was written, look
at how the people of that period lived, and consider the religions that they practiced.[1] Imagine a world where God was not
known, spoken of, or even heard of—a world where children and
elders spoke of "the gods" in fear. It was a time of mythology.
Pagan temples were places of "sacred prostitution," the profession of pagan priestesses. Human sacrifice was common. Little
children were burned alive to appease the gods. People lived in
dread fear of the gods of their imagination. Things that even
non-religious people today would consider disgusting or even
demonic were considered "sacred" in the Near East cultures
of that period. Mythologies developed and came to be written
that perpetuated and gave reason for these practices hundreds
of years before Genesis was composed. We know about these
pagan writings from recent archeological discoveries.

One of the mythologies, for example, spoke of how a god
made the first man by accident during a competition with other
gods while drunk with beer at a party.[2] When the gods realized
how fast these human beings multiplied, they sent plagues, pesti-
lence, floods, earthquakes, etc. to lighten the earth of its load.
Human beings were a mistake; they were forced to serve, reliev-
ing some of the gods' workload. Human beings should practice
contraception and abortion so they do not multiply. Yes, those
things existed even back then! Surprisingly, overpopulation in
ancient times was also a big worry in pagan societies.

The main point of these stories was that creation and human
life were meaningless and worthless. The gods, on the other
hand, were great, important, and powerful. Human beings were

---

[1] For a good summary of how the book of Genesis was written in con-
tradiction to the ancient myths refer to Isaac Kikawada and Arthur Quinn,
Before Abraham Was: The Unity of Genesis 1–11 (Nashville, Tenn.: Abingdon
Press, 1985).

[2] Kikawada and Quinn, 39–45.

kept in degraded slavery before them, serving no purpose but to appease them by any means possible.

Genesis changed all of this. It was a searing light shining in the darkness; it was a completely new world-view. Its ideas were a stark contradiction to the pagan world-view of human sacrifice, abortion, contraception, "sacred" prostitution, low self-esteem, concern for overpopulation, and fear of the gods who controlled destiny and fortune.[3]

A reader from 3,200 years ago would not have to be told that the book of Genesis was written in response to the many creation myths that were all around. He would have known exactly what Genesis was meant to do. It was a revolutionary attack on paganism. Genesis carried on this attack by using much of the same imagery, phraseology, and style as the pagan writings, not to copy them, but to stand in diametrical opposition to the pagan myths.

Consider the dramatic contrast that the book of Genesis offered for the first time in history. The mythologies spoke of many gods, Genesis of one God. This One God created everything out of *nothing*! The pagan gods had always used preexistent material. The myths said that the physical world was evil. In Genesis, God declared that "It was good!" In contrast to the pagan gods, God appears respectable, wise, caring, all-powerful yet not distant. God made man and woman in his image. Their creation was meaningful and was not an accident. He had a plan for them and they were to have a relationship with him and with each other. There was a direction, a design, and a purpose to history and creation. God wanted Adam and Eve to "fill the earth and subdue it!"

Genesis changed the way human beings relate to God and to each other. It did this not by giving us a textbook on biology or

---

[3] For example, one statue of the Baal (god) Moloch was made with an open mouth and large teeth. Fire was lit within. Children were thrown in alive as a sacrifice (Jer 19:5).

geology. Instead, Genesis was to serve as our introduction to the God of Abraham, Isaac, and Jacob. If its goal is to introduce us to God, what does it have to do with evolution, and what does the modern science of evolution have to say about Genesis?

Evolution says that all species develop from previous species.[4] This includes human beings. According to evolution, our physical bodies derived from some ape-like ancestor. Evolution does not explain why the universe started or why the physical laws could lead to the development of life to begin with. Because of this, evolution does not contradict the idea, taught by Genesis, that God is the Creator and author of everything.

Evolution does contradict a strictly literal interpretation of Genesis, however. The literal genealogies of Genesis make the world out to be approximately six thousand years old, while evolution posits that the universe is approximately 15–20 billion years old. Because of apparent contradictions like this, if one believes in a strictly literal interpretation of Genesis, one must reject evolution entirely.

Remembering the essence of what Genesis taught the human race to begin with allows us to avoid this either/or trap. Genesis was not revealed by God to give us science lessons; he left science for us to explore on our own. If we accept both the substance of the Genesis account and the possibility that God created Adam and Eve's physical bodies through the process we call evolution, we are led to the following truths:

---

[4] St. Augustine in the fifth century spoke of the possibility of the physical body developing over the course of a long period of time. But long before Augustine, even before Christ, Greek philosophers spoke of a type of evolution because they were trying to explain why seashells were found on mountains. They observed that the difference in their shape is accentuated as the elevation increased. They concluded that over a long period of time a species changes, but always remains the same species. Until Darwin, the notion that one species becomes another over time was foreign.

- There is one God.

- God created everything, including humanity.

- When God created Adam, he formed him from the earth and breathed into his nostrils the breath of life. Each human spirit is thereafter created by a direct act of God.

- Creation is good, real, has a purpose, an order, and is directed towards God.

- Human life is sacred and must be respected because we are in God's image. There is a purpose to our existence. Therefore we must reverence life in all its stages. We must not sacrifice children, born or unborn.

- The use of contraception is pagan and implies lack of faith in the goodness of life and a purpose to human generation.

- Each human being is given the "breath of life." This means that each human being has a spirit and free will, we are not doomed. We are called to return God's love freely.

- Since human beings have unique souls that God creates we cannot say that the first man had an animal for his father even if that animal was the biological contributor. (One cannot be called a "son" unless he is of the same nature as his father.)

- We all have common parents in the two people the Bible calls Adam and Eve.

- Through Adam and Eve, sin entered our human nature, leaving us in need of redemption.

- Human beings are to tend and nurture creation and one another.

- We are to celebrate the day of rest as a way of renewing the covenant with God and as an expression of the peaceful harmony God wants to have with us and with his creation.

These basic truths are some of the substance of what Genesis teaches us. They are desperately needed in our day. The science of evolution does not contradict these religious truths. There are people who use science to contradict God just as there are people who use God to contradict science. But knowledge cannot betray its originator and neither can God deny his image.

To reduce the book of Genesis to a simplistic scientific-type history of how the world came about impoverishes and destroys a monumental masterpiece. This book has had such an enormous effect upon the very way we think and view reality that we now take some of its most basic teachings for granted and do not easily recognize its substance. But we must not lose sight of these basic truths. They are the building blocks of justice and humanity. We should always keep in mind that there was a time when people were in utter darkness. Genesis helped to change that. What a difference it has made in the world! We need it now more than ever as we are constantly threatened by a new paganism. It is a profound work; read it anew.

APPENDIX F

Science and Faith

The Greeks are generally credited with being the first to begin a systematic study of the physical world. Modern science was created when the Catholic faith was applied to this study. To those nowadays outside the faith, this may seem like a false and arrogant statement. We shall prove this a true statement by following the history of science from its birth among the Greek philosophers, through its adaptation by Christianity, to its modern expression in the "scientific method." We will thereby show that science itself expresses the truths of the Catholic faith.

In the ancient days, there were three religious world-views. There was the world of astrology and magic (the myth-based religions), the world of illusion (the Hindu-Buddhist religions), and the real created world of the Jewish religion. Greek philosophy (in contrast to Greek mythology) was a fourth world-view, but it was not a religion.

The golden age of Greek philosophy took place 100–500 years before Christ. This was the world of Parmenides, Socrates, Plato, Aristotle, and many others, who were developing theories to explain the material world. One theory described the world as a mixture of earth, air, fire, and water. Another theory proposed that matter consisted of basic units called "atoms" that were

---

To read more about this subject we highly recommend any work by Fr. Stanley Jaki, winner of the Templeton Prize, historian and philosopher of physics. Brief essays summarizing his thought can be found in Stanley Jaki, *Catholic Essays* (Front Royal, Va.: Christendom Press, 1990).

indivisible.[1] Amazing discoveries were also made regarding the spherical nature of the earth, its approximate size, and the possibility of a species evolving over a long time.[2]

Nevertheless, this noble scientific endeavor came to a standstill even before Christ walked the earth—all because of an erroneous idea called the "eternal return" that came into fashion and destroyed scientific curiosity. According to this theory, the material world was caught up in an eternal cycle. Given enough time, all the basic elements would, by accident, end up in exactly the same position and the entire world would replay itself once again. Many were convinced that this cycle would continue repeatedly without end. Once this view became widely accepted, the development of Greek science came to a halt. What need was there to seek to explore anything? Everything was just a big circle. The Greeks stopped believing in free will and accepted their destiny with stoic resignation. Thus, although science was born in the framework of Greek philosophy, it looked like it would also die there.

What other world-view could pick up where the Greeks left off? Not the mythological religions. They were engrossed with imaginary gods. To them, the world was real, but not governed by the gods in a unified way. Instead, it was both playground and battlefield for the gods. In this world-view, human beings could rely on nothing to help them understand the world or how things worked.

Neither could science continue under Hinduism or Buddhism (or their derivatives), because these religions taught that both the physical world and the world of imagination were illusions. Anything that could be conceptualized, named, or imagined could

---

[1] "Atoms," as we know them, differ from the Greek idea because they are divisible into smaller sub-atomic particles.

[2] Ever since the golden age of Greece, only the uneducated considered the world flat. In regards to the Greek concept of evolution, they did not yet understand that one species could evolve into another.

only be an illusion. Why "study" a rock, a tree, or an ocean if one believed it was an illusion?[3] No believer in any of these world-views could even begin to pick up a rock and explore it in a scientific way. The concept of "exploration" implies a desire to expand, to discover, and to seek freedom. The belief in circular history and/or a world of illusion, on the other hand, opposes exploration at every turn. Only Judaism and Christianity (the completed faith of Judaism) had a chance to carry on and develop the science that began in Greece.

Christianity brought a completely new and exciting world-view to people of every nation and language. It took centuries for societies to absorb it. What was so original and refreshing about the Judeo-Christian world-view? God's revelation to the Jews gave the world several new starting points. First, the Jews believed that the world is real and that it reflects the goodness of God in some way. Second, they believed that the world was created out of nothing. Finally, the Jews understood that there is a beginning and end to the world *and a purpose for everything*. All of these concepts from Judaism were enough to allow human beings to break out of the prison of fate, astrology, and the eternal return. The human spirit was set free to explore the world around and find meaning, truth, goodness, beauty, and purpose.

Even more importantly, Christianity brought the belief that God became man! Suddenly, the material world became a reflection of the divine. It became natural to seek to understand it and to study it. A wholly new way of living and understanding the world had now been introduced that had not existed since the most primitive human society! Science could begin to advance again because the world had become real again, and it had become important again. The natural world was real because everywhere it reflected the beauty of a single God who spoke to us through it. Because God intended to speak to us in nature,

---

[3] Valuable scientific contributions were made in ancient India and China but these cultures did not succeed in giving birth to science.

the natural world was rational and understandable, and its laws were the same everywhere and predictable.

The "scientific method" simply expresses this Catholic truth. We will explain the scientific method from this perspective. Our explanation is divided into two parts, which are "observation and rational explanation," and "experimentation and tentative conclusion."

Part One: Observation and Rational Explanation

We did not follow cleverly devised myths when we made known to you the power and coming of our Lord Jesus Christ, but we had been eyewitnesses of his majesty (2 Pt 1:16).

The practice of observation and rational explanation means that the scientist at work accepts as real only what he can observe. He is only allowed to describe what he sees. If there is an earthquake, he does not speculate about "angry gods" who might be causing it. He simply records what he sees and uses numbers to describe its severity. Likewise, if an apple falls from a tree, he does not make up or accept any explanation of mythic "gods" who moved the apple. He simply describes what happened and assumes that apples everywhere fall in the same way should they be detached from their tree.

Such an attitude towards scientific study may seem like an obvious necessity nowadays, but it is simply *not* the way that humankind used to think. The scientific outlook requires the belief that the physical world is real and not an illusion. It also requires the belief that materials and energy work in the same way everywhere. To think this way, one must assume that there is one universal set of rules that govern the way that physical things behave. This basic idea is Christian, so whenever a scientist puts faith in natural observation and rational explanations (e.g., theories), he or she passes on a truth propagated by the Catholic Church.

Part Two: Experimentation and Tentative Conclusions

Test everything; retain what is good (1 Thes 5:21).

A belief in experimentation means that a scientist believes a theory only if it can be proven. It must be testable, and the conditions of the test must be able to be communicated to others so that other scientists can duplicate the results. The concept of producing "tentative conclusions" means that even after a theory is tested, it must always remain open to further developments and new discoveries. The scientific community grows by meditating on past research, consulting with current research, and struggling to come up with theories and conclusions that present a united world-view (a view that is "consistent").

The scientific community learned this procedure from the Church community as represented by the Councils. The Councils brought theologians together to explain the faith through ever-clearer formulations. The council members meditated on the faith of the past, consulted with then-current members in the faith, and struggled to come up with statements that were consistent both with the past and with each other.

Even after Christianity in Europe went into division, scientists still kept some Christian unity alive through their struggle for consistency. The scientific community continued the ideal of a common work and a community that crossed international borders. In other words, the scientific community retained its *catholicity*. We could illustrate this principle with nearly any scientist, but let us take the example of Isaac Newton's work on the idea of momentum.

If I have seen farther than others, it is because I have stood on the shoulders of giants — Isaac Newton

Newton's law of the conservation of momentum states that an object continues in the same direction and at the same speed unless, and until, acted on by an outside force. If there is a collision, the total energy that exists after a collision is the same as the total energy that existed before the collision. This all seems reasonable enough, but Newton put this law into a mathematical form so that it could be used when building engines, guns, rockets, or any number of things. Before the genius of Newton could put the idea in mathematical form, however, it had to be first conceived philosophically.

This was done by the Catholic thinker Jean Buridan 350 years before Isaac Newton. Buridan was able to come up with the idea of impetus because he believed in a physical world governed by certain laws and principles established by God. The idea that a body of matter moves in one direction freely and unhindered until it encounters another object became a generally accepted idea by Newton's day.

The story did not end there, however (the greatest stories never do). In the last century, Einstein modified Newton's modification of Beridan's idea. Newton's equation was:

$$\vec{P} = \frac{m\,\vec{V}}{\sqrt{1}}$$

Einstein modified this to:

$$\vec{P} = \frac{m\,\vec{V}}{\sqrt{1-(\frac{V}{c})^2}}$$

From this example, we can see that scientists continue to develop and clarify God's statement to them in the physical world. Doing this, they are imitating the way that the Catholic Church has always developed and clarified the faith that was given her by Christ. One day, complete unity between the two fields of natural science and theology will be restored.

Some Historical Objections

Galileo was condemned by the Church for saying that the earth revolves around the sun. Isn't this enough to show that the Catholic faith is hostile to science?

Sometimes, this condemnation of Galileo is the only thing people know about the Catholic Church in relation to science. That is all we ever hear about the subject in school, college, on TV, radio, magazines, etc. This is pop culture's revenge against the Catholic Church for daring to speak out on moral issues. Again, there is a kernel of truth to this story, but most people hear it with important parts edited out. So, what is the true story?

First, Galileo did not come up with the idea that the earth revolved around the sun. Copernicus, who was a Catholic priest, had discovered this already. If students hear about Copernicus in school, they are seldom told that he was a priest and that his uncle, a cardinal, provided funds for his work in astronomy. Most people did not believe in Copernicus' system, but he was not persecuted because he was a humble man who did not seek controversy. Galileo had the misfortune of being very outspoken and controversial. He was insulting to his opponents in debate, and unfortunately, he became famous at a time when religious wars were in full swing in Europe.

In Galileo's time, every country (including those governed by the pope) sought to avoid further religious factions caused by new ideas. The tribunal that judged Galileo feared that his ideas would cause another new faction to develop. Nevertheless, Galileo was treated leniently—especially considering the punishments used in those days: he was given a villa of his own and confined there under "house arrest," but his confinement was very comfortable, and he was allowed to continue to work and to receive visitors. In fact, Galileo wrote his most famous and profound treatise after his condemnation.

Above all, it should be noted that while the court was wrong to condemn Galileo's work, the general attitude and outlook of Catholicism helped to make such work possible in the first place. Certain specific mistakes do not mean that the Church's general outlook on science is wrong. A person who thinks that any mistake invalidates the whole outlook would never trust a modern medical doctor, just because medical doctors once mistakenly used leeches to "cure" people.

Didn't the Islamic world, during the "dark ages," preserve the science begun by the ancient Greeks and then present it to the West?

This is one of the few ideas that atheistic scientists and fundamentalist Christians agree on. They both believe it for the same reason—namely, because neither one of them credits the Catholic Church with anything good. Because of this, they make a great effort to trace the "enlightenment" from ancient Greece, through the Muslims, and then to the modern world. In this view of history, the era when all Europe was Catholic is derisively called "the dark ages."

There are some kernels of truth hidden within this generally false version of history, however. First, Christianity had to overcome the early persecutions, and then it had to survive the fall of the Roman empire. There were centuries of invasion, looting, and pillaging by barbarian tribes. The Church preserved Christianity through all of this. When the difficulties finally subsided, there was the relative stability that both civilization and science needed to advance. The advancement of knowledge was not idle during these so-called "dark ages," however. Philosophy, astronomy, navigation, mathematics, and biology were all being developed and improved slowly.

The Muslims did indeed re-introduce the philosophers of ancient Greece to the West, but they got this knowledge from the Christians in the areas that they conquered. Islam built somewhat on this knowledge but did not have a religious model that allowed for the continued development and shared international exploration of the truth.

Islam became frozen in time and split by nationality; believers adhered to the simple faith Mohammed had given them, and they were determined to develop no further. Religious faith was reduced to a few fundamentals that had no need of "exploration." The Koran alone would settle all difficulties.

Islamic philosophy also fell into an error from which it never recovered, namely a fatalistic belief in predestination. The belief in God as absolute monarch led to the false conclusion that he is also the doer of all good and all evil. In other words, there is no free will. God himself causes a person to act, whether for good or evil. Such an understanding of the world turns the human being into a mere object. This view destroys any interest in the material order and puts an end to all scientific advancement.

Christians were not the only ones to make great discoveries. Nevertheless, the Catholic world-view was the incubator for science until it was mature enough to be born and take on a life of its own. The scientist's excitement at a new discovery is simply part of the Catholic joy of exploring the beauty and truth that is God.

Conclusion: Science and the University

The word *catholic* means "universal." The university was part of the Catholic Church. Modern science is generally conducted in a university, but this word now means something different than it once did. A university used to be understood as the place where all things were studied, but not in the sense of a buffet where each thing is to be sampled on its own.

The prefix *uni-* means "one." While there were many subjects to study, they were all unified by the realization that God was the ultimate author of each of them. Thus, theology, the study of God, was the queen of the sciences and the one study that unified and directed all the others. Any university campus, therefore, that does not have theology at the center of it does not really deserve to be called a "university."

Scientists who know their history realize all of this, but some of them only think of the Church as the place where science was born. They do not think of themselves as witnessing to the one, universal, and *catholic* nature of truth when they do their work. They are mistaken, however, because the Catholic faith witnesses about the *entire* universe (this means the spiritual realm as well as the earthly realm), while science expresses the Catholic faith regarding only the *physical* universe.

Imagine that science keeps on advancing. Centuries roll on, and humankind becomes supremely powerful (in a material sense). Imagine we can control the weather, colonize other planets, and make this world whatever we want it to be. There still remains the question "What do we want it to be?" Should it be one giant park? Should it be one giant shopping mall? Should there be ten billion people on the planet, or should there be on hundred billion? It is obvious that science will never be able to answer such questions as these, because science is a tool. It can tell us how to get what we want (materially), but it can never tell us what we should want. A wise man once said: "People who know *how* always end up working for the people who know *why*." Science done properly must always be directed by a person's faith.

Because of this, humanity will have to begin asking the deeper questions once again. Why are we here? What is the point we are trying to work toward, as a whole race? What should we do? These are ultimate questions, and they lead back to the Church. Many people thought that these types of questions (and questions about "ethics") had become only theoretical exercises. Advances in the field of genetics, especially, are waking people up to the reality of how important these topics really are.[4] As Catholics, we can find comfort in the fact that God has given us a Church that will guide us even in an age where parents will be tempted to "special-order" their children's genetic traits. St. Paul assures us that the Church is competent to settle all such issues:

---

[4] Interestingly, it was a Catholic monk, Gregor Mendel, who first discovered the modern science of genetics. He pioneered the study of dominant and recessive traits in plants in the garden of the monastery.

Do you not know that the Holy Ones will judge the world? If the world is to be judged by you, are you unqualified for the lowest law courts? Do you not know that we will judge angels? Then why not everyday matters? (1 Cor 6:2–3)

Many people wrongly think that they have to choose between faith and science. Others keep the faith but relegate it to something sentimental. The great secret that has been kept hidden since the "enlightenment" is that God is the supreme author of both.[5] True science and true faith cannot contradict. If they seem to contradict, then a person has either a false idea of science or a false idea of what the Catholic faith represents.

Today, when scientists do science, they are doing something of Christianity without knowing it. Science must presume that the world is real and not an illusion, it must presume that things make sense and not non-sense. A scientist must have an interest in the material world in order to be a scientist. All these are beliefs that have Christian roots. It is ironic that many scientists deny God while also upholding the most basic Christian dogmas. A Hindu or Buddhist scientist does not realize that he is contradicting the dogmas of his own faith and infiltrating the world with Christian notions of reality.

Science took the Catholic Church's world-view and does not remember where it came from, but nowadays we do not hold it against them. In the same way, "Bible Christians" took the Bible from the Catholic Church but no longer remember where it first came from. Because of this, Catholics tend to witness arguments between atheistic scientists and fundamentalist "Bible Christians" with a sad sort of amusement. On the one hand, the atheistic scientist insists that he does not see a Creator's hand in

---

[5] "The Age of Enlightenment" refers to the age of reason when many educated elite in the eighteenth century considered themselves as emerging from centuries of darkness and ignorance which faith had perpetuated. This kind of arrogant attitude continued into the twentieth century and formed the basis of most secular education.

the physical world that he is studying. On the other hand, the "Bible Christian" insists that the world is only 6,000 years old because that is what the genealogies in Genesis make it out to be. We must leave it to the reader to decide which one is being more obtuse.

APPENDIX G

Saints, Images, and Relics

Saints

You are the light of the world. A city set on a mountain cannot be hidden. Nor do they light a lamp and then put it under a bushel basket; it is set on a lampstand, where it gives light to all in the house (Mt 5:14–15).

Understanding this teaching is the key to understanding devotion to the saints.[1] Just as Jesus is the "light of the world," so are his disciples (Jn 8:12, 9:15). Once we understand that the light of the disciples is not separate from the light of Christ but is Christ himself, we will be able to have the right attitude towards the saints.

So why do Catholics pray to saints? Isn't it better just to pray to Christ directly rather than through a saint?

There have been cases where people mixed pagan superstitions with Catholicism. In such cases, saints were wrongly worshipped along with pagan gods. This does not represent true Catholic teaching or practice. We must not worship the saints or the Virgin Mary, but we should honor them because even the Father honors them and because they love us (Jn 12:26).

---

[1] The word *saint* is used in several ways. Originally, it simply meant "holy," or "set apart." In a sense, all the baptized are "set apart" and can be referred to as saints. In this essay, however, we mainly refer to the canonized saints. A canonized saint is a person whom the Church has declared to be in heaven and whose life can be an example for us to follow.

The Catholic Church believes that Christ is the only mediator between heaven and earth. However, Christ shares this role with all believers to some extent. For this reason we are able to pray for one another. All the faithful are members of a royal priesthood (1 Pt 2:9). This means that all are able to mediate and intercede, because all share in Christ's priesthood. This is the reason we can all go to God saying, "Our Father." We do not have to go to Christ and ask him to go to the Father. Nevertheless, whenever we do go to the Father "directly" we are still going through Christ. Likewise, when we pray to the saints, we are praying to Christ and through Christ. Our prayers to them (and their prayers on our behalf) have merit before God only because they are joined to Christ.

We ask the saints for their prayers, but we also ask them for their guidance and help. In this life, we can do more than just pray for others. We also can help. The same is true of the saints. Christ has not made heaven into a constraint or a diminishment of their abilities. Instead, heaven enhances and fulfills them.

But why not go directly to God?

The saints in heaven are "saved," and salvation means that we share in God's very nature (2 Pt 1:4). Praying to a saint is going directly to God because God cannot be separated from the saint. We witness to the great grace of salvation by going to the saint. Doing so shows that we recognize the presence of Christ in others.

Sometimes, a saint brings Christ to people in a more direct way than the written gospel can. Mother Teresa, picking up a dying man off the streets of Calcutta, preached the gospel without saying a word. For that man, and possibly his descendants, her face is the face of Christ. Later, after she died, if he were then to pray to Christ through prayers to Mother Teresa, is it rational to try to claim he is worshipping her as God? No. Rather, each saint's life is like an entire gospel written in God's hand. Ignoring a saint is like ignoring the Bible.

The Bible condemns contact with the dead. Doesn't praying to the saints go against this teaching? Isn't prayer to the saints a form of pagan idol worship?

The worship of idols, the practice of witchcraft, and spirit summoning are all forms of paganism, of course. They are based on the idea that human beings can manipulate or control the spirit-world by practicing some sort of art or ritual. King Saul was condemned for trying to do this when he employed the witch of Endor to call up the prophet Samuel (1 Sm 28:1–25).

In contrast to this episode, Jesus, Peter, James, and John communed with Moses and Elijah on Mount Tabor (Mt 17:3, Mk 9:4). Jesus shows by his actions that he has opened up a new relationship between those who have died and those who remain on earth. In this new communion, we do not worship the dead as gods and we do not try to work magic to manipulate them. We simply relate to them as our brothers and sisters who are alive and in another place. Since they are in heaven, their example serves to inspire us.

The Bible says that the saints have "fallen asleep." Doesn't this mean that they are unable to hear our prayers?

No. "Falling asleep" simply expresses that someone has died. This expression says that those who die in the Lord are at peace with God and hope to be resurrected in a new physical body. Some people try to make this expression mean that the dead are unconscious or that there is some other reason why they cannot hear us. Christ refuted this very idea when he told the Sadducees:

> And concerning the resurrection of the dead, have you not read what was said to you by God, "I am the God of Abraham, the God of Isaac, and the God of Jacob"? He is not God of the dead but of the living (Mt 22:31–32).

> He is not God of the dead but of the living. You are greatly misled (Mk 12:27).

And he is not God of the dead, but of the living, for to him all are alive (Lk 20:38).

As Christians, we do not believe that death is the end, nor is it a separation. The body of Christ is present on earth and in heaven at the same time. Therefore, we are united to our members who are in heaven. There is no "chasm" between them and us, as there is between us and the souls of the damned.

Why doesn't the New Testament talk about praying to the saints?

The majority of people reading the New Testament were pagans who had problems enough understanding how there can only be one God, much less understanding the deep matters of the body of Christ. It would have been foolish to confuse the issue. The writers of the New Testament were wise. They knew that even the performance of miracles among pagans could be risky (Acts 14:12–13). Therefore, the subject of the communion of saints was approached with caution.

This does not mean that nothing at all was said. On the contrary, mention was made of our communion with the "spirits of the just" and of the intercessory prayer of those in heaven.

> You have approached Mount Zion, and the city of the living God, the heavenly Jerusalem, and countless angels in festal gathering, and the assembly of the firstborn enrolled in heaven, and God the judge of all, and the spirits of the just made perfect . . . (Heb 12:22–23).

> Each of the elders held a harp and gold bowls filled with incense, which are the prayers of the holy ones (Rv 5:8).[2]

> Another angel came and stood at the altar, holding a gold censer. He was given a great quantity of incense to offer, along with the prayers of all the holy ones, on the gold altar that was

---

[2] "Holy ones" or "saints" in both references from Revelation refers to all God's people on earth.

before the throne. The smoke of the incense along with the prayers of the holy ones went up before God from the hand of the angel (Rv 8:3–4).

This "cloud of witnesses" supports and encourages the Church on earth (Heb 12:1). Catholics know it as the *communion of saints*. The saints look at us with love, offering prayers on our behalf, so that we might one day join them in heaven. Having reached such perfection, how could the saints possibly forget about all of their relatives and friends still on earth and striving for perfection? The saints look down at us because *they have not forgotten about us.* The prayers of the saints are a valuable resource, as we strive to live good lives. No one should take lightly the power they wield, because, by virtue of their sanctity "The fervent prayer of a righteous person is very powerful" (Jas 5:16).

Images, Statues, etc.

Why do Catholics use images? Isn't this forbidden in the Ten Commandments (Ex 20:4)?

God forbade statues and other images because people so easily fell into the sin of worshipping them as gods. The source of the problem was not in the statue itself, but rather in worshipping it as if it were God. This is clear from the chapters in Exodus when God commands the making of two statues of angels called cherubim, to be stationed above the Ark of the Covenant in the Holy of Holies (Ex 25:18–22). God also commanded Moses to make a bronze serpent and mount it on a pole as a warning for everyone to turn away from sin (Nm 21:9). Although this statue foreshadowed Christ's nailing sin to the cross, the Hebrews before the time of Christ did not know what it signified. They fell into worshipping the snake statue as a "god," and so King Hezekiah had it broken up (2 Kgs 18:4).

Questions about the use of images arose in Christianity after the rise of Islam, which forbade any images at all. Amid great controversy, the Council of Nicea II in A.D. 787 condemned Iconoclasm, which mandated the destruction of statues and icons. The Council concluded that the proper purpose of any religious practice was to bring us closer to Christ. This is a broad principle. It means that any form of art, including music, statues, literature, etc. can have a valuable role in fostering genuine devotion to Christ. If, however, any item or practice leads people away from Christ, then it should be forbidden. With this principle in mind, the Council decided that the veneration and use of statues and icons in the worship of Christ is not idolatry, but could instead be beneficial.

Relics

Why do Catholics have relics? Why are bones used?

When the martyrs were fed to the lions during the persecutions in Rome, the early Christians would save and treasure their bones. Since the superstitious pagans were afraid to go near the cemeteries at night, the Christians would have Mass there. Masses were often said over a martyr's stone tomb, which served as an altar (Rv 6:9–11). The Catholic Church recalls this even today. Nearly every altar in the world has a relic of the patron saint of its particular Church somewhere within it. In such fashion, the Church remembers her beginnings and shows her continual belief in Christ's union with his beloved.

Honoring relics, the Church recalls how Jesus took care to teach us with things we could touch. He made mud with his spittle to heal the blind man's eyes. After he was resurrected, he cooked and ate real fish with the apostles in order to show them that he was not a ghost. In honoring the relics of the saints, the Church shows a special faith in the fact that Jesus Christ once walked among us and touched us and that his touch is continued through the long line of his followers after him.

The bodies of the saints are holy because they have been perfected by their heroic virtue and suffering. Because the saints manifest the body of Christ, their relics, anything they touched, or any piece of their body is revered, not worshiped. Just as we ought to revere the remains of our deceased, we should also revere the remains of the saints, but to a greater degree. Relics bring special blessings because they signify Christ's new creation transforming the old. Here are two examples of the use of relics in the Bible:

> Elisha died and was buried. At the time, bands of Moabites used to raid the land each year. Once some people were burying a man, when suddenly they spied such a raiding band. So they cast the dead man into the grave of Elisha, and everyone went off. But when the man came in contact with the bones of Elisha, he came back to life and rose to his feet (2 Kgs 13:20–21).

> So extraordinary were the mighty deeds God accomplished at the hands of Paul that when face cloths or aprons that touched his skin were applied to the sick, their diseases left them and the evil spirits came out of them (Acts 19:11–12).

God performs miracles and gives graces through the saints and their relics. He does not do this to exalt them as "gods." He does this to affirm their union to Christ. When Christ took on a human body, it was for all time. Those, like the saints, who are members of his body, testify to Christ's ongoing presence in the material creation. When we reverence a saint or a relic, we are honoring Christ for being present therein.

References

Cassidy, Edward. "Press Conference Statement on the Joint Declaration." *Origins* 16 July 1998: 128–130.

Chacon, Frank and Jim Burnham. *The Beginner's Guide to Apologetics*. Farmington, N.M.: San Juan Catholic Seminars, 1994.

Egan, Jennifer. "Why a Priest?" *New York Times Magazine* 4 Apr. 1999: 30.

Hahn, Scott. *The Lamb's Supper*. New York, N.Y.: Doubleday, 1999.

Feuillet, André. *Jesus and His Mother*. Trans. Leonard Maluf. Still River, Mass.: St. Bede's, 1984.

Keating, Karl. *Catholicism and Fundamentalism*. San Francisco, Calif.: Ignatius Press, 1988.

Kikawada, Isaac and Arthur Quinn. *Before Abraham Was: The Unity of Genesis 1–11*. Nashville, Tenn.: Abingdon Press, 1985.

Farstad, Arthur, ed. *Holy Bible: The New King James Version: Containing the Old and New Testaments*. Nashville, Tenn.: Thomas Nelson, 1982.

Flannery, Austin, ed. *Vatican Council II: The Conciliar and Post Conciliar Documents, New Revised Ed.* 1975. Northport, N.Y.: Costello Publishing Co., 1984.

Gibbons, James, ed. *The Douay-Rheims Bible*. Trans. Richard Challoner. 1582 (New Testament), 1609 (Old Testament), 1752 (Challoner Translation) 1899 (Gibbons as ed.). Rockford, Ill.: TAN Books, 1984.

Hartman, Louis F., Patrick Skehan, and Stephen Hartdegen, ed. *The New American Bible.* Washington, D.C.: Confraternity of Christian Doctrine, 1970.

——. *The New American Bible, with Revised New Testament and Revised Psalms.* Washington, D.C.: Confraternity of Christian Doctrine, 1986.

The Holy Bible, 1611 Edition. Nashville, Tenn.: Thomas Nelson, 1993.

Jaki, Stanley. *Catholic Essays.* Front Royal, Va.: Christendom Press, 1990.

Jones, Alexander, ed. *The Jerusalem Bible.* Garden City, N.Y.: Doubleday, 1966.

Jurgens, William A. *Faith of the Early Fathers.* 3 vols. 1970 (vol. 1). Collegeville, Minn.: The Liturgical Press, 1979.

Laurentin, René. *The Truth of Christmas Beyond the Myths.* Trans. Michael Wrenn, et al. Petersham, Mass.: St. Bede's, 1986.

Luther, Martin. *Luther's Works, Weimar Edition.* Trans. J. Pelikan. St. Louis, Mo.: Concordia, 1957. Vols. 4, 22.

Lutheran World Federation, Roman Catholic Church Staff. *Joint Declaration on the Doctrine of Justification.* Grand Rapids, Mich.: Eerdmans, 2000.

Mother Teresa. "Whatsoever You Do. . . ." National Prayer Breakfast. Washington, D.C., 3 Feb. 1994 (http://www.priestsforlife.org/brochures/mtspeech.html).

National Council of the Churches of Christ, Division of Christian Education. *The New Revised Standard Version of the Bible.* Ed. Bruce M. Metzger. New York, N.Y.: Oxford U. Press, 1990.

Neuner, Joseph and Jacques Dupuis, ed. *The Christian Faith: Doc-*

trinal Documents of the Catholic Church, fifth ed. New York, N.Y.: Alba House, 1992.

Noonan, Peggy. "Still Small Voice." *Crisis* 16, no. 2 (Feb. 1998): 12–17.

Official Dialogue Commission of the Lutheran World Federation and the Catholic Church. "Joint Declaration on the Doctrine of Justification." *Origins* 16 July 1998: 130–132.

Ott, Ludwig. *Fundamentals of Catholic Dogma.* Ed. James Bastible. Trans. Patrick Lynch. 1955. Rockford, Ill.: TAN Books, 1974.

Palmer, Edwin et al., ed. *The Holy Bible, New International Version: Containing the Old Testament and the New Testament.* Grand Rapids, Mich.: Zondervan, 1973. Revised 1978 and 1984.

"Passover" and "Septuagint." *The International Standard Bible Encylopedia.* Ed. G. W. Bromily. Grand Rapids, Mich.: Eerdman's, 1986. Vols. 3, 4.

"Overshadow" *(with the original entry in Greek). Theological Dictionary of the New Testament.* Ed. Gerhard Kittel and Gerhard Friedrich. Trans. Geoffrey Bromily. 1971. Grand Rapids, Mich.: Eerdman's, 1988. Vol. 7.

U.S. Catholic Conference. *Catechism of the Catholic Church,* second edition. Washington, D.C.: Libreria Editrice Vaticana, 1997.

Wansbrough, Henry, ed. *The New Jerusalem Bible.* Garden City, N.Y.: Doubleday & Company, 1985.

Weigle, Luther, ed. *Revised Standard Version of the Bible, Catholic Edition.* Nashville, Tenn.: Thomas Nelson Publishers, 1966.

Glossary

Aaron—Moses' brother and the first High Priest (Ex 29).

Aaronic priesthood—Descendants of Aaron. Only members of Aaron's family were allowed in the Holy of Holies (Ex 29). Zechariah, the father of St. John the Baptist, was a descendant of Aaron and therefore an Aaronic Priest. He was ministering in the Holy of Holies when the angel appeared to him (Lk 1).

Abraham—Lived approx. 1850 B.C. The man of faith called by God from Ur of Chaldea. Received God's promise to be the father of nations, one of whom would receive the Promised Land and be God's chosen people (Gn 17).

Adam—The first man, Eve's husband. God breathed the breath of life into him, giving him a spirit and free will. His fall into sin caused our nature to be tainted.

Advocate—The lawyer that takes your side in court. Christ used this word to describe the Holy Spirit.

Alleluia—Aramaic expression meaning "Praise God!" Alt. sp. Hallelujah, Halleluia.

Alpha and the Omega—The first and last letters of the Greek alphabet. When Christ says that he is the Alpha and the Omega, he means that he is the beginning and the end (Rv 22:13).

Amen—A Hebrew word that means "truly" or "so be it."

Angel—A pure spirit created by God. Angels do not have physical bodies. When we die, we do not ever become "angels," since we will receive resurrected physical bodies. Fallen angels are called "demons," or "devils." Angels never become human, but can appear in human form.

Animator—Another name for the Holy Spirit, who animates the Church like our own spirits animate our bodies.

Anointing—Applying oil to cause something or someone to take on a new identity that is permanent. Examples would be the anointing of a king, a priest, or a Christian in the sacrament of Confirmation (Chrismation). Christ was anointed with the Holy Spirit. Sometimes an anointing is medicinal, such as in the sacrament of the Anointing of the Sick. (Anointed = *Messiah*: [Hebrew origin] = *Christ* [Greek origin]).

Annulment—Christ forbade divorce. The only way that a husband and wife are not to be considered married is if their marriage was never valid to begin with. If the Church investigates a marriage and finds that it is not valid, the marriage can be declared "null." This means that the parties to it were never validly married.

Annunciation—The announcement that the angel Gabriel gave to Mary in Luke 1. Upon his announcement, Mary conceived and the Word became flesh.

Anti-Christ—In a general sense, anyone who does great evil in the world. In a narrow sense, one that will come into the world at the end of time to contend with Christianity (Rv 13).

Antioch—The city, (in modern Turkey), where Christ's followers were first called "Christians." Ignatius, Bishop of Antioch was the first on record to use the word "catholic" to describe the one true Church in A.D. 107. It was also in Antioch that the word "Trinity" first appears in a treatise by St. Theophilus of Antioch in A.D. 181.

Apocalypse—Greek for "unveiling," or "revelation." Another name for the last book of the New Testament.

Apocrypha—Books that are not considered inspired and therefore not part of the Bible. Protestants mistakenly call Tobit, Judith, Maccabees I and II, Wisdom, Sirach, and Baruch apocryphal.

Apologist—Someone who argues for the faith, and explains it.

Apostle—"One who is sent." In general, an authorized messenger. Specifically, the twelve eyewitnesses to Jesus. He gave them authority and sent them out to preach the good news throughout the world, baptize all nations, and shepherd his people. Judas Iscariot was removed from their original number, while Matthias was added. The number twelve was chosen to represent the Tribes of Israel.

Apostolic—From the apostles or from the time of the apostles.

Aramaic—Language spoken by Jesus and the apostles. It is a Semitic language similar to Hebrew.

Arianism—The heresy that the Son was created by the Father as a sort of super-angel. Named after Arius, a priest who originated this false teaching in the early fourth century.

Ark—In general, any container or box. The word was used to describe Noah's ark, the ark that Moses was placed into as a baby, and the Ark of the Covenant.

Ark of the Covenant—The box God commanded Moses to make. It was made of wood and plated with gold. In it were placed Aaron's staff, some of the manna, and the Ten Commandments on tablets of stone. When it was completed, it was overshadowed by God's presence (Ex 25).

Assumption—The taking of Mary into heaven, body and soul.

Assyria—Empire that captured the northern kingdom of the Hebrews, called "Israel," in 721 B.C. These ten tribes became the "Lost Tribes of Israel," and the northern kingdom was never re-established (2 Kgs 17).

Atonement—Repairing a separation through repentance, sacrifice, and commitment. Christ atoned for the sins of humanity on the cross. *See* Day of Atonement.

Babylon—Earlier called Chaldea. Babylon conquered the southern kingdom of the Hebrews, called "Judea," around 587 B.C.; the Jews spent seventy years in Babylon in exile before they were allowed to return by the Persian conqueror of Babylon, Cyrus (2 Kgs 25).

Baptism—Immersing someone in water to signify and effect new birth. Baptism makes us one body with Christ.

Baptism by desire—Some accept and have faith in God without having had the chance to take part in a water baptism. Some others may have some sort of faith in God and accept him without knowing him clearly or explicitly. These both might be regenerated through a "baptism" into Christ's body in an invisible way.

Beatific Vision—The direct vision of God. It is experienced by the angels and the saints in heaven (1 Jn 3:2)

Bible—"The Book." It is actually a collection of seventy-three books that the Holy Spirit (through the Church) has declared to be inspired ("God-breathed"). There are forty-six books in the Old Testament, and twenty-seven in the New Testament. The Bible is part of the deposit of faith given by God to the Church; the other part is sacred Tradition. *See also* Inspired.

Biblical—When a statement or doctrine agrees with the Bible, it is said to be "biblical."

Bishop—"Overseer." Greek = *episkopos*. The apostles appointed bishops to take over their governing offices when they died. God established these offices to be passed on from generation to generation until the end of time (1 Tim 3).

Blasphemy—Deliberately saying something insulting to God.

Body—The physical home or house of a spirit, and the tool through which a human spirit acts in the world. A physical body is composed of parts.

Body of Christ—The Church, the spouse of Christ (Rom 12:3–8).

Bosom of Abraham—A spiritual realm where it is supposed that the Patriarchs awaited the redemption won by Christ (Lk 16:20–25). *See also* Sheol, Hades, Paradise of Infants, Purgatory.

Breath—Hebrew = *ruḥ*. Greek = *pneuma*. Both the Hebrew and the Greek use one word to describe "breath," "wind," and "spirit." This means that there are profound connotations wherever they are used, like when God breathed the "breath of life" into Adam. The Holy Spirit is often thought of as the "Breath" of God, just as Christ is expressed as the "Word" of God.

Brother—In Aramaic, the language that Christ spoke, there was no word for "cousins." Therefore, the word "brother" can mean cousin, nephew, or any relative. The reader must use the context to determine which is meant. Christianity followed this Semitic usage of the word brother and applied it to all members of the Church; this usage is followed even today.

Canaan—The son of Ham put under a curse in Genesis 9:25. The land of Canaan was given by God to Abraham and his descendants. It later became the land of Israel, and the Canaanite tribes were either exterminated or enslaved, fulfilling the curse pronounced by Noah.

Canon—Official list of books in the Bible. The Catholic canon has seven more Old Testament books than the Jewish and Protestant canons of today.

Catechism—The teaching that adults were expected to learn before they were baptized into the faith.

Catechist—A person who teaches the faith. *See* Catechumen, below.

Catechumen—A person who is studying to become a member of the Church. In the early Church, catechumens and all un-baptized had to leave the Mass just before the Liturgy of the Eucharist.

Catholic—Greek = *katholikos* "universal." *See* Universal.

Chaldea—Abraham's original home (Gn 12). It was where the modern country of Iraq now is. This region later came to be called Babylon. *See* Babylon.

Charity—Divine love. God's grace expressed in works of divine love is one of the two necessary means of salvation, the other being faith.

Cherubim—Angels before the throne of God. They were depicted in sculpture above the Ark of the Covenant (Ex 37:7–9 and Rv 4:6–9).

Chosen People—The Hebrews. They are the race that God formed from the seed of Abraham to bless all of humanity.

Chrismation—The sacrament by which a person receives the gifts of the Holy Spirit by being anointed with oil. It follows Baptism. *See* Christ, Anointing.

Christ—Greek *Christos* = Hebrew *Messiah* = English "Anointed." Jesus is the one who is anointed. The Father is the one who anoints him, and the Holy Spirit is the ointment. *See* Anointing, Chrismation.

Christian—In a general sense, anyone who professes the Christian faith.

Church—The assembly of Christians, the people of God, the body of Christ, the Bride of Christ, the spouse of the Lamb, the New Creation, the New Jerusalem, the New Temple.

Church Fathers—Early bishops, priests, or devout men who learned the faith from the apostles or from their immediate successors. They left us a treasury of writings that help us to interpret both Scripture and sacred Tradition correctly.

Communion—Taking part in the sacrifice instituted by Jesus at the Last Supper. By sharing in the one loaf, we are made into one body, and joined to God (1 Cor 10:17).

Communion of Saints—The connection we have with one another and with the saints who have died and gone to heaven; this means we can intercede for one another (Heb 12:1).

Confession—In a general sense, testifying to Christ, as if in court. At the same time, we confess our guilt and rely on his mercy. In a narrow sense, it means the sacrament where we do this officially before a priest who represents Christ to us.

Confirmation—*See* Chrismation, Anointing.

Conscience—God's testimony in our hearts about what is right and wrong. God has written his law on the human heart. This is why we feel guilty if we do something wrong (Rom 2:15).

Consecrate—Setting something aside for a special purpose; dedicating it to that purpose.

Council of Jamnia—Jewish council that mistakenly removed seven books of the Old Testament from the canon. Protestant reformers later followed this list to determine their version of the Old Testament.

Counselor—Another name given by Christ for the Holy Spirit.

Counterculture—A trend that goes contrary to the current way of doing things or presents a new way of thinking that goes against accepted norms. The Church has often found herself to be counter-cultural in the sense that she often must stand against worldliness.

Covenant—A special kind of unbreakable and permanent contract that forms a family bond.

Created—Something that is made from nothing; God is the only uncreated being. Since Jesus is God the Son, the Son is uncreated.

Creation—Everything that God has made from nothing, visible and invisible. This includes heaven, and everything in the physical universe.

Creed—From the Latin word *credo* = "I believe." A statement of what must be believed in order to be called "Christian." The most widely recognized Christian creed is the Nicene Creed.

David—King after Saul; ancestor of Christ. Prophecy declared that a descendant of David would be the Messiah and ultimate king.

Day of Atonement—*Yom Kippur.* Once a year the High Priest would enter the Holy of Holies to offer atonement for the sins of Israel and for himself (*see* Aaronic priesthood). Christians believe that Christ fulfilled this offering for all time on the day of his crucifixion (Ex 16 and Heb 9–10).

Deacon—From the Greek *diakonos* = "minister" or "server."

Dead Sea Scrolls—Scrolls found between 1946–1956 in caves near the Dead Sea. Most of them were written before the time of Christ. They contain copies of books from the Bible as well as other literature. They also contain copies of deutero-canonical books from the Old Testament in Hebrew that are contained in the Catholic Bible.

Deutero-canonical—From the Greek: "other canon." A council of Jewish scholars at Jamnia in A.D. 90 removed seven books from the Old Testament, claiming that they were not written in Hebrew, and were therefore invalid. The Catholic Church retained these books in the Old Testament. Protestants adopted the revised Hebrew Canon instead, and call the Deutero-canonical books the "Apocrypha."

Divine—"Of God," "having the nature of God," or "God like."

Divorce—Jesus Christ forbade divorce (Mt 5:32). *See* Annulment. This is understood as an attempt to dissolve a valid marriage.

Doctrine—Any defined truth, whether from revelation, reason, or conscience, that the Church teaches must be believed.

Dogma—The whole faith of the Church whether defined as doctrine or not. The faithful must hold to the entire faith of the Church and not just doctrine.

Elder—From the Greek: *presbyter.* The word had both a broad meaning and a narrow one. Broadly, (in the early Church) it meant any Church leader, even a bishop. It could also mean any older member of the Church in good standing. It later came to be restricted to referring to the ordained priests of the Church. In this sense, presbyter = priest.

Elijah—The Old Testament prophet who ascended into heaven in a fiery chariot. It was prophesied in Malachi that he would return to prepare for the coming of the Messiah. Jesus said that John the Baptist was the fulfillment of this prophecy (2 Kgs 2:11, Mal 4:5, and Mt 11:14).

Emmaus—A village seven miles from Jerusalem. Disciples recognized the risen Christ there when he broke bread with them (Lk 24:13).

Enlightenment, Age of—The belief, made popular in the eighteenth century, that the only way one can know anything with certainty is through reason alone, not faith.

Eternally begotten—This phrase was put into the Nicene Creed to delineate two truths. First, the Son was always with the Father. Secondly, the Son was of the same nature as the Father and was not a created being.

Eucharist—From the Greek for "thanksgiving." It is another name for Holy Communion.

Evangelist—Someone who proclaims the Good News. One of the four authors of the Gospels.

Eve—Adam's wife and first mother of humanity. She was tricked by the serpent into the sin of pride. She ate of the fruit when he promised her she could be a God.

Exodus—The Israelites "exit" from Egypt. Also, the second book of the Bible.

Faith—The virtue given by God's grace, enabling one to believe what God has revealed to be true.

Faith alone—The doctrine of Martin Luther. He taught that we are justified by grace through faith alone, saved, *and then* do good works. The correct teaching is that God's grace gives us faith, and God's grace gives us works of divine love. These two expressions of God's grace justify us; we are then "saved" if we cooperate and persevere in them to the end (*see* Works).

Fall—The original sin of Adam and Eve. Also called the fall of Man. This original sin caused a defect in human nature that is passed on to every human being. It means that we all have some tendency to sin. In the end, we also experience suffering and death, and enter existence estranged from God's friendship.

Father—The first person of the Trinity. From him, every fatherhood on earth takes its name (Eph 3:15). A father is to be the head of, and origin of, the family. He is to love, provide for, and protect his family under God.

Feast of the Dedication—Called "Hanukkah." It is a Jewish festival that recalls the cleansing of the Temple by Judas Maccabeus (2 Mc 1:9). Nowadays it occurs sometime in November or December.

Festival of Booths—Jewish harvest festival that begins in mid-October, five days after the Day of Atonement. It lasts for one week. During this time, Jews live in "tents" or "booths" in order to recall the forty years of wandering in the wilderness of Sinai (Ex 23).

Festival of Weeks—Jewish festival of the first fruits, in Greek called "Pentecost" or "fiftieth day," because it is the fiftieth day after the Passover (Ex 23). On this day, Jews remember the giving of the Law on Mount Sinai that formed them by God's covenant into his chosen nation. It was on this day that the Holy Spirit descended on the apostles and animated the Church (Acts 2). Jews continue to celebrate the Festival of Weeks fifty days after Passover; Christians celebrate it fifty days after Easter.

First-born—Because the angel of death had passed over the first-born of Israel, God commanded that the Israelites should "redeem" (offer a sacrifice) for each first-born son of their household. First-born became an honorary title, giving the child special rights and privileges. To call someone firstborn (as in the case of Jesus Christ) does not imply that there were other children.

Flesh—The material that any living animal is made of. God shows that man is related to the animals and has authority over them by including man when talking about "all flesh." Cf. Jl 2:28.

Free Will—The doctrine that man, being in the image of God, has a certain degree of freedom in what he does. Calvin taught, falsely, that man's free will was totally destroyed (radically fallen) by the sin of Adam and Eve. The correct teaching is that man's free will was impaired by the fall, but not completely destroyed. Modern psychology often tries to reduce man's behavior to be something determined completely by heredity (what we get from our parents) and environment (what we learn). While it is true that these things do influence our behavior, we must believe also in the existence of Spirit in order to say that a man may do things in freedom.

Fundamentalism—Reducing the faith to a few catch phrases and claiming that they are all that are needed for salvation.

General Priesthood—Called "Royal Priesthood." All Christian believers have some share in the priesthood of Christ; this means that they all share in mediating God's grace to the world. In this same way, the entire Hebrew nation had some share in the levitical priesthood (Ex 19:6 and 1 Pt 2:9).

Gentiles—The Jewish name for people who are not Jewish.

Gnostics—Early heretical Christian sects that taught that Jesus only "appeared" to come in the flesh; they believed that matter was evil, so God would not become materially present. They also taught that people are "saved" by secret knowledge (in Greek, *gnosis* = "knowledge"). As a person rose in rank, they would gain access to deeper secrets. Modern sects like Scientology and Masonry imitate this system.

Godhead—Another name for the Trinity that emphasizes its oneness.

Good Works—In discussions about salvation, the New Testament distinguishes among three types, two of which have no part in our justification. Paul makes clear that works of the law, i.e. the Old Testament rituals, do not justify us. Paul also says that works done in the sense of trying to earn one's way into heaven (works "so as to boast") also do not justify us. Both Paul and James, however, make clear that works inspired by God's grace and done in the spirit of divine love, do play a part in justifying us before God.

Gospel—The "Good News."

Grace—Any gift from God. When talking about salvation, we must emphasize that it is a gift from God given to us because of Christ's sacrifice. The sacraments are visible signs of God's grace, making us holy and pleasing to him because they unite us more closely to Christ.

Grace Alone—All Christians believe that salvation comes to us by God's grace alone. This means that we are granted salvation because of Christ's sacrifice, and not because of anything that we do. In this sense, we believe that faith and works join us to Christ; they do not in any way "earn" our salvation.

Greek—At the time of Christ, four languages were spoken in Judea. Hebrew was the language of Temple ceremony, and of the Scriptures. Aramaic was the day-to-day language spoken by the people in their homes. Latin was the language of the occupying Roman Empire, and Greek was the language of education and trade. The New Testament was ultimately passed on to us in Greek, though Aramaic was the language spoken by Christ and the apostles.

Hades—The Greek word for the underworld, the land of the dead. It was not described like the Christian hell; it was a drab, gray world that human beings went to when they died. The Greeks could not imagine mortals going to heaven. In this sense, the Greek *hades* was similar to the Hebrew *Sheol. See also* Purgatory, Sheol, Paradise of the Infants, Bosom of Abraham.

Haggadah—The "story." During the Jewish Passover ritual, the story of Exodus is retold by having a child ask questions of the father.

Hallelujah—*See* Alleluia.

Hanukkah—*See* the Feast of the Dedication.

Harrowing of Hell—An expression that refers to Christ's descent into "hell" in order to preach to the souls in "prison." *See* Purgatory (1 Pt 3:18–20).

Heaven—Spiritual place where God is visible. The angels and saints see him as he is, and reside there in perfect happiness.

Hebrew—The race descended from Eber and continued through Abraham, Isaac, and Jacob (Gn 10:21). Hebrew is a Semitic language, as are Aramaic and Arabic. *See* Semitic.

Hell—The place and choice of deliberate separation from God. Since our true identity and our freedom depend upon our relationship to God, hell is both a loss of self and an enslavement.

Heresy—Doctrine that contradicts the faith given by the Holy Spirit through the Church.

Hierarchy—The visible Church leadership that resides in the bishops as successors to the apostles, united to the pope, who is the successor to St. Peter. The hierarchy makes it possible for the Church to love, teach, and witness in a visibly unified way.

High Priest—Before Christ, this referred to certain descendants of Aaron whose turn it was to make the offering on the Day of Atonement. Christ fulfilled and superseded the Aaronic priesthood at his crucifixion, breaking the barrier between God and Man, and becoming the eternal High Priest (Mt 27:51).

Holy—To be dedicated and assigned a special purpose for God. To be separated from all other purposes. Profane means something for regular everyday use; in this sense, "holy" is the opposite of "profane" or the opposite of "regular." Sometimes the word "reserved" might be a good translation of the word "holy."

Holy of Holies—The Temple was made according to the plan God gave to Moses as depicted in Exodus chapters 25–27. There was a large outer meeting tent. Inside this was the Holy Place, where only priests could go. Inside this was the Holy of Holies where only the High Priest could go, and he could only go in once each year on the Day of Atonement. The Ark of the Covenant was placed within the Holy of Holies.

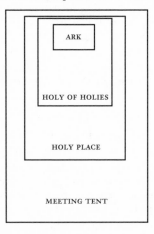

Holy Place—*See above.*

Holy Spirit—The third person of the Trinity, who proceeds as the Love of the Father and the Son. He is the Sanctifier, the Advocate, the Counselor, and the Comforter promised by Christ. He is the Inspirer of the Prophets and the Animator of the Church.

Hyssop—A bristly plant that can serve as a brush or a sprinkler. The Israelites used it to brush the lamb's blood over their doors on the night of the Passover. The Gospel shows Christ is the Passover lamb by describing how hyssop was dipped in sour wine and raised up to Christ as he hung on the beams of the cross (Ex 12:22 and Jn 19:29).

I AM—Hebrew = *Yahweh*. God gave this answer when Moses asked his name in Exodus 3. God is the source and origin of existence itself.

Immaculate Conception—The dogma that Mary was conceived without original sin. Though Mary was conceived by her parents in the normal way, she did not share in the original sin of Adam and Eve. She remained completely pure and free from sin from the very beginning of her existence. This was made possible because God foresaw the redemption of Christ and applied it to her. Since she would be God's dwelling, God did not allow Satan to touch her in any way.

Immanuel—Hebrew = "God with us." The name given to the coming Messiah by the prophet Isaiah (Is 7:14).

In the Person of Christ, *In Persona Christi*—A Catholic priest, when offering Christ's sacrifice in the Mass, stands in Christ's person as the spouse of his Church. At this moment, he is representing Christ's passion on the cross for the sake of his bride. This is one reason that the sacrificial priesthood is restricted to males.

Indulgence—A free gift where (after we repent and are forgiven) Christ and/or his saints take the suffering caused by the punishment for our sins, and in exchange, we receive purifying grace from God for doing good deeds. In other words, we are made more pure by a gift rather than through the normal way, suffering. One should not confuse the eternal suffering caused by unrepentance with the purifying suffering after repentance (Such as a repentant criminal who is still in jail). Sometimes the Church recommends performing a certain deed to gain an indulgence such as prayer, fasting, almsgiving, reading the Bible, etc. How effective this is depends on the nature of grace granted by God, and upon the purity of the individual's intention. Indulgences may be gained for ones' self, other living persons, or souls who are in purgatory. Abuses in the preaching of indulgences led Martin Luther to deny this doctrine, and to deny the very existence of purgatory. (*See* CCC 1471–72).

Infallibility—Jesus promised that all the powers of hell will not prevail against the Church (Mt 16:18) and that the Holy Spirit would guide the shepherds of the Church to all truth (Jn 16:13). A teaching is considered infallible when: a) Any bishop teaches what the Church teaches. b) All the bishops together, in union with the pope, speak on matters of faith or morals. c) The pope alone speaks authoritatively with the intention of addressing the entire Church infallibly regarding a matter of faith or morals that is part of the deposit of faith.

Inspired—"God-breathed." Islam teaches that the angel gave Mohammed the Koran by dictating it *word for word* to him. This is *not* what Christians believe about Scripture. Scripture is "divinely inspired, not divinely dictated." This means that God's grace moved the writers of Scripture to express truth, but God did not override their own humanity to do so. God left the writers free to express things in ways consistent with their own personal culture and history. Therefore, while the Bible is free from theological error, it was produced by both God and men. As such, it must be interpreted correctly in order to be understood correctly, and there can be "errors" in the sense of mistaken details.

Isaac—The second son (the one promised by God) born to Abraham. He is the ancestor of the Israelites (Gn 21).

Ishmael—The first son born to Abraham. He is the ancestor of the Arabs (Gn 16, 25).

Islam—Religion begun by Mohammed around the year A.D. 621 in Mecca, Arabia. It teaches that the angel Gabriel gave Mohammed the Koran as the final revelation from God in order to correct the mistakes of Judaism and Christianity. Islam denies the divinity of Christ and his crucifixion, and rejects the Trinity.

Israel—Hebrew for "contended with God." The angel changed Jacob's name to Israel after wrestling with him in Gn 32:29. The name is also applied to the people descended from Israel through his twelve sons (the twelve tribes of Israel). The name is also applied to the land that God promised to give to his descendants; this is why the modern state is named "Israel."

Jacob—*See above.*

Jamnia—*See canon.*

Jerusalem—City which David captured in 2 Samuel 5:6. God designated that the Temple should reside there forever, and David's son Solomon built it. The Church as the New Jerusalem includes heaven, which is the "Jerusalem above" (Gal 4:26).

Jerusalem Above—The Church in heaven; *see above.*

Jesus—Hebrew = *Yeshu'* = "God saves." The Son of God.

Jews—Descendants of Judah, the fourth son of Israel. After the northern tribes were conquered by Assyria (*see* Assyria), only the tribes of Judah and Levi remained. Since the Levites, as the priestly class, did not have a portion of land that was specifically theirs, the remnant of Israel came to be called Jews. (*See also* Hebrew, Israel).

John the Baptizer—The one who came in the spirit of Elijah to prepare for the coming of the Messiah. (*See also* Elijah).

Judah—The fourth of Israel's twelve sons. Judah's descendant was David, who established the royal line in Israel. *See also* Jews.

Judaism—The Jewish faith, which today rejects Jesus as the Messiah but retains the worship of the God of Abraham through obedience to the Torah (the first five books of the Bible).

Justification—That which makes us acceptable to God and therefore enables us to enter heaven. For Protestants, this is grace alone through faith alone. For Catholics, this is grace alone through faith and works. *See* Faith Alone.

Kaddish—In Hebrew = "holy." Also refers to the Jewish tradition of prayers for the dead.

Kephas—Aramaic for "rock." When Jesus named Peter "Rock," he did so in Aramaic. "Peter" comes from the Greek for rock: *petros* (Jn 1:42).

Keys—Giving the keys of the kingdom or city to someone means to make them the prime minister. When Jesus gave Peter the keys, he was designating that the Church on earth would always have a visible head, a "prime minister." This is the establishment of the papacy, since Peter was the first pope (Is 22:22 and Mt 16:19).

Last Supper—The final symbolic Jewish Passover that was celebrated by Christ and the apostles. Christ fulfilled the Passover observance forever; we take part in it whenever we celebrate the Eucharist.

Levite—Levi was the third son of Israel (Jacob) and therefore a patriarch of one of the twelve tribes. Moses was a Levite, as was his brother Aaron, the High Priest. The Levites were not given any specific portion of land in Israel. Instead, they served as the priestly class, and were responsible to care for the Temple (Nm 1:47–54).

Levitical Priesthood—*See above.*

Limbo—*See* Paradise of Infants.

Liturgy—Greek = "The peoples' work." In reference to the service of the Eucharist.

Lost Tribes of Israel—*See* Assyria, Jews, Judah.

Love—God in our hearts, allowing us to give of ourselves for the sake of another. "No one has greater love than this, to lay down one's life for one's friends"—Jn 15:13. Love is different than desire because it seeks to give, not to receive. God is Love (1 Jn 4:16).

Magisterium—The supreme teaching office of the Church. *See* Infallibility.

Magnificat—The prayer spoken by Mary during her visit to Elizabeth in Luke 1. It begins "My soul magnifies the Lord. . . ."

Manna—The bread that God sent from heaven to feed the Israelites in the wilderness in Exodus 16. It foreshadowed Christ, who is the true "bread from heaven" (Jn 6:31–35).

Martyr—From the Greek: "witness." Someone who witnesses to Christ with his life.

Mary—Hebrew = *Mariam*. The Mother of Jesus.

Masks—*see* Modalism.

Mass—The Liturgy of the Word and the Liturgy of the Eucharist.

Mediator—A representative or minister between two parties. There is only one mediator between God and man; this is Jesus Christ. To the extent that we minister Christ to one another, all Christians share in Christ's mediation.

Meeting Tent—*see* Holy of Holies.

Melchizedek—An ancient priest who made offerings on behalf of Abraham. His mysterious origin and superior priesthood foreshadowed the coming of Christ. Catholic priests are ordained according to the "Order of Melchizedek" (Gn 14:18, Ps 110:4, and Heb 7).

Messiah—Hebrew for "Anointed one." *See* Christ, Anointed.

Modalism—The heresy that Father, Son and Holy Spirit are really the same person who uses different "masks" or "modes" at different times. The correct belief is that they are three distinct persons yet one God.

Modes—*See above.*

Morals—Rules regarding our behavior that teach us the difference between what is right and what is wrong.

Mortal Sin—Sin that is deadly. Since it is a deliberate and complete break with God, a person who has not repented of mortal sin(s) cannot enter into heaven, meaning that if they die in such a state, they will spend eternity in the second death, which is hell. In order to be mortal, a sin must be 1—a grave matter, 2—deliberately committed, 3—done with full knowledge and full consent.

Moses—The prophet who led the Hebrews out of the slavery of Egypt and formed them into a chosen nation.

Mother—"Bearer." A mother is the temple of her spouse and the home of her child. The Church imitates Mother Mary in bearing Christ to the world.

Mount Horeb—Another name for Mount Sinai.

Mount Moriah—One of the hills on which Jerusalem is built.

Mount Sinai—The mountain on which God appeared to Moses. It is where God entered into a covenant with the Israelites (Ex 19).

Mount Zion—One of the hills on which Jerusalem is built. The Temple was built on Mount Zion, an ancient fortress.

Muslim—One who "submits" to the will of God. A person who subscribes to the religion of Islam.

Mystery—A truth that reveals itself and constantly unfolds but can never be fully understood. An example is the fact that every time we read the Bible or pray, we always get something new from the experience. God is Mystery. Mystery is also another name for sacrament in the Eastern Catholic churches.

Nature—What a thing is. Jesus has two natures. He is human, and he is divine, but he is one person. *See* Person.

New Ark—The Virgin Mary.

New Creation—The Church.

New Eve—The Virgin Mary.

New Jerusalem—*See* Jerusalem.

New Testament—The twenty-seven books of the Bible that explain Jesus Christ as the fulfillment of the Old Testament laws, types, and prophecies.

Nicea—Town in what is now Turkey where all the bishops of the world met in A.D. 325. This council of bishops condemned Arianism and began formulating the Nicene Creed.

Nineveh—Capital of the Assyrian Empire. *See* Assyria.

Nirvana—The state of perfect non-self that a Hindu ultimately seeks to obtain. Once achieved, the concept of self disappears entirely. This version of "heaven" is not consistent with Christianity.

Old Testament—The forty-six books of the Bible that predate Christ and look forward to him with types and prophecies. *See also* Deutero-canonical.

Omega—*See* Alpha and the Omega.

Organization—The way that many parts are able to be unified, like the organs of a body. Those who seek spirituality without organization are really fleeing from authority and commitment. This attitude contradicts authentic Christianity.

Original sin—The sin of Adam and Eve that tainted our human nature, giving us all a tendency toward sin, suffering, and death.

Overseer—Greek = *episkopos*, English = bishop. *See* Bishop.

Overshadowed—Word used in the Old Testament to describe the Spirit of God filling the sanctuary and the Ark of the Covenant in the form of a cloud (Ex 40:35). This same word is used in Luke 1 to describe the Holy Spirit filling Mary, conceiving Jesus Christ within her.

Pagan—Someone who believes in many gods.

Paradise of the Infants—(Also referred to as Limbo.) There was a tradition in the Church that children who died before the age of reason but without baptism might be granted by God an existence of eternal natural happiness without the Beatific vision. The Church has never pronounced definitively on this matter. *See also* Purgatory.

Passover—The ritual meal that God commanded the Israelites to keep forever. It recalls their escape from Egypt when the Angel of Death passed over them (Ex 12). A lamb was sacrificed and its blood smeared on the doorposts; death passed over any house where this was done. Christians see in Jesus Christ the "lamb of God, who takes away the sin of the world." As such, he fulfilled the Passover ordinance for all time. *See also* Last Supper.

Patriarchs—The biblical men of ancient times with whom God entered into a Covenant.

Penance—Works assigned by the priest to a person after he confesses as an outward sign of an inward repentance.

Pentateuch—The first five books of the Bible, called the Torah in Hebrew.

Pentecost—*See* Festival of Weeks.

Person—The "Who." An intellect having the possession of self, free will, and power to act.

Personal Relationship—To interact with someone "face to face." Jesus repeatedly taught that we can have a personal relationship with him through our actions and relations with our fellow man. He told parables showing that people who have "direct relationships" to him while ignoring the plight of their fellow man in fact have no relationship to him at all (Mt 25:31–46).

Peter—Originally named Simon, Christ changed his name to the Aramaic *Kephas*, which means "Rock." In Greek this has been translated *petros*. This can mean "small rock." The Greek word for large rock (*petra*) was not used because it is feminine. By giving Peter this name, and giving him the keys to the kingdom (among many other things), Christ designated Peter as the first pope (Mt 16:13–20).

Petra—*See above.*

Petros—*See above.*

Pharisees—A Jewish religious party at the time of Christ who believed in very strict observance of the Mosaic Law. They believed in the resurrection of the dead. The Sadducees were another party existing at the time that denied the resurrection of the dead. The two parties often contradicted each other, and both of them were critics of Jesus and of Christianity.

Pope—Coming from the Latin *papa* = "father." The apostles handed down their governing and teaching authority in general to the bishops that followed them. Peter, the first pope, was martyred in Rome, and he passed on his specific office as the visible head of the Church on earth, to the bishops of the See of Rome.

Prayer—Response to God. This can be in the form of praise, meditation, contemplation, thanksgiving, petition (requesting something from God), offering, repentance, or affection (love).

Presbyter—From the Greek for "elder." *See* Priest, Elder.

Priest—Someone who mediates between God and Man. In the Old Testament, this was reserved for the Levites and the sons of Aaron, even though all Israelites shared in their priesthood in some way. In the New Testament, Jesus fulfills, completes, and replaces the Old Testament priesthood. Catholic priests share in Christ's priesthood, and only the ordained clergy can stand "in the person of Christ" in order to offer the Eucharist. Though the sacrificial priesthood is reserved for the clergy, all believers participate in Christ's priesthood to some degree (1 Pt 2:9).

Primacy—The idea that the pope is the highest visible authority in the Church; as such, a bishop that is in communion with the pope is known to be connected to the one, true, original Church established by Christ through the apostles.

Prophet—A person sent by God with a message. This message can be a command about the present, or a prediction of the future, or both together.

Protestant—A branch of Christianity begun by Martin Luther in the sixteenth century. It "protests" Catholicism. Its teachings, as far as they are different from Catholicism, are: The belief that justification is through faith alone, revelation is through Scripture alone. There is no sacrificial priesthood, and there is no apostolic succession. The pope is not the visible head of the Christian Church. Man is radically fallen, and incapable of any goodness. There is no purgatory, and prayers for the dead are useless. Prayers to the Virgin Mary and the saints are also useless, and may be idolatrous. The four main branches of Protestantism are the Lutherans, the Calvinists (these branched out into various evangelical groups such as the Baptists, Presbyterians, and Methodists, and lately the "Non-denominational Christians"), the Anglicans (in the U.S. called "Episcopalians"), and the Anabaptists (whose ideas are imitated by modern Pentecostals). Today, there are thousands of different denominations.

Purgatory—From the Latin word for "cleansing." When we die, most of us will still have some stain of sin on our souls. When we enter heaven, we will be perfect. Purgatory is defined as the change that takes place between death and entrance into heaven. This change is accomplished by the grace Christ has won for us. This change is painful, since it is painful to us to give up our sins (1 Cor 3:15). The suffering we endure in purgatory can be lessened by the intercession of our brothers and sisters in Christ. But the soul about to see God also experiences over-whelming joy. The suffering of purgatory has always been presented as different from the suffering of hell; the CCC speaks of it only in terms of being a purification (nos. 1030–32).

Rabbi—Hebrew for "Teacher." Literally, this word meant "Great One" or "My Lord."

Real Presence—The Catholic Dogma that the Eucharist is really the body and blood of Christ. What remains after the consecration is bread and wine by appearance only. In reality, it has become Jesus Christ's body and blood.

Reconciliation—The sacrament whereby our relationship to God is re-stored after we have sinned. *See also* Confession, Penance.

Redeemed—Something that is reclaimed after paying a price for it (the idea is similar to one used by pawn shops). Jesus redeemed us after we had sold ourselves into sin.

Reformation—This word is often specifically applied to the Protestant movement begun by Martin Luther. In general, it means to rededicate or reconstruct something that has departed from its original beauty. Ignatius of Loyola was, in this sense, a Catholic Reformer.

Reincarnation—The idea that human souls exist before their physical conception, and that they return to new bodies sometime after their death. Hindus and Buddhists seek to free themselves from the cycle of death and re-birth. Christianity teaches, in contradiction to this idea, that God creates a person's spirit new at the moment of conception. Belief in reincarnation also contradicts the Christian doctrine of the resurrection of the body.

Relationship—*See* Personal Relationship.

Religion—The way that we are related both socially (as a body) and as individuals, to God. Religion is our relationship to God. For Christians, religion = the way that one is joined to Christ Jesus. This includes the action of the Holy Spirit expressed as visible signs in the sacraments, and the governing, moral, and theological teachings of the Church (*see* CCC 2104, 2105 on the virtue of religion).

Re-presented—In the sacrifice of the Mass, Christ is not sacrificed over and over again. Instead, the one eternal sacrifice that he made once for all is made present for us. For this reason, it is called an "unbloody" sacrifice.

Resurrection—When a physical human body is re-constructed, glorified, and rejoined to its proper spirit it is said to be "resurrected." The Resurrection refers to Christ's rising from the dead. In Christ, we all will be rejoined with our resurrected bodies when he returns in glory.

Revelation—In a broad sense, truth revealed by God. General revelation was completed and finished by Christ. The New Testament contains the disciples' witness to him as the final general revelation. While individuals may still receive personal revelations from God, it is absolutely certain that there will not be any new general revelation adding new information necessary for the salvation of the world. This is why the canon of Scripture is now closed. As regards Church teaching of doctrine: this is understood as an ever-deepening declaration of the deposit of faith given once for all by Jesus Christ to his Church. The Church does not add new truths. Instead, it continues to understand better and better the truth already given it.

Sabbath—God established the last day of the week as a day of rest, the day wherein mankind should rededicate creation back to the Creator (Gn 2, Ex 16:28–30). In the Old Testament, this is Saturday. When Christ arose from the dead on Easter Sunday, it was the dawning of the New Day. All Creation is made over again in Christ's risen body. As such, the Church observes Sunday, the first day of the week, as the fulfillment of what the Sabbath represented. Jews and some semi-Christian sects continue the observance of Saturday as the Sabbath.

Sacraments—The seven visible signs of God's grace given to people through Christ's body, the Church. Jesus established these as the means by which we would be joined to him by becoming one with his body. They are: Baptism, Communion, Confirmation/Chrismation, Reconciliation, Marriage, Holy Orders, and Anointing of the Sick. The sacraments are also referred to as the mysteries among Eastern Christians.

Sacrifice—Giving up something good for a higher good. Jesus Christ made the ultimate sacrifice on our behalf. Any other sacrifice, in order to be effective, must be joined to Christ's sacrifice in some way.

Sadducees—*See* Pharisees.

Saint—In general, a "Holy One." Any Christian. One specific meaning is applied to "those who are now in heaven." An official, canonized, saint is someone whom the Church has declared led a life of exemplary virtue, is now in heaven, and may be venerated.

Salvation—To be delivered from evil. For a Christian, this means to be joined to Christ forever, since Christ separates us from our sins and from the consequences of our sins, allowing us to avoid hell and enter into heaven.

Samaritan—People of mixed race who lived in and around Judea and

Samaria at the time of Christ. The Jews of that time considered them unclean and would not associate with them because they mixed pagan practices with Judaism. A few hundred descendants of the Samaritans still live in the Holy Land.

Sanctification—To be made holy, and worthy to enter heaven. For Catholics, this is a process that leads to salvation and entrance into heaven. For Calvinistic Protestants, this is a process that occurs after someone has already been "saved." Both Catholics and Protestants believe that it is through the application of the grace won by Christ that we are sanctified or made holy; i.e., it is through Christ's sacrifice that we are made holy.

Sanctuary—*See* Holy of Holies.

Sanhedrin—The governing council of Jewish religious leaders at the time of Christ. Two factions within the Sanhedrin were the Pharisees and the Sadducees. The High Priest ruled.

Satan—The fallen angel (Lucifer) who wished to be God. He is the one who tricked Adam and Eve. He was cast out of heaven by the archangel Michael (Rv 12).

Saved—Jesus redeemed the world but a person must remain in the faith and continue to cooperate with God's grace in order to be saved. Although we cannot be certain whether we will "endure to the end" until we die, we ought to have confidence in God's mercy.

Scripture—*See* Canon, Bible, Inspired.

Scripture Alone—The heresy that God's revelation comes to us through the Scriptures alone. The correct teaching is that his revelation comes down to us in the form of Scripture and sacred Tradition. Christ did not write anything, and the apostles did not write down everything he communicated to them. This sacred Tradition has been passed down from successor to successor within the Church. *See* Tradition.

Semitic—A family of languages and/or races that are descended from Noah's son Shem (Gn 5:32).

Septuagint—"The seventy." Greek translation of the Old Testament that was made before the time of Christ. Christ and the apostles quoted from it, and it contains the seven Old Testament books that are in the Catholic Bible that Protestants mistakenly call "apocrypha."

Sheol—*See* Hades.

Sin—Deliberate wrongdoing that separates us from God. Because we are physical, changeable beings, every sin alters our identity in a negative way, because human beings tend to become what they do. God's grace, won by Christ, allows us through co-operation to undo the damage. This process is called "sanctification."

Solomon—King David's son. Reputed to be the wisest human being who ever lived. He built the first Temple based on the plan given to Moses. In his later life, he fell into sin and idolatry because of his many foreign wives.

Son—To be descended from and of the same nature as one's parents. Jesus was the Son of God because he was the Son of the Father in heaven. He was the Son of Man because he was the Son of Mary.

Son of David—Jesus' title showing that he was reckoned as the descendant of David and therefore the inheritor of the Kingship.

Son of God—*See* Son.

Son of Man—*See* Son.

Soul—The word is often thought to be the same as the word "Spirit." Theologians tend to differentiate the two, however. A soul is the sum total of a person's background, ideas, and emotions; a soul is dependent upon one's history and place in the world; your family, country, nationality, language, personal habits, etc. are all part of your "soul." Your "Spirit," on the other hand, is the part of you that has free will and "decides." Using these specific definitions, angels are spirits, but do not have souls. Animals might have souls, but do not have free will, and therefore do not have spirits. Each human being possesses a soul that is also a spirit.

Spirit—*See above.*

Spouse of Christ—One of the titles of the Church, since she is Christ's bride.

Tabernacle—"Tent." God gave Moses a plan for the "Meeting Tent." Solomon used this plan when building the Temple. *See* Holy of Holies.

Temple—The dwelling of God built by Solomon according to the plan God gave to Moses. *See above.* It was destroyed and re-built several times. Jesus revealed that his body was to become the final Temple and dwelling place of God (Jn 2:19–22). His body, through the Eucharist, is expanded to be the Church. The Church is the New Temple.

Ten Commandments—A summary of the Law that God gave to Moses. God wrote it himself on tablets of stone (Ex 20). God replaced them after they were broken, and they were kept in the Ark of the Covenant. As such, they are a symbol of Christ, the Word, within Mary, who is the New Ark.

Torah—Hebrew = "Law." The Hebrew name for the first five books of the Bible.

Tradition—While this term is commonly used to describe venerable practices that have become part of the identity of a society or a family of societies, it also has various theological meanings. One meaning in particular is in reference to the unchangeable apostolic teaching that is infallibly handed down by the Magisterium. *See* Infallibility, Magisterium.

Trinity—The word first used by Theophilus, Bishop of Antioch in A.D. 181. The Father, Son, and Holy Spirit are three divine persons, but one God.

Twelve Apostles—The Twelve witnesses chosen by Christ. He chose twelve to symbolize the beginning of a New Covenant that would fulfill and replace the Old Covenant with the twelve tribes of Israel. *See* Apostle.

Twelve Tribes of Israel—The descendants of the twelve sons of Israel (Jacob) (Gn 49).

Unbloody Sacrifice—*See* Re-presented.

Universal—Greek = *katholikos*. A word first found being used by Ignatius of Antioch around A.D. 107 to describe the one true Church that is present everywhere, includes all nationalities, and is rightly descended from Christ through the apostles. The fundamental concept is that there may be many "local" churches, but they are all part of the *one* Church.

Universe—A word that emphasizes the "oneness" of all created things. Every created thing is included in it. Since the Church is the New Creation, the Church is, in this sense, the New Universe.

University—A campus designed to imitate the Catholic nature of truth, i.e. many disciplines all united and dedicated to the unified worship of God, and to understanding him through his Creation. In a true "university," theology is the discipline that unifies and directs all the others to this goal. Therefore, a university that does not offer theology cannot truly be said to be a university at all.

Venial Sin—Sin that is not "deadly" because it does not totally break one's relationship with God. In some sense, all sin tends toward death, since not even the slightest sinfulness can enter heaven. A soul that dies in venial sin, however, will be cleansed in purgatory before entering heaven, so that soul will not experience the "second death." For deadly sin, *see* Mortal Sin.

Virgin—In a narrow sense, this word means someone who has not had sexual relations. In its broader sense, it means something that is unspoiled and/or something that has been set aside for a higher purpose. In this sense, it is synonymous with the word "Holy." The Virgin Mary is so called for both of these reasons. Christ and the apostles always presented virginity for the sake of God's kingdom as a special grace, a virtue pleasing to God (Mt 19:12, 1 Cor 7:32–38, and Rv 14:4).

Word—Both the Old Testament (Gn 1, Is 55:11, among many other places) and the New Testament (Jn 1) present God's word as Creative, and as a form of binding Law (Ps 119). The New Testament goes beyond this, revealing that God's Word is the living person of the Son, and cannot be distinguished from God.

Works—In regards to salvation, there are three types of works discussed in the New Testament. Two types play no part in our salvation. These are: Works of the Law, and works "so as to boast." Works of the Law are Old Testament rituals such as circumcision. Since Jesus Christ fulfilled all purity and sanctification, all such laws regarding ritual purity are no longer in force (Rom 3:21–30). The second type that is ineffectual is "good deeds," so as to "boast" (Rom 4:1–6). This is the idea that one can "earn" one's way into heaven by doing good. The mistake here is to think that one can attain true holiness apart from Christ through one's own efforts. The last type of "works" does indeed contribute to our salvation. These works are works that are inspired by God's grace, operating through faith. These are works of Divine Love, or charity. As such, they reveal communion with the Holy Spirit. These are spoken of in (Rom 2:10, Gal 5:6, and Jas 2:14–16, among many others).

Yahweh—Hebrew = "I AM". *See* I AM.

Zion—The ancient fortress built on a hill that protected Jerusalem. King David conquered it by invading through the aqueduct. King David's son Solomon built the Temple on this site. Henceforth, Zion would become synonymous with the Temple, Jerusalem, Israel, and the people of God in general.

Index

*Bold page numbers refer to glossary entries.

*We would like to know how this book
helped you in your journey of faith.
Please address all emails to
solidfoundation@catholicexchange.com*

Order Form

CATHOLIC WORD
Bringing You The Best in Catholic Publishing

Ascension Press, Basilica Press, Lilyfield Press,
St. John Press, Company Publications, CH Resources, My Soul to Keep

W5180 Jefferson St.   Phone: 800-933-9398
Necedah, WI 54646   Fax: 608-565-2025
                    E-mail: familytrad@aol.com

PO#:_____ Date:_____

Bill To: **Ship To:**

Name:_____ Name:_____
Address:_____ Address:_____
City:_____ State:___Zip:_____ City:_____State:___ Zip:_____
Phone:_____ Fax:_____
E-mail:_____

QTY.	ISBN	Description	Unit Cost	Total
	193-031-4043	Building on a Solid Foundation $14.95 NEW!		
	193-031-4035	Surprised by Truth in Spanish $14.99 NEW!		
	096-592-2847	Amazing Grace for Those Who Suffer $12.99		
	096-592-2804	Did Adam & Eve Have Belly Buttons? $12.99		
	097-035-8903	My Life on the Rock $14.99		
	096-592-2820	The Rapture Trap $11.99		
	096-592-2812	Friendly Defenders Catholic Flash Cards $11.99		
	096-592-2812	Friendly Defenders EZ Ring $14.99		
	096-592-2863	Friendly Defenders in Spanish $11.99 NEW!		
	096-592-2863	Friendly Defenders in Spanish EZ Ring $14.99 NEW!		
	096-426-1081	Surprised By Truth $14.99		
	096-426-1006	Pope Fiction $14.99		
	096-426-1065	Making Senses Out of Scripture $14.95		
	096-426-1022	Nuts and Bolts $11.95		
	193-031-4078	Scripture Studies - Galatians $14.95		
	193-031-4000	Bible Basics $19.95		
	096-426-109X	Any Friend of God's Is A Friend of Mine $9.95		
	096-426-1030	Springtime of Evangelization $14.95		
	193-031-4019	Lessons from Lives of the Saints $12.95		
	096-714-9215	Philadelphia Catholic in King James's Court $12.95		
	096-714-9223	Philadelphia Catholic Discussion/Study Guide $3.95		
	093-898-4047	Holy Innocents: A Catholic Novel $16.95		

Subtotal

Shipping

Total

otes: _____
_____

ll For Bookstore & Parish Discounts.

clude $4.60 for the 1st book and $1.00 for each additional book or
ll for exact shipping.

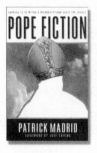